Morgan Spring

Morgan Spring

Life and Wildlife near the Edge of the Grid

M. RALPH BROWNING

Foreword by Alan Contreras

RESOURCE *Publications* · Eugene, Oregon

MORGAN SPRING
Life and Wildlife near the Edge of the Grid

Resource Publications
An Imprint of Wipf and Stock Publishers
199 W. 8th Ave., Suite 3
Eugene, OR 97401

www.wipfandstock.com

PAPERBACK ISBN: 978-1-7252-9861-3
HARDCOVER ISBN: 978-1-7252-9862-0
EBOOK ISBN: 978-1-7252-9863-7

04/27/21

Photographs by the author and Linda Ray-Browning

Dedicated to Linda, to neighbors down the road
To Don and Phyllis
To trees, birds, the elk, and their spirits
To the life-giving water that is Morgan Spring

Contents

Foreword

When I first read *Morgan Spring* in draft, I could almost smell the forest and I could certainly imagine the birds—and the neighbors. This part of southwestern Oregon has a lot of pine and mixed forest above the summer-hot Rogue Valley floor. The residents are an independent collection, all told, a unique mixture of pot growers (now legal), survivalists busy sorting their guns and canned food, naturalists enjoying the rich texture of wildlife and plants, Hollywood people wanting a private retreat space, staff and owners of the expanding wine industry and many others.

Ralph Browning came to these hills as both a homecoming and a new start. He grew up thirty miles to the south near Medford and went to school at what is now called Southern Oregon University in Ashland. These years and his career as one of the nation's preeminent avian taxonomists are set forth in detail in his book about birds and birding, *Rogue Birder*. The adventures at Morgan Spring pick up more or less where *Rogue Birder* ends.

What happens when a young retiree marries his childhood sweetheart and, unlike most of us who think we want to, actually *does* move to a cabin in the woods? A lot, as it turns out in this loping adventure in the towns and forests of Jackson County, Oregon. Ralph's morning welcome could be (and was) the local black bear with her cub. It could also be the discovery that unless he got a trim he'd be indistinguishable from the bears.

Leaving behind the giant cockroaches of Washington, D.C. for the mountain lions, bears and skunks of the southern Oregon forest is a trade-off between one kind of wildlife and another. The house at Morgan Spring was basic—the door latch was locked partly out of habit and partly because the skills of black bears are constantly expanding. The Brownings gathered tools and domestic objects from chainsaw to birdhouse as their new life took shape. Transplanting flowers turned out to include transplanting toads.

Ralph is an ornithologist and the story is infused with facts about birds and also with simple enjoyment of birds, as in the time that he and his wife

Linda used a trail-of-seeds to make sure that the local juncos knew about the new feeding station that had just opened. Yet this was not just about feeding—how exactly did these small finches interact with each other in the feeding zone. The term "pecking order" applies to more than chickens. The technical aspects of fly-catching come in for review via the beaks and gullets of nighthawks, phoebes, warblers and more.

A compact history of the region adds a layer of time to the Brownings' experience. Mining, cattle and forestry left the land a patchwork, but Ralph notes that leftovers are better than nothing even while chasing off hunters who casually leap the fence in pursuit of venison. Those who hunt and those who don't have in common the need to feel their way through a complex web of land ownership. In addition to learning about the humans, we learn about the trees, mushrooms and, most prosaic of all, the dirt on dirt.

It is said that all good things come to an end, and this book does, as does Ralph's time at Morgan Spring. I hope you enjoy your visit.

Alan Contreras

Preface

Morgan Spring, surrounded by conifers at the edge of a meadow in the low Cascade Mountains in southwestern Oregon, provided Linda, my life mate and partner, and me an opportunity to not only experience the region but also to cherish it. Morgan Spring gave us time to build on our past and learn how to live near the end of the electric grid, beyond the geographic possibility of newspaper delivery, even daily postal mail, and cable communication. It was a time to discover ways to live in the country and to appreciate insights and contributions from our few neighbors. Morgan Spring offered time to contemplate both tame and wild life, to draw upon creativity and to build a life once nearly smothered by too much civilization. The potential of living at Morgan Spring offered more than we initially understood. Living there soon exposed our curiosity if not our physical being to scratching the surface of geology, history, wildlife, and environment.

While living at Morgan Spring, we quickly developed a sense of belonging. In no time, we felt a strong affinity for Morgan Spring and tried our best to be good stewards for the privilege of living in such a wondrous setting. Morgan Spring was a place to love, a place for love, and a place that nourished our very fiber.

Each day was a time to begin exploring our surroundings. As time progressed, we met our neighbors, who in this chronicle remain anonymous with respect to their privacy. Their friendliness and their seasoned residency not only made us feel welcome but safe, should we need their help or expertise. Morgan Spring might just be a dot on a map and hardly a sentence in history, but stories were there to be discovered, to be lived and shared.

M. Ralph Browning

Acknowledgments

Morgan Spring would not have been without sharing it with Linda Ray-Browning, who am eternally grateful. Special thanks to Don and Phyllis Nelson for their introduction to Morgan Spring and for their welcoming friendship. Appreciation goes to our neighbors, who out of respect to their privacy shall remain anonymous. I thank Alan Contreras for his decades-old friendship and encouragement. Alan, Hendrick Herlyn, and others read and offered appreciated comments on earlier drafts. Heartful thanks goes to Joshua Little, Matthew Wimer, and other members of the Wipf and Stock Publishers for their patience and help.

Abbreviations

ABA—American Birding Association

ATM—Automatic Teller Machine

ATV—All Terrain Vehicle

AOS—American Ornithological Society

AOU—American Ornithologists' Union

DBH—Diameter at Breart Height

BLM—Bureau of Land Management

ELC—probably Elk Lumber Corporation

IRS—Internal Revenue Service

MIDI—Musical Instrument Digital Interface

ODF—Oregon Department of Forestry

ORD—Open Range Deficit (a made up abbreviation)

OSHA—Occupational Safety and Health Administration

SICS—Insect Control System (a made up abbreviation)

UV—Ultra violet

Illustrations

Introduction

Early retirement translated to a major problem. Reduced income would not allow continued residency in the Washington, DC, region. Where would Linda, my soul mate and friend since age nine, live? Should we stay somewhere on the East Coast, perhaps a little house on the prairie, or return to our roots in Oregon?

What and where would our lives be after retirement? We discovered a publication listing caretaking positions that included a gamut of activities such as periodically starting vehicles to keep batteries charged to feeding domestic animals, even being a maid or butler. In exchange, the position might offer free housing, maybe more, possibly a small stipend. There were many choices, including a couple of jobs we thought of taking. In the end, we decided on our home turf where our parents were living their last years. We would live close to them, but not too close. We would help serve their needs including transportation to doctors and other help as needed.

The place we found to live was beyond our expectations, exceeding our dreams and enjoyment that we thought not possible. Our new location, remote and near the end of the grid, was surrounded with nature and reasonably close to our parents. It was perfect. All our friends, our parents and other relatives easily recognized our elation, our enthusiasm of living at Morgan Spring. In a short time, even our neighbors realized, I think, that the new kids on the block were a happy pair.

Our neighbors consisted of six families scattered in the woods. When rarely encountered, they usually had good news, a tidbit or more about our region including an occasional idea about living near the end of the grid. Living at Morgan Spring required splitting wood, lots of it, and being alert to our surroundings, being ready to be snowed in and not starve, and watchful for wildfires. One parent warned us to be especially on guard for possible quicksand and cougars. As young children, we had sometimes lived in remote regions and our loving parents had taught us how to live independent of restaurants and take-out. As adults, we had raised families, doctored the ill, worked in the woods in National Parks, and more. It did not take us long to learn most of the ways of Morgan Spring, but there was always more to know. What we did not know was answerable, especially from neighbors down the road.

Living at Morgan Spring was a chance in a lifetime. Living there inspired attempting to learn about its rich history, geologically and humanism. Morgan Spring inspired learning about and caring for the environment. Even personal creativity in the forms of visual art, writing, and composing music was inspired by the spirit that is Morgan Spring. What pleasure. Morgan Spring filled in any missing pieces that life brought. Morgan Spring was love.

Lessons learned from Morgan Spring and how its perfections treated us are experiences that we will never forget. Finding our Morgan Spring when my mate and I did was our great fortune. A different Morgan Spring must be out there, somewhere, for others to live. Everyone should look for their Morgan Spring and allow it to intertwine with one's own fabric. As for us, we are thankful we did not let something so crucial slip away and grateful to live to tell the story of Morgan Spring.

CHAPTER 1

First, A Word from the Nation's Capital

Linda and I could hardly wait to escape our crowded urban habitat for what we imagined Morgan Spring might offer. After a bittersweet departure from Smithsonian where I had worked and a westward journey, our arrival at Morgan Spring became a dream, but would or could we live in such a remote place? After our first day, the answer was clear. Morgan Spring would be home as long as possible. At the time, we had no idea what tomorrow might bring, but we were anxious to foster our new home and learn from its lessons.

Any explanation as to how Linda and I had the privilege to be students of Morgan Spring cannot be simple. Our earlier journeys, our past experience, influenced our perception of what was to shape the how and why we felt about Morgan Spring. Having Morgan Spring in our lives was an accident, but not exactly. The story begins sometime before we ever heard of Morgan Spring. The seed, the turning on the light bulb, the great idea that directed our thinking toward living at the edge of the grid might have begun sometime in our youth. When old enough to walk, we explored the out-of-doors as far as our little legs allowed. We did not plan Morgan Spring. We did not discuss our love away from four confining walls of our school room since we were too young to communicate our real desires. Although numerous parallels in our early history might suggest we were somehow genetically connected, we, thankfully, were not. Still, nature, as much if not more than human nurturing, was and is our good friend. Finally, at age nine, the birth of our meeting, we could share our thoughts. Of course, being kids, we did not share inner thoughts the way we do today. I wonder if either of us had an inkling about what the future might bring. It seems likely we did, even though we did not realize it at the time. I am not sure. The notion of a Morgan Spring might have been there, but at the time we had no suggestion of the power of such an idea. The idea evolved and did, to our good luck and amazement, become the nurturing place we called Morgan Spring. How? Perhaps analyzing such good fortune is for another day. Though we accept that every event in life influences other events, what guided us to Morgan Spring cannot be fully understood or known. What ever the reason, the history, the force, or luck, the nature of our nurturing during the long journey that brought us to this place was foundation for appreciating Morgan Spring.

Skipping a few decades of nature and nurture is currently prudent. Thus, the story might begin by informing that, in 1995, Linda and I were living in a 202 unit 10-story high-rise apartment in Arlington, Virginia. How that happened, the circumstances leading up to our mature lives, an explanation to fill in the previous 50 some years, all that is perhaps best set aside for another story. This story, the story of Morgan Spring, began while contemplating a change. So, in 1995, Linda practiced nursing in adjacent Alexandria while I worked across the Potomac River on the sixth floor of the National Museum of Natural History building in Washington, DC. The national headquarters of Hospice, an organization familiar to Linda who, as an accomplished Registered Nurse, helped start a hospice in Oklahoma City, was in the area. My primary doctor always told me to find a mate who is a registered nurse. He was correct, and having a nurse as your best friend cannot be beaten. And the museum could not be a better second muse. Even in the thick of the national capital, the even thicker traffic packing every byway, the politics and politicians, the expense of daily living in the region, the crowds and more, equaled a sum that made our lives happy. Could we be having too much learning and fun?

The seed setting the state for the fun began during my first visit to the Division of Birds in 1962. That was the year Linda and I graduated from high school, and the year I made a long trek around the United States in a used VW Beetle looking for as many species of birds as I could find. For about a week in October 1962, I rummaged through the Division of Birds library where I met former Secretary of Smithsonian and legendary ornithologist Dr. Alexander Wetmore and several of his colleagues. Fast-forward almost a decade. I returned to the candy store, not as a green visitor but as an only slightly less naive employee working in Smithsonian's Division of Birds for the Department of Interior's Biological Survey. The place, the concept, it all made me feel both old and at the same time young. Actually, I was a babe in the woods, but eager to learn and contribute. Much about my youth and my time at the museum is chronicled in my earlier book, *Rogue Birder*.

After my years of joyful work in the Division, Linda joined me. The glow of museum life surprised her due to the dedication happily practiced by the pool of so many people surrounded by the disparate politicians and lobbyist. Museum folk also stood out visually from most government employees, the IRS, Commerce, and other employees shackled by mundane dress codes. Staff at Smithsonian wore everything from t-shirts and shorts to ties and jackets, skirts or pants, and that is just in the summer. Lab coats are rare. During winter, anything from mukluks to dress shoes was just fine. I recall George Watson, principal consultant on the first edition of the National Geographic field guide, wearing wingtips to Birds. My footwear of choice came down to sandals in the summer and boots or loafers in winter. Flannel tops, sweaters and denim bottoms were cold-weather coverings. Life at the museum was nourishing, occupying most waking hours and inviting, whether on a regular workday or a holiday. Except for a few hours late at night and very early morning, someone, often me, was soaking in birds at the museum. The Division of Birds was open to employees 24–7, and it was hard to resist.

In a blink of an eye, new changes were presenting themselves with more questions that eroded some of the lure of working at the museum. Could we have more fun away from the museum? Could we leave? We loved Washington, DC, the city on the river. The region, full of history and culture was home to many friends and invaluable opportunities. Not so many years ago, leaving the National Museum of Natural History was incongruous. The museum is a bastion of scientific thinking, a place for leaders in their field, a working home of countless discovers of ideas, and contributors to an enviable bulwark of literature documenting their findings. I was darned lucky to be a small part of that. Regardless, certain crucial events would soon unfold that would catapult us westward. Beginning in 1995, an idea surfaced. The government was offering early retirement. The thought of retiring was never entertained before Linda and I reunited after a more than three-decade hiatus. No, we had not been together for the last way-too-many-years, although we secretly hoped of running into one another during one of many of our separate pilgrimages to visit our respective parents living in the Rogue Valley in Oregon. During the last three plus decades, our aging shyness and being married to different people at different times prevented direct contact. Life kept using up our good years. We did not directly communicate until meeting following our 25th high school reunion. Sparks were still there. Finally, a long-distance phone call reignited an unstoppable flame that began with our first childhood impressions of each other. At least, our good years

were not over yet. Linda and I realized our time together was and is precious. Early retirement meant more quality time to share. Of course, we had
to be practical and asked, would taking an early retirement provide enough
income to afford the time together?

While thinking of retirement, the government shut down because the
policians could not pass a budget. That had happened other years during my
career, but the duration of the current closure was longer. Such a circum-
stance is not a good thing, but for Linda and me, the shutdown was more
than inspirational.

And then it snowed. And it snowed some more. Lots of snow! So
much snow accumulated that not only was it impossible to get to and from
work, it was not possible to travel to most anywhere else. We had to walk
to the grocery store. Sidewalks were buried. The mail barely made it to our
high-rise. Luckily, the lights and heat stayed on. What a time to cultivate an
idea.

CHAPTER 2

Turning the Corner

Although retirement was definitely inevitable, we had not decided where we might relocate. Should we move to some rural setting? If that was our destination, what then would be our employment opportunities should we need them, access to libraries, and, of course, the basics, a decent grocery store and, just in case, medical care. We opted for something to take us away from metropolitan living to some place where we could reconnect with nature. Our main concern was to find a place where we could have more time together and less time with the maddening crowds of city living. A rural setting was definitely a prerequisite to the future. We discovered people were looking for help at a fish hatchery in the Appalachians in North Carolina, a couple of organic gardeners, one in Michigan and one in northern Georgia, needed hands and offered a free place to live in return. There was also the Jack and Jill of all trades needed at different places, one in Vermont, one in Texas, and another in Montana. As time for retirement was closing in, we ruled out any eastern location. Those long hot and humid summers and more than annoying chiggers in Georgia, even outside the Washington, DC, beltway, did not cajole a favorable response. On the other hand, Montana sounded good until we acknowledged that we were not Jacks or Jills of all trades. Would it be some place in our home state of Oregon?

Exploring the possibilities began and in about two months prior to retirement, Linda and I flew west. We had learned of several possible places to retire, some of which involved caretaking a piece of land in a few western states. One site was in eastern Oregon in a placed called Christmas Valley where we would be expected to start a pickup and other vehicles periodically to maintain their batteries and avoid motor seals from drying. We would also be expected to keep watch over the place and report any trouble such as fire or vandalism. Other expectations were minimal but just a bit worrisome, especially the one about being a security presence. A little research told us the region was hot in the summer and cold and snowy in winter, that it was essentially treeless and the local sand dunes attracted lots of ATV fanciers. We decided the weather was not a too serious impediment, but noisy ATVs and no trees was a clear reason for taking Christmas Valley off of our list. After ruling out of other potential sites, we were beginning to shave down our short-list to dangerously few choices. Of course, our post-retirement locality did not have to be in Oregon. Our home was with each other regardless of location, but a roof and some walls somewhere would be welcome.

We had an offer as caretakers and consultants with the US Forest Service in the Columbia River Gorge at the boundary of Oregon and Washington. The offer included free lodging at one of two locations. One abode sat in the fierce and almost constant wind blowing along the shore of the river and through the cracks in the walls. The other residence was away from the wind but only a few car lengths from a busy Interstate highway. Noise levels seemed to approach those near a jet runway. Any birds that might have been around the substantial house and bird-worthy grounds were invisible and certainly inaudible. Still, the offer of free lodging was momentarily enticing. The Forest Service staff meant well, but free versus loud decibels banging our eardrums or piercing wind only local wind-surfers could love were not that welcoming. The payback for free rent was considerable. It would probably be a 40-hour grind and then some. The Forest Service's ambitious proposal included devising and operating an interpretive program in the Columbia River Gorge, an area approaching 300,000 acres. Linda and I had worked all of our adult lives, worked as teenagers, worked during college, and worked well over the forty hours per week during the last three decades. We were ready for a reprieve. Besides, why interrupt our ongoing honeymoon? We told the welcoming staff we would consider their proposition, but as we drove away, we doubted we would be residents in the Columbia Gorge.

Once back in the southwestern part of the state and close to our parents, we began scanning the local newspaper for a place to live. Every house and apartment hunter knows that, besides size, location, safety, and cleanliness, the place has to feel right. We visited and rejected several prospective properties. We tried to ignore our desperation, but time was running out, both for our western stay, and the date of retirement.

Three days before we would have to return to our eastern apartment and respective jobs, we spied a small ad in the newspaper that sounded enticing. A person on the other end of a phone call provided directions and an invitation to check out what the promising ad described. The location of the property seemed to be rural enough for our taste. We drove and drove, with ridge after ridge appearing in our rear-view mirror. This was new territory. Our final turn was just as described when we phoned about the place. "Watch on your left for a large wooden sign with the address painted in red." There, leaning from a large splintery fence post was the dusty sign with five, not one, two or three and certainly not four, numbers indicating the address. The five digits told us were in the country. Somewhere beyond that sign and up a narrow driveway was our destination. Was the steep gravely driveway even passable? Of course, it had to be. Linda and I found what we instantly knew was to be our new home. Morgan Spring felt exactly right.

The first look at our future home, the house at Morgan Spring.

We flew back to Washington, DC, and for the next three months, we prepared to relocate across the continent. We had taken pictures of our new home to remind us that we would not be hearing sirens, jets, jackhammers, and the general roar from thousands and thousands of people. We also had a photocopy of the floor layout of the dwelling and began making plans about furniture placement, what might go in each closet, and imagining being there. During our brief inspection of Morgan Spring we realized we would be almost engulfed by nature. Morgan Spring would be a treat and we wondered what wildlife might be sharing our new home. What kinds of birds would be nesting there? We heard Western Tanagers and Cassin's Vireos singing. The vireo was known as Solitary Vireo when we moved to

Morgan Spring. As any good birder would practice, Linda and I had our binoculars at the ready and observed Steller's Jays noisily dancing from branch to branch on nearby trees and saw a Northern Flicker calling from a bare perch while a Red-tailed Hawk sailed over the meadow adjacent to our prospective home. Would there be juncos, Golden-crowned Sparrows, and more visit in the winter?

There was much to do before enjoying nature at Morgan Spring. Finding what we hoped would be a reasonably priced moving company was no easy task, but Linda skillfully negotiated the deal. Weekends and evenings were spent gathering boxes for the big move. Boxes from the local CD shop were helpful although some of the best boxes came from liquor stores. Of course, larger boxes, smaller ones, boxes of all kinds, sizes, and shapes were needed to move our accumulated belongings. Moving is a good time to pare down, to get rid of stuff. We had too much stuff. At least we did not have so much stuff that we had to rent a storage unit for any overflowing stuff. Nonetheless, we had way too much stuff. George Carlin was correct. We all have too much stuff, and the longer we live in one place the more stuff we collect. Gradually, 1,000 square feet of living space becomes crowded. We wonder how much stuff is need by two people living in a house with floor space exceeding 3,000 square feet. Not that many people need space for ballroom dancing.

Our apartment in Arlington was smaller than the house that awaited us at Morgan Spring. We did not want our new home cluttered, so we began paring down by getting rid of some of our present clutter. That did not mean books, twenty pounds of cherished LPs, but it did mean getting rid of clothes not worn since bell-bottom days, kitchen pots not used in years, and related items collecting dust since Watergate. We also decided, partly because of what commercial movers charge, to sell our hide-a-bed couch, which was in the hernia weight class. The stereo system I purchased a few years before entertaining any promise of Linda and I reuniting cost as much as a mid-sized sedan. It had to make the trip to Morgan Spring. Of course, the most integral part of any stereo is music, and there were 100s of CDs. The collection included token recordings of the Beatles, King Crimson, and some good jazz, but most were of classical composers primarily from the Romantic Era. There were even a couple of recently purchased CDs from the local Tower Records of recordings by a couple of composers we heard for the first time at the Kennedy Center. Besides the music and memories of the Washington, DC region, most of the apartment's furniture would go to Morgan Spring, including our dining room table where on Sundays we listened to the string quartets of Shostakovich and placed raisins on the outside window sill for the local Northern Mockingbirds.

Right up to moving day, we were packing and sealing boxes with miles of fiber tape. Well into the nights was heard the rattling of packing material, mostly waded paper and sometimes those clear packing bubbles, the ones it's hard to resist popping no matter how tired you are. After stuffing a box, we shared the ripping noise of the fiber tape reeling off its roll. Anyone passing down our hall would then have heard the felt-tip marker "squeak-squeak" on a label placed on the sides of a box that indicated what was inside and what room the boxes should be moved. We later discovered that our movers were not much into reading since kitchen boxes ended up in the bathroom and bedroom boxes were stacked in the living room.

Packing occupied a huge portion of our nights and weekends, with some reprieve when we both continued to go to our respective places of employment. There is no such thing, as far as we know, as leave or time off for moving. Nurse Linda was out the apartment door well before I sleepily thought about Constitution Avenue or birds. My working hours at the museum focused heavily on my departure, including trying to tie down any loose ends. I did not want to leave any problems for someone else to clean up.

Retirement day from the museum turned out to be an event. A huge party was thrown by friends from the Division of Birds, the library, archives, and other departments. There was sadness at the end of the last day at the museum. Leaving, we say we will write or phone. I think we will. The concept of email, something most of us at the museum had little exposure to because budgets kept the staff always back in time, might help keep us in contact. Of course, getting online at Morgan Spring was not at the moment on our minds. Driving the thousands of mile to Morgan Spring was very much our near future.

According to plan, we said good-bye to our close personal friends from years of support, laughter, and love, and left our little apartment for the west one day after Labor Day. The traffic was light after the last summer holiday. The car, a mid-sized sedan, was heavy after loading the trunk and back seat to the brim. We sped from the urban sprawl, westward and away from the Potomac River, ascended the foothills east of the Appalachian Mountains and turned southward through the Shenandoah Valley. We were still on familiar ground as we rolled into the sleepy little college town just at the edge of Virginia and Tennessee where my daughter was living. She asked about the retirement party. My daughter knew most everyone there from her many childhood visits with her old dad. The next day, Linda and I rushed through Nashville and onward, westward ho, to an unforgettable night in East Memphis. Elvis may have liked it but where we wound up staying was a motel not fit for any king. With the next morning's sunrise at our backs, we bolted away, reaching our next stop, Oklahoma City, where we visited our Swedish friends, and Linda's son. The home-grown terrorist bombing had occurred just a little over a year ago. I recalled that day by a phone conversation with Linda. Since TVs and radios are rarely if ever played at the museum and I had not turned on the news once I got home, I was completely unaware of the horrific event. Early in the conversation, Linda told me she was alright. She must have detected my clueless tone and told me what had transpired. Linda's firsthand memories of the aftermath and nursing triage were not welcome recollections.

Leaving the flat terrain of Oklahoma, we remained true to our passions for birds by maintaining a list of birds seen along the route. Our trip list began with a Turkey Vulture in Virginia. Was that a bad sign? Perhaps not, since our second roadside species was Mourning Dove, a bird of peace and well-being. Ironically, that species is also a game bird in many states and is often blasted from the sky. Anyway, as we motored ever westward, we finally spied a Great Egret in Arkansas and Scissor-tailed Flycatcher in Oklahoma where we saw our last Eastern Bluebird. We knew Western Bluebirds would be a summer bird at Morgan Spring.

We motored across the Great Plains according the plan that the moving truck should be a day or so behind us and our anticipated arrival at Morgan Spring. That should allow us to detour on our transcontinental journey for some scenery. After dodging cars in Denver and reminiscing about working on birds in the Pawnee National Grassland and at the collection in Denver and Ft. Collins, we drove into Cheyenne, Wyoming, for the night. The next day, we toured part of Yellowstone National Park from the southern boundary north to Old Faithful. It had been years since either of us had been in the park. My last visit was during five glorious days in Yellowstone in mid-June 1962 while on a nine-month birding trip during my days of portraying a young Danny McSkunk, all wet behind the ears, fresh high school graduate. It was bone-chilling cold during that spring when there were trees everywhere. I did not have to view fire-ravaged scenes left in 1988. That was when a total of 793,000 trees once forming a lush carpet of green conifers growing innocently on 1.2 million acres in and around the park were, according to one report, "scorched" by 42 lightning-caused fires and 9 human-caused fires. The region that burned is an area larger than Rhode Island. The fire was one of 28 of the 50 fires in Yellowstone National Park that that were allowed to burn that year and ended up costing tax payers $120 million. Periodic wildfires occurring in Yellowstone from 1881 to 1987 have been relatively small compared to the very noticeable fire in 1988. Eight years later, Linda and I observe some of vegetation is reclaiming the past and gradually changing what is mostly a stunted and bare landscape.

That evening, Linda and I splurged by spending a night at an inn on the shore of Jackson Lake. The youngest range in the Rocky Mountains, the barren crags of the Tetons, our favorite range of mountains, loomed magnificently in the sharp background of rocky peaks, the lake, and green conifers. This was a far cry from East Memphis. We slept peacefully and woke with the sunrise warming the granite cliffs towering above. Before departing Grand Teton National Park, we visited Jenny Lake, a small emerald jewel even closer to the rough cliffs of the Teton Mountains. I first saw the lake during the 1962 birding tour. Jenny Lake and the stupendous mountains offer the same awesome sights seen with disbelief so many years earlier. It feels good to witness the indelibleness of the scene, to know that the Park Service is preserving such awesome beauty.

We motored through Jackson Hole, Wyoming, saw a western species of a blackbird, Brewer's Blackbird, and, with the Grand Tetons behind us, we began the trek across southern Idaho. Roadside birds added to our list, with Prairie Falcon being the highlight. Along the route, we checked in with the moving company. We were told by a dispatcher that we were still ahead of them, but actually, we were not. What we did not know could not hurt us and we continued to believe our stuff would arrive at Morgan Spring after we would. Even if not, we could drive only so fast. Soon leaving Idaho behind, we entered arid eastern Oregon where a Golden Eagle, California Quails and Sage Thrashers were welcoming us. Our route took us through Burns, just north of the famous Malheur National Wildlife Refuge. My last time there was early June in 1962. September would have been an interesting time to visit the refuge but we pushed on to Lakeview in south-central Oregon.

Looking back, our trip list of birds beginning in Virginia with Turkey Vulture also included Blue Jay, Carolina Chickadee Northern Cardinal, and Chimney Swift. Somewhere in the country's mid-section we stopped seeing the eastern swifts and began looking for Vaux's Swift. We even picked up a couple species of owls along the way, but they were the easier-to-find Barred and Great Horned owls. Black-billed Magpie and Ferruginous Hawk foraged in Wyoming. East of the Cascades in Oregon, we identified Clark's Grebe and observed another grebe that probably was a Western Grebe. At that point in time and space, traveling onward was a greater urgency than a large trip list. The need to reach our new home, Morgan Spring, became our paramount goal.

How many more hours will we need to complete the journey? Tired that night in Lakeview, we told ourselves it is not much longer.

CHAPTER 3

The Arrival

Anniversaries are times for celebration, for remembering an event that was life-changing. Everyone hopes the remembrance is of a happy time, the beginning of joy and enriching experiences. Our 13 September 1996 arrival is one of those wonderful beginnings, the day we arrived at Morgan Spring, the day beginning with our final approach to our new home in the Cascades of southwestern Oregon.

The bright morning of that day was uneventful as we departed Lakeview, Oregon, a little town near the high desert and perched in the edge of the mountains just a few hours east of Morgan Spring. Lakeview, once a logging town, is now a picturesque stop along the route known as "Winnemucca to the Sea." The Winnemucca part refers to a town in northern Nevada. The route is the one to take should you live in northern Nevada and yearn for the Pacific Ocean, aka "the Sea." A visitor might continue west to the smell of salt water or they might pass through Lakeview to drive northward on the pavement to Malheur National Wildlife Refuge or travel south into northeastern California where the highway crosses the Applegate Trail of the mid-1800s. California was but a few miles away, but Malheur refuge would require close to 140 miles of driving. It takes over two hours of stern driving northeastward to reach Malheur and about 5 hours west to view the sea. We are not certain of the actual miles remote Lakeview is from everything since travel in the West is most often measured by time, not distance. Fortunately, our westward time behind the wheel today would only be slightly over three hours.

The morning began with a crisp blue sky, but as we rolled onward, the sun soon dimmed in a sky awash with gray clouds. We traveled west on Oregon State Highway 140, first passing the flats outside Lakeview, and then through conifer bedecked slopes and up and over Quartz Mountain Pass. The meandering highway eventually spilled into a valley of marshes along the Sprague River and again entered mountains of pine and fir. The hard pavement eventually took us through a brownish barren dotted with smaller trees and chaparral on rounded hills, and finally the road straightened on flatter terrain to Klamath Falls. This was the first town in almost 100 miles with more than one traffic light. Of course, that is not necessarily a positive condition since our destination would be many welcome miles from traffic lights and the hordes of people needing them.

Our route today left behind the browns and sullen yellows of grasses dried from the long and hot summer of rainless days and took us beyond the parched coniferous trees of second-growth, remnants of long past virgin forests. Winter rain and snow would soon whet the appetites of the grasses, chaparral, a smattering of junipers and thirsty pines. On we sped. Large tracts of agricultural land, now harvested, were yellowing in the wait for winter. West of Klamath Falls, we entered the lush green coniferous forest seen standing tall along the twisting highway climbing over the crest of the Cascade Mountains. The height of the mountains, at least 4,000 to 5,000 feet in elevation, causes moisture-laden clouds sweeping from the Pacific to move higher and higher until the upper air's coolness causes rain or snow to fall. In the Pacific Northwest, precipitation generally occurs from about September, but usually from October to May. Rain is a rare commodity during summer. Eastern Oregon gets much less precipitation during winter because the Cascades create a rain shadow. The summit of the Cascades marks a major biological difference between the west and east slopes of the mountains. Eastern Oregon (as well as eastern Washington and northeastern California) is relatively drier than western Oregon. Once we arrived on the west slope of the Cascades, the lushness of the forest deepens, with Douglas fir and true firs dominating the pines that were more common to the eastern slope.

Geographic changes in the amounts and timing of precipitation, temperature, and distribution of plants and more that ecologists love to study also reveal differences in the distribution of birds. Today, crossing the Cascade Mountains, we leave behind the range of Brewer's Sparrow and, in the western valley beyond, we should find California Towhee. Our journey toward Morgan Spring enters the western segment of the breeding range of Nashville Warbler. Again, the ecology of eastern North America is unlike that of the western part of the continent, and the two populations of Nashville Warbler are allopatric, that is, the breeding ranges of the two are not connected. Eastern and western Nashville Warblers are barely discernible in the field, but they sing different tunes. Have the two populations responded to their two respective environments and succumbed to evolution? Have they changed their genes? We briefly entertained an idea—are there actually two species hidden in what we collect under the name Nashville Warbler?

We peered down the asphalt meandering around ridges and skirted a lake or two. We were nearing our destination. This was the final leg of our journey from our home in Arlington, Virginia, to our new home at Morgan Spring. We sped onward, not stopping to listen to the sound of the September wind humming like no other sound as it passes around the billions and billions of pine and fir needles. We counted on hearing that unique soothing sound at Morgan Spring sometime before sundown.

The three hour drive from Lakeview to Morgan Spring seemed interminably long. Our aging day was becoming one of those drizzly times when our windshield wipers' noisily skittered across an almost dry glass one moment and then silently glided across wetness a second later. The highway spilled us from the 5,000-foot summit of the Cascade Mountains westward and into the Rogue Valley, a wide valley ranging in elevation from about 2,000 feet to around 1,300 feet. The cool, almost cold temperature, with a fresh clean dampness today does not interrupt the scene as we soon travel back roads to bypass the bright lights and bustle of Medford. We would go to that big city later but only when we needed supplies to stay up at Morgan Spring. We stopped less than forty minutes from Morgan Spring to phone my father who lived south of the heavily peopled Medford, the principal city of the Rogue Valley. The ubiquitous cell phone had yet to become a member of our family. The call to my father was to let him know that we would not be stopping by as earlier planned. He was alone; my mother was visiting her sister in Arkansas, and he could have used the company. We told him we would see him next week. He masked the disappointment that I heard in his voice as he welcomed us to Oregon. It was late afternoon. The sun was now low in the west and we did not want to arrive at Morgan Spring in darkness.

Thick moisture-laden clouds filtered the waning afternoon sun so much that at times it would have caused birds to scurry for a dry perch to roost. It is as if dusk occurs three times but three times is interrupted by slight revelations of bright silvery linings from a sun not wanting to give up the day. The windshield wipers swiped away reappearing lumps of sprinkles and heavy cool humidity condensing on the glass. Sunset was around the corner. The headlights lit the way as we turned onto a road that would take us to yet another road before driving up to Morgan Spring.

Our next to the last road to travel, Oregon State Highway 62, fondly known as Crater Lake Highway, snaked northeastward and upstream along the Rogue River. The wide valley behind us, foothills of the Cascades invaded the banks of the cold river and soon we found our final road of the long transcontinental drive. Our final route is on Elk Creek Road, a county road up Elk Creek, an 85,363 acre watershed of which about two-thirds is owned by the Forest Service, Bureau of Land Management (BLM), and Oregon State. The watershed is about twice as large as Washington, DC, and thankfully without traffic circles and motorcades. Elk Creek Road was at first every bit as good as, and even somewhat better than, state highway 62 connecting near Medford. We began our ascent up Elk Creek a little over 1,600 feet in elevation, just yards from the confluence of the Rogue River and Elk Creek. Once around a few miles of attention-grabbing curves above the creek, the road narrowed through a valley occupied by small ranches and a few houses probably owned mostly by commuters. For the next couple of miles, the creek and surrounding ridges almost merge. Here, huge Douglas firs tower over the creek and the road long ago protected by prohibitions of cutting trees in certain riparian areas. There are no shadows at this late hour. The heavily falling clean mist drenched the dark overhanging green bows of the trees and the little road less traveled.

There is enough daylight to view a sudden turn where the pavement crossed Elk Creek, and in a steep and windy path, wound upward on the side of what Linda and I called Button Creek Canyon. Its narrow length was short. On one side of the road was a steep cliff about 30 feet above, on the other was the canyon, replete with rock walls at least 30 feet down to an unseen creek flowing just below a waterfall of about the same height. The bare rock and precipice to the creek reminded us of a scene from some old western, especially when imagining the road without asphalt. Horses pulling a stagecoach struggle up the hill as the driver snaps his whip in the dry dust of summer. Stiff wagon wheel spokes strain from shattering as the coach rattles upward, all the while thoroughly shaking the bones of its passengers. Today, the paved section of road from the bridge crossing Elk Creek passes the waterfall and continues up Button Creek, named for elk buttons. Our route upstream from the top of the falls was wider than the older asphalt. There was even a center line in the last paved section of Elk Creek Road, which, because of the steepness and blind corners, was a good thing.

By now, we were becoming weary of sitting in a car for miles and miles, and more anxious to complete our journey. Another stretch, this time on the lightly graveled Elk Creek Road, crunched under the tires that, until that time, had barely encountered a graveled road. Our upward route was wide enough for two vehicles to pass if they slowed their speed. No one was on the road. On the way up Button Creek, we drove northeast, passing two driveways belonging to our neighbors. We could barely see their houses. We gained around 400 feet in elevation over 1.5 miles from the road above Button Creek Canyon to our driveway. From Elk Creek Road, our car lurched up for 250 yards and another 100 feet in elevation on the strictly one-lane dirt-and-gravel driveway. Our final destination was just short of 2,500 feet in elevation. Since the Potomac River, which borders Arlington and Washington, DC, is tidal, we would be living almost a half-mile higher in our new home. Our first thought about our elevation was how lucky we were that snow had not covered these last few yards of our long journey. The narrow driveway was bare, and our heavily packed sedan had to shift into its lowest gear for the climb from the road to the house. Excited and relieved, Linda and I took in the driveway's every turn to memorialize our drive home.

The low part of the driveway did not permit seeing our house. The tires of the front-wheel-drive slipped now and then on the steep ascent through scattered oaks and occasional ruddy-barked madrone. By now, the dimming light caused most colors to lose their definition we had seen on our maiden voyage last summer. In the growing darkness, green was becoming almost a shade of dark gray. Our new home was not visible until we exited a cathedral-like section of thick and straight dark trunks of conifers. The trees, Douglas fir and ponderosa pine, flanked the driveway's very edge. There, the driveway is level. On one side of the level part, a bank rises about three to four feet high. The other side drops off perpendicularly down to what we dubbed Morgan Creek sitting about 50 feet below. A bed of long pine needles covering the level section dampened the sound of our car to near silence. There was no room for any driving error.

The top end of the "cathedral" abruptly opened. Dim light filled in a few details, including a view of the woods surrounding Morgan Spring, the trees around the spring and our source of water, a meadow, and, by taking a hairpin turn hard to the right, the welcome outline of the house. Our home. Morgan Spring at last.

Unfolding ourselves from the car after the long drive, we were happy to turn the key and be inside our little abode. We were also relieved that the electricity was working, something we were to discover later was not always functioning. Since we had been told we were geographically ahead of the movers, we expected empty rooms. Sleeping bags in the back of the car would be just fine for a couple of days. However, the moving van's schedule was not behind our agenda. Although the giant moving van had been unable to negotiate the driveway, a much smaller truck had to have brought our belonging to our new home. Even so, a few small trees bordering the driveway had some of their bark freshly scrapped away. Linda and I were most grateful to Linda's mother, who lived in the Rogue Valley. In advance of a Murphy's Law situation, we had mailed her a key, which allowed the mover's access to our home. Linda's mother also purchased an electric stove and refrigerator on our behalf. Both appliances were in position and faced toward the meadow beyond the sliding glass door. The fronts of the two items were black, the color we requested since wildlife would less likely spot us walking in front of the appliances. Camouflage appliances were not available.

Boxes and furniture covered the floor of almost every room.

Linda and I opened the front door and were confronted by our furniture and dozens of boxes stacked on almost every square foot of floor. Although we had labeled the room destination each container ought to end up in, the boxes were everywhere. The movers already had our not small sum of money and more or less dumped 100-plus boxes, sprinkling them in helter-skelter fashion in each room. It was chaotic, and it was our chaos to begin dealing with tomorrow since, to paraphrase George Carlin forecasting the weather after sunset, it is dark at night.

Looking out the large east window on our arrival day gave us a view of a meadow stretching upward; its summit over 100 feet above the house. Had the meadow not turned to its fall color of pale straw, it would not have been visible in the near dark sky. The meadow, which someone said was a natural feature and which occupies around 11 acres, is shaped like a giant goose or duck, with the head at the top and it breast closer to the house. Except for water overflowing from Morgan Spring during winter and early spring, grasses of the meadow were at the mercy of the natural climate. There was a barely visible watering hole, actually an old freezer without its lid, that receives a trickle from a small spring a few yards into the woods near the top of the meadow. Gently sloped, except near the far section, the meadow curved around a peninsula of trees that surround Morgan Spring not far from the bottom of the meadow. The lowest part of the meadow is beyond the kitchen window. Fencing marked the boundary of the meadow, with its easternmost fence above the slope near Alder Creek. For those that might be confused, and I apologize for that, Alder Creek flows nearby before joining Button Creek. Beyond are trees and the ridges of forests. We are only 250 yards from the boundary of the national forest. That might have been true at the time, but I am getting ahead of myself. Meanwhile, in the darkening view, several unsuspecting turkeys walking along the edge of the meadow froze in position. They had seen us, and we had seen them. These truly wild birds, officially known in the annals of ornithology and birders as Wild Turkey may not have been too happy to see us. Linda and I may have interupted their last forage for food prior to going to roost and would encounter these large birds many more times.

We managed to find our bed among the boxes. Astonishingly, it was set up and in the correct room, but where were the sheets? We slept well that night, except, of course, for an unexpected sound at the back door.

CHAPTER 4

Day 1

Day one, 14 September 1996, was the day of a new beginning that started sometime after midnight when Linda and I managed to break away from a deep slumber. "What was that sound?" Every house has its creaks, groans, and pops, which are usually in tandem with changing temperature and humidity. The sound was not in tandem with anything we understood. It didn't sound like the sound of weather-induced expansion and contraction of a house. The sound seemed to be emanating from the back door, our new back door.

We had to investigate and relied on a faint star shine barely lighting our bedroom to begin our trek to the back door. The even darker adjoining hall between the bedroom and washroom separated us from the unidentified noise outside the back door. At least we were reasonably certain the sound was not originating from the inside surface of the trusty door. Negotiating the piles of cardboard boxes, potential land mines to a bare toe, we finally locate a window. Outside that window and to the right, a few feet away from the back door, stood a black bear. It was one of an estimated 12,000 to 13,000 bruins in western Oregon. Ever alert, our bear must have seen our surprised faces peering out a small window next to the door. Without ceremony, the adult bear nonchalantly loped away from the house and out into the meadow. A smaller shadow followed the larger dark parent. The adult and cub increased their pace as they walked hurriedly towards the pitch black of the trees. They traveled in the direction of the spring seeping its clear liquid about 500 yards northeast of the house.

We would hear other night sounds while at Morgan Spring. Almost all were welcome sounds, including the bear. We didn't care much for the unnatural man-made sounds we would hear during future nights. The noise from humans was rare after sundown, but even a vehicle motor faintly accompanying the crunch of gravel under the tires on the unseen road below was annoying. The occasional foraging mammal padding under an open bedroom window kept us alert with curiosity but never fear or anxiety. At last, no more fleets of rushing car tires humming on busy streets, no more sirens blasting from emergency vehicles, or other man-made cries in daylight and in the darkness. Sounds from Morgan Spring were welcome sounds. The sighing of the wind in the trees' needles, the quiet moon, singing frogs, the bugling of elk calling each other, or coyotes and screech-owls that would later lull us to sleep.

Beyond the nightly interlude of the visiting bears, scratching and all, was the morning. The air was cool and heavy from the misty rain that fell most of the night and continued into the day. Large drops gathered on the long needles of nearby ponderosa pines standing tall as if to guard our home. After running down the needles, the water drops fell, only to spatter in all directions. The sound of their life-giving splashes lightly filled the crisp fall air. We also heard drops splashing on the roof as they let go of pines hanging over the house. The sound caressed our senses. Each drop, every minute, and throughout the day made us aware we are privileged to experience nature. Of course, we realized that our new environment did not contain old-growth forests, that the ax and chainsaw had once left its mark here, but time had allowed a modicum of return of what might have been. For us, Morgan Spring offered degrees of naturalness far beyond our years of dwelling in urban torn environments. Holding on to each other, we celebrated the good fortune of residing at Morgan Spring.

We also were grateful for our dwelling. Except for the ample windows, the 1993 rectangular structure was covered by roughly hewn wooden siding. The brown painted surface was not something to rub up against but was wholly suitable for a remote house in the woods. The pale-colored composition roofing had a few long brownish pine needle bundles resting on its not terribly steep surface. We reasoned the pitch of the roof would have been steeper if great quantities of snow were expected. Two tall windows, each about eight feet in width, exposed the northerly and easterly sides of the house. Both bedrooms had two standard-sized windows each, while the kitchen, bathroom, and even the utility room had single windows. All the windows had white vinyl frames and each window was capable of being opened by sliding it horizontally. Just inside was the living room that opened, wall-less, to the kitchen. The sturdy front door opened to the living room. Almost directly opposite the front entrance was a door to a utility room barely large enough for a washer, dryer, and hot-water heater. Beyond those appliances was the back door, which was apparently bear-proof. There was little wall space between the east living room window and a glass sliding door at the boundary of the L-shaped kitchen. The bedrooms were past a closet and to the right. The master bedroom was about 12 X 13 feet in addition to a closet maybe eight feet wide, with its walls and ceiling painted off-white, as was the remaining interior of the house. A smaller second bedroom was, well, smaller. The single bathroom was adequate in size and actually larger than the one in our apartment back in Arlington. Storage closets abounded. The rooms, including the closets, added up to about 920 square feet. All but the front entrance-way, kitchen, utility room and bathroom was carpeted. It would not be a great problem keeping the country home floor clean, since we habitually removed our shoes or boots before entering most homes.

From the large and much appreciated window facing east, our eyes traveled up the meadow, over the surrounding trees and ridges beyond, and back to the meadow. The natural light of the sun plying its way through the opaque clouds revealed a straw-colored meadow with hints of greening from the fall rains. Only irrigated meadows and fields stay green during the rainless summers in Oregon. Our meadow was on its own during the dry season while at the mercy of the sun and without the benefit of water. Sometimes from September to October, bountiful rains begin to powder Oregon down to the roots of every plant. By this mid-September, our first September, the dead stems of the meadow were interspersed with a scattering of blades of green, but most of the meadow's grasses were prostrate from age and the summer drought. Soggy clouds beyond the meadow were hanging low over the ill-defined, although not distant, ridges some 800 feet above our home. The ridges not engulfed by low-lying clouds were under muted light and painted a grayish-blue. Further down the ridges, green, the color of life, gradually dominated the grayness, revealing the dark waxy leaves of distant madrone and a mixture of coniferous Douglas fir and pine growing up to the edge of the meadow. Closer to the house, we could see the depleted grass stems, their pale straw hue speckled with dark grays and blacks, the sign of microbes breaking them down to complete the life cycle. The smattering of new green grass spotting sections of the meadow lay low to the ground, ready for snow that would eventually follow the quenching rain.

It was difficult to rein in our eyes, to not stare out the window and wonder about what we could not see. It was so close, just through the window and beyond, we could almost feel the view, but first there was work to do. Regardless of tasks at hand, we managed to catch glimpses of four species of birds on our first full day at Morgan Spring. Three of the group of species were woodpeckers, including Northern Flicker, Hairy and Pileated woodpeckers. Perhaps three species of woodpeckers were to be expected. After all, our new home was in the woods.

The view from the large northern window framed an area wide enough for an average vehicle to turn a tight circle and graveled enough to prevent personal communication with the mud that would otherwise spin tires or be tracked indoors. The northern side of the gently sloped region ends abruptly over the driveway. A forest of trees looms high on the left just beyond a concrete slab poured for a garage soon to be built. The light, dimmed by thick wet clouds, revealed a green metal gate and a narrow lane aimed into yet more trees and slightly to the east, we viewed the edge of the meadow. Long brown needles, some exceeding six inches in length, dropped from overhanging ponderosa pines litter the edge of the rain-soaked gravel. Although evergreens, coniferous trees replace their needles and some of them fell on the car. The car. It sat on the left side of the picture window and it was loaded to the brim with what did not go on the moving truck. I slipped on a jacket and positioned the rear of the little sedan-that-could close to the front door. A covered concrete stoop at the front door kept me and the car's contents mostly dry. It took awhile to empty the crammed vehicle. We should have down-sized more.

Inside the windows, our foreground, within the walls of the house, were the boxes to unpack. They had not disappeared since yesterday. No magic elves had come during the night to unpack. Perhaps the bear scratching on the back door had scared them. The boxes had not moved, remaining stacked, jammed against walls, close to doorways, and generally impeding a steady gait. Walking had to be erratic—Monty Python style, a mix of two normal strides, a lunge to the right, a two-step to the left, two wobbles to the right, a waltz step, only backward, and frequent stops to avoid tipping over. That was just getting to the bathroom.

A bathroom is the first room to enter after a long night's sleep. It is possibly the most important room in a house because specific activities performed there are not generally possible elsewhere. It is the room, that in movies, the actors never run to upon waking. Actors apparently reabsorb whatever collected in their bladder during the night, or so we might believe. Our Morgan Spring abode has only one bathroom, much to the chagrin of some of our acquaintances and relatives who would later come calling. How is it possible that we could function with one bathroom? After all, it is the room of rooms.

Somehow, having one bathroom was not a problem, even when we had the rare overnight company. Somehow, our folks managed to raise a family of two or more tykes in a house with only one bathroom. Our growth was not stunted. How was it possible that a family could survive with one bathroom? Neither of us recalls peeing on ourselves, or worse. Maybe having one bathroom available is a problem today because of all those diuretics we soak up daily. Too much coffee, beer, soft drinks, and insufficient fiber seems to point to why people believe they need a second toilet. Of course, maybe we have become a society of poor planning?

Once inside the small but adequately sized bathroom, it became apparent that even the movers had been thoughtful by not scattering boxes on its floor. Perhaps it was not a selfless gesture. Perhaps they were planning for themselves. Regardless, the bare floor was a welcome result. I could go on about the room of rooms, but I will leave the rest to imagination.

Once fortified with long and longing looks out the windows and a good breakfast, we surveyed the boxscape. We also surveyed the landscape, although it was from inside our window. The great out of doors beckoned. Almost mesmerized by the lush panorama of coniferous trees and ridges half seen through the shifting mist of foggy clouds, we congratulated ourselves for the good fortune of this momentary view. Our scene from the house evolved in beauty every day, and we knew we were lucky to experience it.

Today, we were new to our meadow and trees that surrounded it and tree-covered above and below. What we saw and what might lie behind the next ridge, what kind of view might be seen from the summit of the peak to the right or to the left, what kinds of animals we might observe, and what to explore beyond was more than intriguing. Moreover, the sooner we unpacked the sooner we could explore Morgan Spring country. We took time to grab a handy pair of binoculars to confirm what we guessed was a Say's Phoebe on a distant fence wire. Adding to our furtive observations of woodpeckers was a kestrel on patrol and Steller's Jays fussing close by. The woodpeckers reminded me of a project that is neatly hidden in one of the too many boxes waiting to be unpacked.

That phoebe was just the beginning of our birding at Morgan Spring, along with the first of many regular visiting Wild Turkeys. That was our first bird when we ventured up the driveway upon our arrival on 13 September. We would add more and more species, including in a couple days later when we saw Golden-crowned Kinglets that did not notice a Red-tailed Hawk and four Turkey Vultures soaring over the meadow. Our first day at Morgan Spring did not include a Northern Goshawk chasing a small unidentified bird that graced us a week later. It was September, and we believe the goshawk was a migrant. A couple of days after Day 1, we hung a hummingbird feeder outside the northern living room window. A male Rufous Hummingbird took a few sips before disappearing to its winter range south of the border. A few days later, we realized the Morgan Spring region is host to many juncos, Spotted Towhees, Golden and White-crowned sparrows,

Chestnut-backed Chickadees, and Red-breasted Nuthatches. We can hear them by stepping just out the door and see them from our windows. Just above Morgan Spring, the spring, was a covey of at least eight Mountain Quail. It was time to think about more bird feeders and wonder what we might lure our way.

CHAPTER 5

Why Here?

Our initial unpacking, the important part when toothbrushes and toilet paper are located, took a while. Meanwhile, a couple of bags of groceries picked up at the closest grocery, only 20 miles away, would keep us from starving. In the meantime, we began thinking of how to describe where we lived. Even before we could unpack, we had been asked why we would want to live in such a remote location. That might be difficult to explain. Driving directions would explain where we live, but Morgan Spring is more than a location. Someone is going to ask the why question. Why do you want to live so far from shopping areas, so far from whoever is asking, and really, why? It is a state of mind, but so much more. Could we explain why we lived at Morgan Spring?

People once asked, "Where are you planning to live?"

"Up Elk Creek." A smile usually accompanied our answer. The smile usually translated somewhere from wry to contrived, one almost showing teeth that fades into a look of puzzlement, fortunately, none like Jack in "The Shining," and a smile that seemed to say "how wonderful, but really?"

After our visitor fumbles their smile, the easier question comes.

"How far?"

Gleefully, we would answer, "About 15 miles from the main highway, not far from the end of the grid."

For us, where we lived was a badge of courage. It seemed natural, but not to those we decided were outsiders, the lowland sibling, the valley cousin or parent that came to see for themselves. Until actually witnessing our new home, we would hear, "Morgan Spring, where is that?" You could almost hear them scratch their heads over the phone. Morgan Spring was on some maps, but were we actually talking about water bubbling out of the ground or a state of mind?

Another question related to the name of the spring. Morgan. Our first thought was that the word "Morgan" was a misspelling of "Morgan's" that would indicate someone named the spring in honor of a person named Morgan. We had dismissed the idea the spring was named for a pirate or a type of horse that might have once roamed the meadow and drank water from the spring. We discovered a Harvey F. Morgan once owned the property encompassing the spring and it seems reasonable to surmise he or someone knowing him named the spring Morgan Spring. Mr. Morgan did not live at Morgan Spring, but somewhere east of Squaw Prairie, where he left decades of refuse to be cleaned up by the new owners in 1987. Although thankful all that refuse was not dumped near our spring, we continued to wonder about the etymology of Morgan Spring. Perhaps our spring was named in honor of some other person named Morgan. Maybe it was named Morgan because, after all, the spring was probably once part territory of the local native people and in typical pirate fashion, the spring was taken from them. The spring was pirated from the original owners. Yeah, that is it, maybe. In the meantime, we vowed to accept the term Morgan for our spring. From a map published in 1970, land owned by Harvey Morgan was surrounded by the Forest Service and properties labeled as belonging to the ELC Corporation and T & L Incorporation. Who these businesses were was not pursued although ELC surely is an abbreviation referring to Elk Lumber Company formed in 1946. Linda and I heard a few stories about Harvey Morgan, but that may be another story for someone to tell.

Telling someone we lived at Morgan Spring, regardless of the origin of the name, was too much detail. Sometimes we would say we lived near the end of Elk Creek Road, or that we were closer to Crater Lake National Park than to Medford, the only national park and principal city of southwestern Oregon. Actually, all of the above is accurate, although not completely. We tried to describe we were living away from ambulances hurrying to a hospital, fire trucks blaring their rough horns at intersections, and police rushing to the next crime. All of that was the soundscape on the Virginia street named Quincy running between us and the Arlington County Library where we once voted and read, and was reasonably near the museum where I worked. We were living without the deep whirling sound of early morning street sweepers, those Zamboni-like vacuums of pavement that attempted to void the crammed habitat of its human detritus. We were looking for and found clean air, crisp stars not dimmed to invisibility by artificial lighting, and precious silence interrupted only by our breathing, a confident cricket, and perhaps the reassuring trill of a screech-owl.

We lived in north-central Jackson County, Oregon. Our driving directions might add that the road climbs abruptly to follow the north side of the tributary called Button Creek. If the directions are followed, we could be found a few yards from Morgan Spring, a trickle of clear water to quench thirst, and for cooking and cleaning. That was where we lived and how we lived. There is plenty more about the how, but I am getting ahead of myself.

We were not in Kansas anymore where roads often run north to south or east to west. Way too many mountain ridges interrupt the possibility of straight-line transportation. Somehow, realizing the remoteness, the rough topography, the difficulty and time for travel and so much more made us happy and at the same time challenged us to live differently than ever before. Certainly, we had lived in some remote areas, but mostly as children. We, as seasoned adults had enjoyed that freedom. Perhaps freedom was the more important part of living at Morgan Spring. Maybe analyzing the issue should be avoided. We knew that Morgan Spring was not just a picturesque locality but also a way of life. That is the why of Morgan Spring. Yes, it is a state of mind.

The why of Morgan Spring had a beginning, but that why originated elsewhere. The why that drove us to our present circumstances has roots and a history that helps explain current conditions and drives the future. The story of Morgan Spring, that is, our story of Morgan Spring, began decades ago when we realized how much we loved nature, and that love then followed us for years and thousands of miles. Our adult lives were lived in many places east of the Rocky Mountains. Worse, our collective adulthood included residing in several large eastern cities. Our collective eastern residences ranged from upstate New York to the flat windy midsection of Oklahoma, Texas, and cities like Philadelphia, Washington, DC., and Baltimore, or Ballmer, as they say there. There were some welcome stays in Arizona and Washington State, but most years were more east than we wished. It was a learning experience but there was more formality than we liked. We had little enthusiasm about the erstwhile spaces filled to the gills with houses, apartments, office buildings, shopping centers, golf courses, and parking lots. There were and are too many people.

Of course, living east of the Rocky Mountains among the pulsating accouterments associated with denser eastern populations had its positive and negative points. Some circumstances were enjoyable such as being able to find something you need. It was a pleasure not to go through life having to detail to a clerk what you needed since requesting a particular item would cause the entire store staff to think you are crazy for even asking. Some clerks in the western establishments may not have heard of something commonly sold in eastern stores. Easterners, at least most of those we met, luckily had been exposed to more than just their own back yards. They had been around the block and paid attention during the trip. There is more in stock. If you just have to have Prokofiev's complete ballet the "Stone Flower" that a particular orchestra performed, it is possible to find a copy. Many places in the west will not have that recording or even a recording of any of Prokofiev's music. That might not be a problem for those yearning for country-western recordings. Of course, time, computers, and more and more people in the West have changed things since we first moved to Morgan Spring. In the mid-1990s, the East also provided plenty of platforms to jump into educational outlets such as museums, concerts, and all kinds of places for book and poetry readings, and thousands or millions of people of a multitude of cultures with whom to exchange information and ideas. The bigger eastern cities offered the most educational opportunities, greater prospects for finding Prokofiev's "Stone Flower" recordings or a particular spice or book, and the most people. People often bring opportunity, but ultimately they cause opposite outcomes that we did not welcome, that we knew were an accidental blight on the land. All those people. Who knew that the number of humans and their greed would be so destructive.

Our last eastern location, Washington, DC, was a great place to live and learn. However, our hearts beat to distant drums somewhere far away to the west. Our frequent but short visits to parents back in Oregon alleviated some of the need to be west of the Rockies. The pilgrimages to Oregon were like booster shots. On the other hand, returning east made us appreciate concerts and museums. We experienced a bit of cultural shock, whether arriving at our western destination or our eastern one.

Most displaced westerners probably believe that if they return from their eastern lives they can bring with them what they learned from living east of the Rockies. One thing we could bring is a renewed appreciation of nature. Also, owing to the severely humanized and often permanently altered regions east of the Rockies, we could bring an apology for those contributing negatively to the environment. No one is perfect and it was our plan to not remake Morgan Spring into some image we might have experienced in the east. In a sense, we gathered more eastern experiences than most couples who lived far and away from the west coast. The eastern city residences had been good to us, and it taught us a lesson. Our plan was to take the better lessons and leave the rest behind.

So, why here? Why Morgan Spring? Why did we pick such a place or did Morgan Spring chose us to be its caretaker? It soon became obvious. Being at Morgan Spring was almost spiritual. It is the feeling of informality, an enthusiasm for open spaces, nature, and not too many people. It is freedom. It is so many things, with too many to enumerate and more to feel. Morgan

Spring is a place to embrace and love, not molded to meet human needs so much as to let it nourish our new beginning. It is a place of beauty and love. Morgan Spring is the realization that life is undeniably good and we would make last as long as possible.

CHAPTER 6

The Trim

Several days had gone by since my beard and mustache had a thorough grooming, and a haircut loomed overhead. What? It is just that we wanted to make a good impression. We were not moving into a downtown apartment where it is easy to maintain anonymity. We were moving to a rural location, a place near the end of the grid where everyone is going to know your name. We wanted to fit in, but not so much that we lost our own identities. People hearing our last name usually retort, "like the gun." A question mark sometimes followed, but that was optional, and another answer might be, "Like the poet." The latter was usually our reply before leaving the East Coast, but we moved to Morgan Spring to assimilate so our answer was sometimes "like the gun." Length of hair and presence or absence and style has historically and geographically been problematic at times, both to the viewer and the wearer of said hair. Over the years, I had gone from teenage flat-tops to hair hanging down to the middle of my back, sometimes in a braid, and from an exposed mug to a beard. My hair was probably befitting almost anyone anywhere in late twentieth century America so long as over the ears is acceptable. You never know. A snip here and there might put me in better stead with the locals. Maybe it did not matter. My facial hair had slightly gone astray, but today Linda and I would witness just how far my beard could, but should not, go.

We were not ready for a mountain man beard such as the one witnessed on our third day. It began with the usual coffee and breakfast when we heard something coming up our driveway. A rather worn vehicle parked near our car. A short individual climbed from his four-wheel steed and before he could knock, we opened the door. Our first neighborly visit began with an apology for just showing up. Maybe he was concerned we might be worried he was up to no good. We were not and invited him inside. The man stood near the front door, hat in hand and curious eyes looking over the newcomers. His short stature sported a relatively long and unkempt beard. The clothes he wore were way overdue for washing and luckily he said he just wanted to just say hello before getting back down the hill.

The sight of our guest must have reminded Linda that I was overdue for a trim. Yes, my hairy self was beyond most neatness and fast approaching an expiration date. Perhaps I had been too busy twirling my mustache or pulling on my beard during deep consternation about the nomenclature of geographic locations. The trim also left plenty of time to ruminate over thoughts other than which hair to cut. After all, I had been trimming and snipping my hairy growth for decades. So, as the scissors snipped boredom began creeping into or was it out of the folds of my brain just inches from the trimmed hair. That affliction known as boredom was quickly replaced with questions. I began thinking about the history of the place, the gravel crunching from a vehicle traveling the road below, and what are those birds, wait, those kinglets doing in the nearby Douglas fir? Reality, in this instance, glorious reality returns and I get back to the trim.

What is so important about facial hair? I sometimes ask that question myself. Usually, I come up with the same answer: it is as much a part of me as my skin. Before growing my beard, I grew a mustache. The Navy owned my skin then but allowed mustaches. My mustache was wholly above the lip and, with the help of mustache wax, extended one-inch outward on each side of my face like curb feelers. To the benefit of younger minds, curb feelers were flexible metal devices that stuck out beyond the width of a vehicle. Their purpose was to warn drivers by their loud scrapping racket if the vehicle was approaching too close to a street curb and thereby might scuff their sidewalls. What? Sidewalls of tires were optionally white and regarded as something to behold by some fanciful drivers, who, of course, purchased curb feelers to protect their investment if not their vehicular pride. The outer lengths of my mustache definitely warned me of sidewalk curbs and put me in competition with most cats and dogs. Eventually, the mustache had to be corralled by curling its ends. All this fuss was a lot of work, but it was worth it since my superiors did not like the look. The longer and more outlandish, the more it irritated the chiefs and most officers, but it was militarily legal. After all, part of my duty in the military was to keep those chiefs and officers on their toes. I was committing a hairy protest and getting away with it. Around the time, I was also volunteering at Smithsonian's Division of Birds where I noticed several bird people wearing beards. Over in the Division of Mammals, mammal people sported beards. Male members of the Division of Herpetology, the snake and frog people, also joined the beard brigade.

Beards were everywhere. The beard is the mark of scientific endeavor since so many Smithsonian males at least wore beards and happy smiles. I wanted a beard, but the Navy then was not offering the opportunity to grow a beard, or smile, for that matter.

Beards have almost become as commonplace as they were during Oregon's Centennial in 1959. Were beards popular a hundred years ago? History indicates that white settlers brought their beards with them. On the other hand, native people in southern Oregon were not bearded. The consensus from several sources indicates native people are genetically not predisposed to the slavery of shaving. What few facial hairs that raise their ugly heads were dutifully plucked. Owing to the egregious treatment of native people , not having to shave may be their singular piece of luck.

Youth prevented growing a beard for Oregon's Centennial. My beard would sprout a few years later during the Navy days. Beards were taboo in the Navy during my first part of my indenturetude where I found myself reluctantly serving as an enlisted sailor boy. I had turned down the prospect of a commission and elected to be as anonymous as possible. My beard didn't become a full facial feature until the day Admiral Zumwalt announced that he would allow his sailors to grow one. Zumwalt was then the Chief of Naval Operations and I was one of his many chief bottle washers at the Pentagon while serving my part of the Vietnam War.

Admiral Zumwalt, who I had met on occasion, was about the only guy I respected during my stint competing with Donald Duck for fashion king. He, Zumwalt, not Donald Duck, successfully improved the lot of the sailor, and in doing so took some heat from his fellow Navy people. For an admiral to look a lowly sailor in the eye and smile was not normal. What was he thinking?! Officers and enlisted are not to fraternize, they are not to hybridize, not to upset the entrenched class system prevalent in the late twentieth century military. I did want to thank him for the beard but did not. Had I attempted this, his nervous, by the book assistant, Lt. Fretful, would have put a stop to my forwardness. Admiral Zumwalt was respected not just because of the beard, or his 121 memoranda, known as Z-grams, that promoted equality in the traditionally stifling Navy, but because he opposed the Vietnam ground war. His opposition of at least that part of the war was better than no opposition, especially considering his high profile. He must have made life at least a little difficult for the old farts that were so enthralled with keeping the Vietnam War fed with dollars and bodies. After retiring, Admiral Zumwalt became a stalwart champion of veterans with health problems.

Once out of the Navy, my beard lost its status as a symbol of rebellion and gained utilitarian importance. The hairy edifice couldn't be penetrated by pesky mosquitoes. Those horrible females on wings could no longer suck my face and leave itchy welts. Shaving was limited to the neck. A good pair of scissors was enlisted to trim wayward hairs and thereby avoid competition with such luminaries as the members of ZZ Top.

Three days before arriving at Morgan Spring was the last time for beard pruning. Even more time had passed since tending my locks. A lot can happen with facial hair in that short time and I didn't want to get the porcupine look or have to resort to a mustache cup. In addition to normal growth, there was, of course always that rogue hair that decides, with no warning what-so-ever, to spring out in the wrong direction, rebelliously curling skyward or straight out from those well-behaved hairs pointing in the intended direction. Those mavericks were definitely not team players.

The care and feeding of a beard is a routine practice for all but the scraggliest and it was time for a trim, the first of many at Morgan Spring. Not wishing to rain bits of messy beard hairs over the almost pristine bathroom sink, I set up a mirror balanced on a fence post just outside. The rain had let up and the clouds thinned to let more sun flow over the meadow. The snipped wayward beard hairs and drooping mustache particles fell where they may. No cleaning up the aftermath of facial hair; our bathroom would remain a virgin to the mess. The process continued under the perfect light that was almost too perfect since it revealed facial lines that had developed in life.

I had walked through beard maintenance 101 repeatedly for over two decades. My mind wandered all the while the scissors snipped away. Oregon. Yes, the last time I returned to live in Oregon was before the beard growing days in the Navy, and the time following high school when I birded around the country for nine months. More beardless time had passed and now, bearded and back in Oregon, I contemplated the past and present while wondering what would be next.

Hardly anyone in Washington, DC would recognize me without my facial adornment, and almost no one except relatives living in Oregon would recognize me with a beard. Only the people who really know me, as my present bearded self, would be stopping me on the street. It is likely I missed one or two people that I might have liked to renew acquaintance, even for a bit of small talk if it wasn't too small. On the other hand, who would recognize whom after decades of wear and tear? Wrinkles may cover the field marks of old friends more than do beards.

Linda likes my beard, and I, therefore, like my beard. I like it because it reminds me of the sixties both in a good and a bad way, it protects me from certain wildlife and reminds me that I was and still am a scientist. Not all scientist have beards, but the majority working at Smithsonian had either mustaches, beards, or both. These and other thoughts zipped through my aging gray matter in a semi-cathartic journey. Finished, the trimmings from my beard blew down the hill to mingle with the ponderosa pine and Douglas fir needles as I scooped the mirror off the top of the fence post, gathered my scissors and comb, and glanced up the meadow. A Red-tailed Hawk soared quickly out of sight, hidden by the conifers. From far up the slope, unseen because of distance and vegetation, came the repeated "wuck" call-note of a Pileated Woodpecker. Steller's Jays, ubiquitous in our new surroundings, scolded and Chestnut-backed Chickadees whispered their locations as they foraged nearby. What a great place to trim a beard.

Trimming hair did not stop that day. After all, hair grows and someone has to cut it. Linda and I both practiced the art of the trim. Linda was brave to allow my scissored hands to hover near her. Linda was much better trimmer than I, and I freely admit her haircuts were far more enjoyable than those interminable visits to a barber. That is where the hair trimmings went down your neck and the conversation was limited to sports and hunting. Oh, that reminds me of a couple of stories, but I will save them for a later time.

CHAPTER 7

Nesting

Humans and other animals are often similar in behavior. Creating a space that is free from danger of predators or other things that can kill you or make you sick, and that can bear the brunt of the most inclement weather is imperative for animals, including humans. We felt secure in our new home and knew the water from Morgan Spring was safe to drink. Most often, a nesting place is also a place for birthing. In our case, there were to be no little Morgan Springlets. We had been there, done that. Our place, our nest was for adults only, but nieces, nephews, and grandchildren were welcome to visit.

Despite our efforts during day 1, we still could hardly see the floor of our burgeoning nest for the remaining boxscape. During our earlier tour in June, we were assured the floors of the then empty rooms would be clean and free of what most nesters do not want. Bugs. Part of the concern was that the short-term occupant of our dwelling had trapped and skinned a few mammals while at Morgan Spring. We were first surprised that anyone claimed to be a trapper in our present time slot. Having worked in a museum and in a laboratory designed for specimen preparation, I knew there was considerable effort expended to control insects that favor nibbling on prepared skins of vertebrates. There was no reason to worry since, as promised, the house was spic and span and clean as a whistle. Perhaps all those years living in Washington, DC, with its humid summers made us paranoid. Did we bring any stowaways to Morgan Spring? Had our packed boxes become hosts to undesirable critters picked up from the belongings of at least two other households we were told would be riding along in the moving truck? We had known many people that had been plagued by awful roaches and other creeping six-legged organisms. We did not want to live with anything that could infest our food or clothing, anything that would leave its mess behind, or that would bite us. We needed to have a nest, with fewer than six legs.

Anyone who ever lived in the tropics or the southeastern United States knows that insects can bore into boxes of food and carry away nuggets of grains and sugar. Major problems with bugs came while conducting some bird work on St. Kitts, a small violin-shaped island in the Caribbean Lesser Antilles. Roaches were so large that it was possible to hear them rattling the dishes in a darkened kitchen. I am not making that up. Washing the dishes was routine before and after eating, and almost all food items, even the cornflakes and sugar, were dutifully stored behind a heavy refrigerator door. Salt and pepper shakers were hermetically sealed in a mayonnaise jar. Insects may be problems in rooms other than kitchens. While in the military during the late sixties but in WWII barracks just a five-minute walk to the Pentagon, were showers loaded with roaches. Adjoining the shower roach feeding area were the no-stall commodes. That area of the military bathhouse is where we guys practiced our military training by having to take care of business in front of your fellow victims who was concurrently taking care of business. Large shower roaches frequently scuttled around the commodes. This creeped out even the most fearless sailors, all except a couple of whom I felt best to keep at a long arm's length.

Next to the dank bathroom habitat of the military quarters was the sleeping area. This consisted of numerous bunks in a long, dingy, rectangular building containing all sort of people, more roaches, and some biting critters that lived in the beds. Experiencing insects or just reading about them is enough reason to carry out some Superior Insect Control Skills (SICS). It was a surprise to us when we were guests of the married adult offspring belonging to some old friends where we saw more bugs than in an insect zoo. We hate to admit this, but our bug-free friends' offspring never cleaned their rooms growing up and continued on the same trajectory as adults. We will not say who, when or where this misadventure transpired to protect the innocent, even though the actual innocent are actually Linda and yours truly. Obviously, our friends' adult kids, who will do the darndest things, were not innocent. Anyway, their SICSness fell short compared to our old friends, the parents of our hosts. In a short time of not cleaning, the offspring had created a habitat of filth that no insect in its right mind could possibly pass up. And, as the insects, large and small, scurried from microbe-infested nooks of grease, dirt, and grime, they left their own trail as they soiled their way. That's right, they did their business. Little nuggets dubbed frass, poop, if you will, were everywhere. For the uninitiated, frass is a polite term for bug poop, which is another word for. . . well, it should be obvious. Frass may dry and become airborne or add to the darkening trail where the floor and wall meet. Linda and I tried to pretend we were camping. In case our own children are wondering, the aforementioned offspring are not fictionalized versions from our loins.

Long past and recent experiences helped hone our practice of ICS. Those experiences prepared us for being stewards of Morgan Spring. The past made Morgan Spring be important and appreciated. Our Morgan Spring nest would be critter-free, or at least as much as possible. Mites, up to a point, have their place, even the ones everyone has residing on their eyelashes. As for the larger invertebrates, we performed a capture-and-release program. Ladybugs and other such creatures were politely given the door. Spiders that even resembled black widow or brown recluse spiders, both of which are now found almost everywhere in the contiguous United States, were killed. Most other spiders were allowed to roam the premises. Ticks were, of course, terminated. We hoped nothing larger than insects would invade our nest, not any other creatures, not even a mouse. If that happened, we respected their territories, but discouraged home invasions.

Thankfully, the packing boxes in our new home looked as clean as the day we stuffed them back in Arlington. Nothing was crawling out of them. At least, we could not see anything crawl out the boxes, all of which appeared frass-free. So many boxes and so little time was daunting. We got down to the task, trying to pick out the most critical boxes to unpack first. There was a stalemate for kitchen stuff vs. bathroom stuff. After all, what goes in must come out. A medium high priority was finding the appropriate cables to get the TV going. We hoped the TV antenna strapped to a fence post just outside would bring us some news of the outside world. We had already discovered that the multitude of ridges between the nearest radio tower and us prevented decent radio reception. Receiving PBS was not always dependable.

Perhaps we were experiencing a little culture shock. We loved the tranquil sounds of nature at Morgan Spring. Still, we needed some twentieth century sights and noise. Connecting the TV to the antenna was no easy task. Although the TV had a relatively average screen size, it was heavy and awkward to move. At the time, we would have appreciated what would become the light weight of a flat screens. We quickly discovered that receiving a picture to accompany the intermittent sound was nearly impossible. One of us would watch for the picture to improve while the other pivoted the 20-foot antenna leaning on the fence post a few feet from a sliding glass door. Touching the wire fence and the antenna concurrently was not helpful. Sometimes we were successful in receiving a signal but most of the time we were left with garbling ghosts and television snow. Even when the sound and picture were palatable, the situation lasted only frustrating seconds. The signal, originating at least 50 miles away, was too far away.

The next step to acquire a bit of the twentieth century was to hook up the stereo. The towering speakers, a sub-woofer large enough to serve dinner for two on, and the amplifier should improve our mood. Technically called ribbon speakers, the pair stood nearly six feet tall. They were less than an inch thick and were easy to move. On the other hand, the amplifier was much heavier. The weight of the sub-woofer was so great I felt like the skinny guy in a Charles Atlas ad who gets sand kicked in his face. Many over 50 years of age remember that beach and Charles. Soon, we could sample some of the music we brought, a library of classical compositions of the nineteenth century and, of course, the twentieth century. Music soothes the savage beast. It is the universal language. The 600-plus CD collection is nourishment. However, where were the recordings of Prokofiev's Symphony no. 5, and the jazz anthology we packed only days ago?

Music has power and it definitely helped us bit the bullet and get the job of unpacking behind us. Actually biting lead could eventually cause one to go crazy. We were not going to let the boxes drive us crazy but we knew if we did not get them empty soon we would go crazy, along with collection of bruised shins and stubbed toes. We also wanted to avoid floundering about looking for some needed item or wasting time because something was put away in an illogical location. Coffee cups should be on the cabinet shelf within easy reach and close to the coffee pot. Towels should go near or in the bathroom. Office supplies should go near the computer, which was somewhere and yet unpacked. We could have gone crazy but thanks to previously identifying the contents of each box with a label that included a room it should go in kept life sane.

Gradually, ever so gradually, the boxscape became piles of cardboard, flattened and tied in bundles that would fit in the now empty trunk of the car. We eventually hauled the cardboard bundles to the local grocer about 20 miles away. Management agreed we could freely add our defunct boxes to his cardboard collection, which he sold to a recycler. It was a winning situation for everyone.

We had to remove more than cardboard. Any plastic and paper product had to be taken away by us. Morgan Spring was well beyond the distance for garbage pickup and recycling other than corrugated cardboard. We had a garbage compactor, an electric appliance about 12 inches wide and about three feet tall, that alleviated the problem of a weekly garbage pickup. Part of the interior of the infernal machine slides out exposing a hard plastic container, which was lined with a heavy-duty plastic bag. Our emptied cans, plastic bottles, even glass, paper and food packaging such as non-corrugated cardboard went into the bag lining the plastic hopper. Periodically, one of us turned a switch that started a plunger that compacted the contents of the hopper. It took days if not weeks to stuff the compactor so densely that I strained my milk lifting the bag out of the compactor. The bag was ferried down the hill to one of our parent's uncrowded garbage cans. Our garbage capable of rotting was dumped into the pit for composting.

We could have burned paper and cardboard during the winter; burning in the summer is prohibitive because of the danger of starting a forest fire. Somehow polluting our air, or anybody's air, with the smoke from our refuse was not an option. Some people burn everything, including plastics. Many have what they fondly call their burn barrel, a discarded, and sometimes rusted out, 55-gallon metal barrel. Placing a wire screen over the top to prevent hot embers flying out is apparently a whim. Others burn their accumulated pile of detritus wherever it might be located, often allowing the wind to spread the ashes. By others, we hoped to exclude the residences living nearby. We hoped they were as respectful to our immediate region as we attempted to practice.

More and more cardboard from unpacked boxes accumulated as the floor of our abode was uncovered as box after box was emptied during too many days. Finally, the day came when we could see the floor, walk from room to room without stumbling, and be able to locate the different items that made the trip from Arlington. Only one box that contained a few breakable items contained glass shards. Of course, there were a few nicks on things but since we did not bring our large furniture, there was less damage. We would later realize the stereo was not what it used to be, and was likely a victim of being dropped on its head.

Accompanying our toil was a slow cool drizzle filling the air and coating the landscape. We were beyond the edge of wetness. Pale gray moisture-laden clouds so close to us as to appear shapeless, steadily filtered our daylight. Shadows did not exist. The temperature remained between the mid to high 40s day and night. As time advanced, there seemed to be the ever so slowly greening of the meadow.

Every day inside was a day we yearned to be out exploring. About the only venture outside had been to unpack the car, and to mark territory. Dog owners know what that means, but in this case, it was probably more an excuse to get outside than to put down scent. I recalled a Smithsonian colleague once saying that he wanted to live where he could pee anywhere without someone observing or worrying of arrest for exposure. It is all about freedom. After too many days our stuff was stuffed in drawers, cabinets, on shelves, and other hopefully serviceable places. Our nest was at last shaped and lined. No horse hair or feathers were used. Sure, we likely needed to move something from one former place to a more utilitarian location, but the nest was completed. The next step would be living in that nest. Would nesting in our relatively isolated pleasure point fulfill our dream? Today and tomorrow the answer is a resounding yes.

CHAPTER 8

Morgan Spring 101

L inda and I did not go far on our first expedition away from our home. We ventured beyond the green metal gate near the house and walked up the narrow lane on the west side of the meadow. Morgan Spring, hidden by vegetation, was just yards to our right.

Morgan Spring begins near the base of the trees near left of center. The spring would soon overflow as rain and then snow saturated the ground, creating the headwaters of Morgan Creek.

Overhanging trees noisily dripped collected mist onto the large leathery leaves that fell from the smooth-barked madrones and adjacent conifers. The only other sounds were those larger drops loudly spattering on leaf litter and the calming descent of small droplets from narrow needles of firs that landed in a whisper. The leaf litter was soaked and here and there grew fungi. In no time, we counted a dozen different shapes and colors of large and small mushrooms, but more on that later. We were about halfway to the top of the meadow, a distance of 200 yards from the house. Here, we cut 100 yards northeast across the top of the meadow and began looking southward to find our home about 125 feet lower in elevation. We were almost nine stories, nearly the height of our Arlington high-rise, above our Morgan Spring home. There, in the southwestern corner of the meadow, below ponderosa pine and a smattering of Douglas fir, painted brown to blend into the tree trunks, stood our nest. Finishing out the day, we found more fungi, a veritable mushroom city, and tracks and scat of elk. For those interested, scat is another name for mammal frass, which, by the way, is another name for poop, one of the hundreds of synonyms for toilet fodder. Of course, any learned poopologist knows the term frass is traditionally used for insect offerings.

Our day was much too short. Earth had nearly rotated to the degree that the sun was beyond our horizon. The soggy, steely-gray clouds absorbed much of the remaining light. Sooner than we liked, darkness would come. We negotiated our way to the fence nearest the house and entered our nest to renew for another time.

Living at Morgan Spring presented many facets of daily and nighttime activities we did not know about from previous experiences or reading. The things we did not know presented the most excitement and, rarely, frustration. Learning, even learning the hard way, is fun so long as injury is kept at a minimum. Of course, our parents' knowledge, some of which we soaked in and some that we should have paid closer attention to for the details is helpful no matter where we might be. Our fathers independently grew up in rural environments, and a good deal of what they learned rubbed off on us. Both were adept at building and fixing things. Our mothers taught us more than we realized. Linda and I were at least partially prepared for our new place on earth. We had lived in a wide array of settings, some of which were barely tolerable to pretty decent. Thankfully independent of Linda, before we reunited and to no fault of hers, I once temporarily lived in a filthy, crime-ridden apartment building that was very much ghetto ready. That is altogether a different story, but it might be worth mentioning that the windows of my horrible apartment framed a grassy hillside and a dozen or so deciduous trees. That view of nature was cathartic. Likewise, the natural surroundings of Morgan Spring were good medicine that made each day better than yesterday and promised outstanding tomorrows. Living at Morgan Spring would not always be easy. There was work to do ranging from clearing snow from bird feeders, composting and more as well as sometimes waiting for electricity to come back online. Truly, it is difficult to think of genuine difficulties that actually fell into the realm of work. If there were, the trees, the mountains, wildlife, and lessons from our parents and others smoothed away any rough edges.

One thing we learned on our own was to lock our doors, a habit that kept us secure no matter our location. Some may believe that our remote location automatically translated to safety, but common since and history told us otherwise. Morgan Spring ought to be safe, but why invite trouble and break a good habit turning the lock. Who knows, that bear might come back and, thumbs or not, turn the door knob. Our parents locked their doors, but usually only at night when the family went to bed. That time was usually after hours of darkness. They rarely locked vehicle doors, night or day, whether at home or on some errand. People on the news might have been scared out of their wits or worse, injured or killed by intruders, but that would never happen to our parents or even their neighborhood. There was little reason to keep the doors locked or check who was knocking before opening a door. In addition to securing our home, Linda and I routinely locked vehicles, and we did not respond to a knock without first confirming who was on the other side of a door. It was a habit, almost an automatic response, to keep doors locked. Why not? The time we expended for our security was minuscule compared to the time that might involve police, ambulances, insurance agents, etc. A locked door might prevent all that disturbance. Because we knew crime was not limited to urban communities, we locked our doors. Of course, Morgan Spring and our neighbors bestowed a feeling of safety, but circumstances beyond those boundaries called for caution.

Morgan Spring presented several projects that we thought we might want or need to change. Fortunately, the interior and exterior of our new home were in good order; everything worked without leaking, squeaking, or falling in the realm of malfunctioning. Beyond the outside walls was a different story. The coming winter could be a problem. How much snow would we have? Would we need a snow shovel? What other tools might be required to weather the winter? We ignored the fact that chains could be a necessity and we decided against a snow shovel. After all, those flat-bladed snow shovels are for sidewalks, something happily scarce at Morgan Spring. We knew kitty litter could provide traction when stuck in snow. However, we were not sure it would be helpful on our gritty driveway, especially owing to the route's steepness. At the moment, denial of problems from snow seemed the best plan. We would rely on our good sense of keeping the cupboard stocked, hope we were never away from home when it snowed at Morgan Spring, and if it did, we would rely on the front-wheel drive of the sedan to pull us up the driveway.

As winter knocked at the door, we kept gloved fingers crossed that the electricity would be around to power the heat pump. On rare sunny days, the easterly windows let the sun warm us. However, the bedroom remained shaded and cold. At night extra blankets kept out the frigid temperatures. The worst ordeal was when not being master of your bladder required getting up in the middle of the night for a bathroom tinkle. The best part of such an expedition was coming back to bed. Because of being aware of each other, the person not getting up temporarily rolled into the spot left empty in order to keep it warm. Returning to bed was a cozy reward.

Early morning departure from bed became a ritual that included dressing as rapidly as possible. Multiple layers were thrown on and buttoned and zipped before performing a jig around the coffee pot and standing in front of the warm air noisily wafting from the heat pump. Dancing before coffee did help our bodies and dispositions, but we hated the noise of our infernal heating machine. Any respectable bird or mammal would want to flee from the alien sound of the electrical engine. Nonetheless, that blower was warming and we were grateful the electricity was on.

That heat pump was our only source of heat, other than the electric kitchen stove. The pump was not one of those sitting outside on a concrete apron familiar to most heat pump field guides. It sat in a wall, much like a window air conditioner. It reminded us of the type of unit in many motels. Would it keep us cozy during winter? Southwestern Oregon has a mild winter climate, but we could not but wonder if our elevation would be colder rather than mild. Fortunately, the little heat pump did its job, but not at the other end of the house where we had to depend on our own coziness. We were not thrilled by the noisy roar it made but hoped it would not suddenly stop because of an electrical outage. It might be at any moment, and we knew that a wood stove was what might save the day. We wondered how a wood stove might fit the limited floor plan. It seemed unlikely that a wood stove had a place anywhere. We also realized any kind of wood stove, real or imagined, would have to wait for a future winter.

Meanwhile, the need for tools grew as we grew with Morgan Spring. We had arrived with a few basic items, mostly for emergencies related to the car. My past employment in service stations, those bygone locations that sold gasoline and actual service, was not for nothing. Knowledge about flats, leaking radiator hoses, changing oil and more sat rusting in my wheelhouse. Additional needed tools would require dipping into our budget or we could accept tools from my generous dad. Over the years, he had collected two or more of almost any tool imaginable. Screw drivers of all flavors, hammers (claw, ball peen and rubber), wrenches including sockets, ratchets and more were his to give, and on every visit he was always ready to gift us tools, maybe a lamp, a nice jacket he picked up at a thrift store, or possibly a book or kitchen utensil was in the offering. He had way too much stuff, but at least he was down-sizing until he went to another garage sale. Linda and I became well supplied. A chainsaw was our only major purchase. We found an old $10 lawn mower for our few square feet of grass. The mower was the human-powered kind, the type that did not scare away wildlife and that did not stink up the clean mountain air with smokey exhaust. Somehow, a wheelbarrow arrived and became useful for, well, wheeling things from place to place. I am reminded that the use and abuse of all those tools were accompanied by more than satisfying views of the surroundings that we called Morgan Spring. What a pleasure.

With the next season in mind, we sprang into a late winter project of building birdhouses. From our visit to Morgan Spring last summer, we were confident in attracting Western Bluebirds. Years earlier, I had given myself a project on the species. I decided to construct several birdhouses and place them in locations I was sure Western Bluebird frequented at a ranch in the Rogue Valley where I worked. That, in itself, was amazing despite the fact that my father had helped build a house in the days when relatives and friends got together to support each other. I was then too young to do anything but watch the process. Later, I had little interest in nails, hitting my thumb with a hammer, breathing all that sawdust and, luckily, my father no longer had the hard labor of carpentry or working in the lumber industry. Somehow though, I cobbled together three Western Bluebird houses that might attract Morgan Spring birds. I also built a larger house to entice our local Western Screech-Owl to grow owlets.

When our first winter was over, the tiny lawn between the house and three strands of the wire fence began to grow. We reasoned that by spring we might be able to grow a few flowers and a have a vegetable garden, some-thing not included in the landscaping near the house. Soil in the immedi-ate region of the house could grow grass, but it was otherwise limited to a half-dozen kinds of diminutive wildflowers, the kinds requiring a hand lens to see their private parts, morphological characters that aid in iden-tifying the plants. Again, in company with the hammer and nails, the saw and that pesky sawdust, we constructed a couple of long enclosed troughs that became plant boxes that should provide a place to begin a gardening project. Later, we constructed a single-wire fence a few feet beyond the main three-stranded fence near the house. Remember, the meadow was sometimes a pasture for a small number of horses and a couple of mules. One of the horses, which to protect its innocence must go nameless, and I made some sort of connection. Since the herd was sometimes kept in another meadow, we both avoided attachment so as not be missing each other. Anyway, my favorite horse was as guilty as the rest of occasionally reaching over the main fence for perceived greener grass. Our new single-wired fence enclosed a no-hoofed animal zone, which translated into a safe space for a small vegetable garden. With the help of a neighbor's once heavily used but very reliable pickup, we hauled sand from Button Creek and rich forest floor soil to bolster the health of the flowers and to grow a few vegetables. I knew Linda's green thumb would not fail.

Setting up a new fence to prevent horese from knibbling the planned garden. Looking up the meadow from near the house. The spring is in the trees on the left and Cat Peak is on the right horizon.

Once the plant boxes were constructed, holes were drilled in the bottoms of the wooden boxes, followed by a smattering of small rocks for proper drainage. Then, the ingredients for a recipe of soil was gathered from the nearby forest floor and was added to the plant boxes. The fertile soil apparently contained seeds that grew into flowers and was perfect for transplanting sword ferns. To help things along, we added more humus, cooling moss and quenched any suspecting thirst. We must have inadvertently transported a small toad that quickly became as big as my fist. Linda and I identified it as a western toad or *Bufo boreas*, a species with a distin-guished, nearly white strip down the middle of its back that separated spots and blotches of black and orange. It sometimes came out in daylight, but otherwise stayed silent and hidden in the cool moss of the long planter at the northerly side of the house. Other smaller planters contained varieties of flowering plants, including domestic petunia and marigolds, the latter which were transplanted along the boundaries of our small vegetable gar-den. Rows of red and yellow gladiolus were planted at the northern end of the narrow lawn. Near the other end, we, or actually Linda, cajoled deep purple and yellow iris to bloom not far from a climbing red rose that Linda started from a plant at my parents' home, the same one I grew up in, and the same rose that I looked after during my teenage chores. The rose rested against the fence and stretched toward the platform bird feeder.

In addition to flowers, our garden grew a bounty of tomatoes and other vegetables.

Other plants were kept on the southeastern side of the house near our retirement party gifted hammock and where the greenery was protected from the sun. Among this staging area were a few selected vegetables, es-pecially tomatoes, which would grow and produce an abundant crop. By now, it might appear that our lawn and gardening efforts were an attempt to displace nature for nurture. To a degree, we did alter our environment. However, any change would be on the minimum end of the scale. Whatever we did, we tried to leave as small of a footprint as possible.

Summer was warm, but it was not the hot muggy weather of our former residence in Arlington, Virginia. Morgan Spring gave us a dry heat, yet not as dry nor as hot as the Rogue Valley. Mornings at Morgan Spring were quite cool, but by afternoon, the thermometer was reading somewhere in the 80s to the 90s. It did not become hot enough to turn on the cool mode of the pesky heat pump. Not long after sundown, air from the surrounding upper slopes cooled and began draining down the meadow and past the house. By dark, we often opened windows on the east side to catch the clean cool breezes. In order to snag more of the agreeable air, I put together a couple of boards and, with hinges, attached a kind of shutter that, when opened on the northern bedroom window, would direct some of the night's draining air to the interior of the room. No reason to waste what nature offered. The cool night breeze became a hot and dry exhale from the valley below during daylight. That was when we took advantage of our isolation that allowed regulating the amount of clothing to be optional, but that might best be told on different pages.

Much to my surprise, we discovered that autumn is the principal time when ponderosa pines lose their needles. A breeze would increase the pace of needles falling to the ground. There were so many pale brown needles that they had to be raked off the graveled area between the driveway and the house. Otherwise, the needles would become slippery, especially if covered by snow. Raking the 10-inch long needles, which came as three to a bundle, differed from gathering deciduous leaves that I remembered were gathered by applying essentially a random direction to each sweep of the leaf rake. A random direction was not the best answer for those pesky needles. The most efficient method of raking was to first rake in one direction. That gathered about 50 percent of the fallen needles but left the other half all pointing in the direction just raked. Step two was to rake the remaining culprits in a direction perpendicular to the first raking. I hope everyone is following this since supplying a video is not an option. Needles also fell on the roof of the house. A straw broom did the trick, but thousands of needles had to be removed one handful at a time from the gutters. Collected needles were hauled a few feet from the house where they were scattered across the forest floor. The pines were more than excused from the work they caused.

Living at Morgan Spring was far more than trundling a load of mulch to the garden. Our mornings, no matter the season, began like any. There was the dash to the singular bathroom followed by waiting over the coffee pot for the first mug of brew. What made all mornings at Morgan Spring different from any other was Morgan Spring. Looking past the steamy mug of coffee, we surveyed our surroundings and scanned the meadow. Would there be elk, deer, maybe a coyote loping across the grass, or maybe an eagle or hawk soaring above? What was the weather and what would it become? Every morning began with questions. What would we see or hear? What might we learn? During late fall, would we find more fungi and, in winter, should the ground be covered by snow, what tracks might be left near our door? From spring through early fall, we were amazed by wildflowers and, that the number and species were not always the same each spring. During any season, we naturally searched everywhere for birds.

Actually, we were on the lookout for everything. So, on a routine day, usually after a simple breakfast, we decided what chores must be done and what could wait. We hoped it was not a day to go to the valley for grub and supplies and to check in on our parents. We loved our parents, but going to the valley, which would include shopping, was not our choice of a good time. It was not fun standing in long check-out lines, staring at the back of someone in front, noticing their rough and gray-white elbows that needed a good scrubbing, or hearing a child in its terrible-two phase testing their vocal powers by exceeding impossible decibels. Most days we did our chores that might range from cleaning house to feeding birds, splitting and stacking wood, and working in the garden. More than likely, actually most days, we packed a lunch and headed into the forest.

One of our favorite hikes was skirting the west side to the quarry, then to a wire gate in the upper corner of the meadow. We would follow the remnants of an almost overgrown road that we dubbed Skunk Road since it frequently had the scent of essence of skunk. Along the route of Skunk Road, we had the option of going on yet another eroded and nearly overgrown road that would take us to the slopes of Alder Creek, and, along the way in the summer, past MacGillivray's Warblers. In the same area during winter, chances were that around early February, and if the ground was not covered with snow, blooming snow queens, a diminutive purple flower, that would be hugging the cold ground. Snow queens were our wedding flower. Most frequently, instead of turning toward Alder Creek, we trekked down a brushy gully, an intermittent tributary of Squaw Creek. Luckily for us, but not necessarily for the ecology of the region, another road paralleled the gully. Near the lower part of the route, we could admire flowers or fungi, depending on the season, and anytime, we could check the few yews struggling in the once-upon-a-time forest among the memory of trees. It was always a relief to see that the yews had not been illegally hijacked for their medicinal properties. From the yews, we usually turned southwest and picked up an animal trail heading into heavier forest (animal trails are often good routes to follow and frequently lead to happy natural surprises or easy ways to reach a location). We then hiked along a ridge above Squaw Prairie, a sizable open flat estimated to occupy about 60 acres, with part of it

abutting Elk Creek Road near the old guard station. Stunted oaks and grasses filled Squaw Prairie, and at its upper drier boundary, thickets of brush
included pale green manzanita, a familiar species favoring some foothills of
the Rogue Valley. Small, almost tiny, pale pink manzanita flowers grew in
prominent, tightly bound bundles from gnarly branches. Their sweet aroma
attracted an audible number of honey bees. The prairie was only a little over
a third of a mile from Morgan Spring. Forest and ridges made distances feel
greater than in actuality, which, if not kept in mind, might cause someone
to become lost, something neither Linda or I experienced. There was an old
road along the side of the ridge, and other than creating our own trail, we
followed the byway to see where it might lead. Our route eventually began
paralleling Elk Creek Road and taking us through a less disturbed, mixed
forest of Douglas fir, pines, and madrone. In no time, we were walking a
slight incline northward above Morgan Creek. Although our home was essentially just across Morgan Creek, anyone walking could not see the house.
We hoped any hunter would refrain from shooting our way. The present
road faded away, just as do all old forest roads eventually; we crossed a fence,
the fence enclosing the meadow, made a right turn and, opening the upper
gate, came full circle. Depending on one's own viewpoints, the route taken
was either long or short, eventful or boring, or to be avoided or welcomed.
We looked forward to our hike, found it eventful since by only looking, we
found new and different things, and easily spent considerable time along the
way. It was not always easy, but we tried to make it home before dark.

Learning to live at Morgan Spring fed our zeal to acquire more information, learn how to live near the end of the grid while being unable to see
your nearest neighbor, learn how to accomplish life away from the fast lane
and to soak in the environment. Each day, every night, was an opportunity.

CHAPTER 9

The Juncos are Coming, the Juncos are Coming

E ver since the first days while Linda and I busied ourselves with the attempted art of living at Morgan Spring, we also were thinking about feeding birds. Over 55 million people in these United States operate some sort of bird feeder and we planned to join the crowd. Feeding birds may sound like a funny thing to do, but it is a good way to attract birds to your home and help the birds out at the same time. Just what kinds of birds might frequent a bird feeder at remote Morgan Spring?

Most bird feeders adorning human residences across the country are in service during winter only but some people keep bird smorgasbords going year-round. Bird feeders range from elaborate platforms with anti-squirrel devices to hopper feeders, trays, shelves, logs stuffed with seed and suet, feeders attached to windows, on poles, hanging from trees, food placed on window ledges, or food simply tossed on the ground. Some people call the locations of bird feeders feeding stations. Food offered to birds is quite variable and ranges from an orange slice impaled on a nail to prevent the whole from being carried away to different kinds of seeds, suet, peanut butter, and more. Of course, the food is placed where we can view arriving birds, but it should also be placed where the birds are not in added danger.

Birds eat fast. They have to ingest the food before a predator eats them or one of their conspecifics beats them to a seed or some other morsel. Each species is very competitive with members of the same species. However, all birds, regardless of their identity, may be competitive with one another at a feeding station. A jay, an Evening Grosbeak and a cardinal might want the very same piece of food at the same time. Which bird eats or steals that morsel may vary. We humans don't usually worry about someone stealing our food. Nonetheless, how many times have you seen people eyeing what you were eating or you eyed what someone else was eating? Birds do that too. They'll be eating earnestly at a particular spot at the feeder until they notice another bird eating more and faster. Could the other bird be eating better food? If the other bird is smaller or somehow is not dominant to the bird observing it, there usually is a confrontation. The larger individual may be the victor of the spoils. Which bird gets the food depends on which one is dominant, a factor determined generally by size, age, sex, or rank within a flock.

The rank is what we ornithologists scientifically call pecking order. It is another way of saying dominance hierarchy. Looking at the big picture, we might use the term 'food chain,' which, of course, translates to the biggest and baddest organism dominates any creature unfortunate enough to be unable to defend itself before it becomes breakfast, lunch, or dinner of the dominating organism. The top of the food chain includes at its apex not necessarily the biggest, but the baddest, *Homo sapiens*, the top of the pecking order. Around the turn of the twentieth century, the top animal in studies in the formulation of the modern concept of pecking order was called the despot. Those animals on the lower side of the pecking order might conclude the term despot was accurate. Thus, the top rank of the pecking order is the pecker while the rest are peckees. Woodpeckers, for example, are dominant birds at a feeding station. Diminutive juncos and other species might peck at each other, but being pecked by a woodpecker is a different situation. Domestic mammals such as cats, dogs, horses, and cows, humans, wildlife of thousands of species including birds all practice a pecking order or king of the mountain, the game kids practice and adults continue. The battle of dominance is part of the entertainment humans enjoy at feeding stations.

Although binoculars help to make a far-away bird seem closer, we naturally savor the chance to see our feathered friends up close and more personal. To see who was winning the pecking order, the color and pattern of plumage, the texture of feathers, and even a bird's bright glistening eye, ever alert to a bird higher in the pecking order, including predators – these are some of the delights humans gain from feeding birds. It is also a good way to determine what species of birds might be lurking about. Of course, not all birds frequent bird feeders, but many birds are curious. Some individuals and species that are not the least bit interested in a bird feeder fare will sometimes check out what all the fuss is about. What are those Purple Finches doing hanging around a house? What are those jays eating? I am pretty sure some of the birds we added to the checklist of Morgan Spring were species simply curious about the local crowd.

Anyone paying attention might wonder what happened to the story of the first juncos. Just to be clear, the juncos coming are technically Dark-eyed Juncos or *Junco hyemalis* for those speaking the language. The juncos in most of the west sport black hoods whereas other taxonomic groups have gray hoods. Our resident black-hooded juncos were once known as Oregon Junco and the eastern gray-hooded birds were called Slate-colored Junco. Both were colloquially snowbirds to those ignoring us bird people. Regardless of taxonomic dispositions, the junco is another example of having different and well-entrenched English names. By entrenched we mean we found it sometimes impossible to convince certain people that the snow-bird (or is it Snow Bird?) and the Dark-eyed Junco are actually the same species. It is no wonder the public might think there are more species than the American Ornithologists' Union (AOU; now AOS [American Ornithological Society]) Check-list admits. Some taxonomists, including myself, continue to wonder what is the truth. There are other taxonomic groups of juncos, but I will refrain from boring diatribes on the befuddled taxonomic status of these birds. Instead, I will save boring diatribes for later chapters. For now, most groups of juncos are considered to represent one species, but that may be wrong. Suffice to say, had it not been for the juncos coming to feeders at Morgan Spring, the parade of other species they attracted might have stayed hidden in the bushes. Certainly, the juncos did not wittingly attract other species for our viewing pleasure, but the end result was our delight.

It is doubtful whether a Hairy Woodpecker would have come out of the woods to enjoy the suet feeder had it not noticed the more easily entice-able juncos. A California Scrub-Jay, a species common much further down-stream, might not have stopped by, or at least we might not have detected it, had not our resident Steller's Jays been so raucous while noticing the juncos at our bird feeders. Even warblers and flycatchers sometimes watched birds near feeders. Once upon a time in the Rogue Valley, an Orange-crowned Warbler became a regular consumer of peanut butter dabbed on a limb of a plum tree. I believe it was attracted to my bird feeding area because of the commotion from sparrows and juncos already eating seeds thrown on the ground. Besides people observing birds foraging at feeding stations, mammals and other kinds of birds may watch with envy. Mammals, especially domestic cats, often salivate at the prospect of a kill and birds of prey, including Cooper's and Sharp-shinned Hawks, like the parade of birds at a feeder. Luckily, we were not visited by either cats or bird-eating hawks. Or were we? More on that later.

Anyone interested in jays may notice that the birds we then called Western Scrub Jays have either become extinct or have changed their names.

They definitely have not gone extinct. The jays have changed their names, legally and became identified under the moniker California Scrub-Jay. Birders are possibly more confused by the change in names than any intelligent jay sporting the generic name *Aphelocoma*. Actually, birds could care less. When birds arrive at a feeder they are not cheered by everyone knowing their name. Birders and other humans want to know just as I did when I first was diagnosed as a birder back in the day when we were dubbed 'birdwatchers.' In those dark ages, the subject jays were known simply as Scrub Jay, aka *Aphelocoma coerulescens*. They came missing the almost ubiquitous hyphen required by the powers to be of the AOU for certain species. That is a wholly different matter that I am electing to fend off. Suffice to say, or in this case, suffice to write, the Scrub Jay of yesteryear and scrub-jay of more modern nomenclature was later split into three species. One occurs in Florida, the Florida Scrub-Jay; a second population recognized as a new species is the Island Scrub-Jay that resides on Santa Cruz Island, California; and a third species was called Western Scrub-Jay, the moniker for the birds breeding in, surprise, the remainder of the west. That great jay rift went down in 1995, a year before Linda and I moved to Morgan Spring. Over twenty years later, Western Scrub-Jays were further split into a mostly coastal mainland California Scrub-Jay primarily west of the Sierra Nevada and Cascade Mountians, and a more interior species blessed as Woodhouse's Scrub-Jay. John Tomer, retired chemist and one of the biographers of Woodhouse the man, roamed the Division of Birds during part of my stay there. I recall having discussions with him about the adventures of Samuel Washington Woodhouse, who, of course, collected the first specimen of Woodhouse's Scrub-Jay. He did not name it for himself. Spencer Fullerton Baird named *woodhouseii* as a species in 1858. Although the taxon *woodhouseii* was relegated to a lowly subspecies for decades, it turns out Baird was taxonomically correct by only 158 years.

We certainly benefited from the juncos attracting so many other species to our feeding station. Getting the juncos come to our door in the first place had not been easy. Sure, we had fed birds at other residences including our last guests, Northern Mockingbirds coming to our apartment for soft and juicy raisins placed on the narrow window ledge. Those vociferous visitors had less fear of humans and human structures, even high-rises, the busy library across the street, or the sirens and other calls of passing emergency vehicles. Mockingbirds even imitated city sounds, and nesting mockers sometimes attacked pedestrians on sidewalks in the busy business districts of downtown Washington, DC. Attracting wild juncos on the other hand, was not easy.

One of the first species of birds we observed near the house at Morgan Spring were juncos. At first glance, docile juncos were no mockingbirds, but we knew they would entertain and their activities at the feeders would attract other species. For their enjoyment, I hurriedly cobbled together some scrap boards for a feeding station. I nailed the station to the top of a fence post. Getting the juncos to notice the seeds placed in the station could take more time than we wished to pass. In order to hurry the processe, Linda and I developed a Hansel and Gretel plan. The plan meant we would be the witches and the junco stood in for the two kids. Noting where the wild flocks fed, we created a trail of seeds back to the house and to the waiting bird feeder.

The little flock of juncos foraging in the shadows of the conifers at the edge of the meadow near the house was coming, but when will they accept our hospitality? When would they come to the grand opening of our feeding station? Our birds slowly followed the growing shadow that progressed between the conifers and the afternoon sun. These softly twittering Dark-eyed Juncos were much too far away to see their dark eyes. The small flock moved in what seemed an unorganized fashion as it remained in the dark shadows. Perhaps keeping in the shadows was a way of avoiding detection by predators. The juncos stayed in the deep shade of the pines and rarely ventured into sunlit parts of the meadow. Being somewhat impatient for birds to partake the offered smorgasbord, I waited inside for the flock to leave. Once they departed, with a bag of seed under my arm I scattered handfuls where the juncos had been foraging. Linda and I waited. In about 30 to 40 minutes, the juncos returned to the shadowed slope. They appeared in a feeding frenzy as they had discovered a new abundance of food, the bird seed I planted. The seed was scattered on the slope where I left the juncos a narrow trail of seed that terminated on the ground below the platform feeder. As the birds depleted the food left on the slope, they began following the trail of seeds towards the house. At last, the juncos entered the back yard. Linda had momentarily left the living room. Excited, I began calling to her, announcing in Paul Revere fashion that "the juncos are coming, the juncos are coming."

Linda and I watched from inside the almost darkened living room. Individually, the foraging juncos kept a distance from one another, which was a length just out of reach from its nearest foraging neighbor. When a bird moved too close to a neighbor the individuals stopped foraging. We are not sure what this distance might be since it changed, but it was well after any one bird could see the dark of the eyes of their compatriots. The space before firing a barrage of bird body language was only inches. The confronting birds, often only the trespassee, went into action. The bird would spread its wings slightly and crouch, with its pale bills open and aimed at the other bird. During the crouching, the tail opened slightly to expose white outer tail feathers. In addition, the bird would vocalize during the confrontation. Frequently, there would be clashes between birds when they would lunge at each other, beaks pointed as if to shoot and emanating brief indescribable, yet pleasing vocalizations. Those sounds were pleasing to us, but certainly not to the birds. The vocalizations might best be translated as "get back or I will peck the guano out of you" or something like that. Sometimes the trespasser would reciprocate the behaviors, part of the behavioral suite, or it would merely move away. We wondered when the flock would cross the fence line and actually invade our yard and bird feeder.

Months later, after our autumn arrival and after the juncos became regular bird feeder customers, we learned that Dark-eyed Juncos nest all around Morgan Spring. Did some of those birds breeding around our home winter in the valleys below? Two yeses are important here. First is, yes, I am getting ahead of myself, but there is a point here that is tied to the second yes, that it is most probable that some of the juncos breeding around Morgan Spring move down into the valley below and some of the juncos remain at Morgan Spring for the winter. After all, individuals of the species are elevational migrants. To prove their movements, our summer birds would have to be banded with Fish and Wildlife Service bird bands, then we or someone would have had to recapture the same birds during the winter. Still, Linda and I were reasonably sure the juncos we were baiting with the trail of seeds were birds familiar with the territory, were confident permanent residents and birds that would need cajoling if expected to come closer to a building, our home, that had only existed for four years.

Juncos at feeders in urban regions we observed were rather fearless to the extent that they would fly only a few feet from an approaching human. Our juncos were not the juncos we knew at feeders we saw at urban or even suburban settings. We guessed that was one of the reasons why the flock near the house was hiding in the deep forest shadows. Unlike other juncos at feeders, our juncos were wild juncos. We admired their wildness. The juncos skulking in the shadows certainly did not consider humans as major sources of food. In fact, they behaved as if we thought of them as a source of food. They were taking no chances.

The bird feeder perched on the fence post at Morgan Spring must have seemed strange to our juncos; birds that, because of lack of experience, wouldn't know a good bird feeder if they saw one. Our created trail of seeds from the shadows back to the house and to the base of the bird feeder had done the trick, but would juncos go to the feeder? We had earlier seen a junco or two perch on some of the fence posts, so we sprinkled seeds on the tops of several posts near the feeder. Nothing happened at first. On day two of this remarkable experiment, we observed a few individuals daring to come out in the open, away from the shadows, where they nibbled at the baited trail. Most animals are opportunistic and juncos are no exception. The bait, as we had plotted, was more than they could ignore. The seeds were easy food and they went for it. Eventually, a daring individual flew to the feeder's bark roof and with slow hesitation, hopped inside where a pile of delicious birdseed waited. Juncos at last! There they were, their dark eyes and busy whitish beaks just feet from our window where we congratulated ourselves for hosting our first guests at the Morgan Spring feeding station.

It was a great beginning. Without the pioneering juncos, the wide palette of other species might have gone unnoticed. Thankfully, the juncos came.

CHAPTER 10

Catching Flies, Fly-catching, and Flycatchers

Part of the spirit of living at Morgan Spring came to us in observing nature and people. We soon began to learn that the sights and smells, and the feel of clouds gathering on a ridge or sweeping down the meadow was the life of that spirit. With open minds, we attempted to learn.

CATCHING FLIES

It was on or around 3 October. The above date is not an exact one; the precise date was changed to protect the perpetrator. It was not changed to protect the innocent because the first group of animals that is concerned with flies and catching them is not innocent.

This animal is human. And it was there to practice the first of the behaviors concerned with flies and catching them. This was the Catching Flies group and includes people who have little if nothing to contribute, the person whose principal activity is nothing more than Catching Flies. If you haven't experienced someone catching flies, you probably have seen someone pretend to be catching flies in a movie. They can be interesting fictional characters, but in real life, not particularly desirable. The person catching flies stands or sits, with nothing to do or say, and all the while their mouth is open. We had very few visitors in our pre-Morgan Spring days who were Catching Flies; we like to keep a conversation going so there was little time for an open mouth that might be Catching Flies. When there was an open mouth, it was brief.

There were several people we left in the hustle of Washington, DC., and other friends elsewhere in the eastern United States, who may have wondered if we might squander time Catching Flies. We didn't. We brought many, perhaps too many, accouterments of civilization with us, along with our ideas and aspirations, not to mention that we lived in the wooded mountains, to have time to be Catching Flies. In fact, many days were busier than those before retirement. Even so, we learned to rest and enjoy our time, a time that was, at last, our own. We were responsible for ourselves; we did not require a bean-counting supervisor looking over our shoulder and directing our work. We had been there and done that, but hasten to add that at least our last places of employment were happily bean-counter free. What might be regarded as downtime, when we were not conducting some maintenance task, when not researching, writing or composing music, or when we were not traveling to the valley either for grub or for care-taking ailing family members, we were playing. Even writing had play elements since I had been asked to contribute taxonomic information for a book on Oregon birds. The research was enjoyable as was composing music. Now and then I would play a finished prelude, a concerto or one of my symphonies from my regrettably private collection primarily tonal compositions. The only flies we caught were accidentally by mouths while gasping for air during a hike. We were busy living life. There was no time for doing nothing. Catching flies was too dull and with eyes wide open, gratefully impossible at Morgan Spring.

Part of the learning was searching for other animals concerned with flies and catching them. It wasn't long before we observed one of these kinds of animal.

FLY-CATCHING

On 14 October 1996, to be exact, we observed fly-catching. The animal concerned with flies and catching them was practicing a routine method of obtaining food. That is correct. The practice of Catching Flies usually amounts to only wasting time although some unsuspecting people have also caught and sometimes swallowed a fly during their endeavor of Catching Flies. Surely swallowing a fly was a giant waste of time for the Catching Flies practitioner, but to them, it did not matter. For that person, wasting time is more than a hobby, it is a way of life. What we observed today was bona fide, tried and true, behavior known as fly catching. This behavior is carried out with deadly precision by many species of birds, but not here including flycatchers that have their own category beyond.

The fall performance of fly-catching involved two fly-catching Yellow-rumped Warblers flitting from the fence near the house to the air, where, as if by magic, they pulled an insect, unseen by us, from the cool air. These small winter warblers had lost their striking hues of spring and summer; the yellow of their throat, head, shoulders, and rump was subdued in the somber autumn light. The yellow on one of the birds was barely yellow, and the back was browner and less grayish blue compared to its fly-catching companion. We were watching a female with a brighter male. Possibly they were mates or siblings from the summer. Both birds uttered distinctive "chips" as they flitted and fed. The call notes were a means for them to locate one another. They were very good at fly-catching.

There are many other species of birds that are well known for their fly-catching behavior, their prowess of grabbing a flying insect from the air with such agility, that early naturalist might wonder if these birds were flycatchers, the family. Before jumping off the limb to grab a snapshot of the flycatchers, credit should be given to those non-flycatchers, the other fly-catching species we saw at Morgan Spring.

By March of every spring we observed some of the best species at fly-catching, members of the swallow family. Our first swallow each spring at Morgan Spring was the Tree Swallow. Two to six individuals nested near Morgan Spring every summer. Eight species of swallows breed in North America north of Mexico; there are 90 species around the world. In addition to the breeding Tree Swallows, we were visited sporadically by long-tailed Barn Swallows, Cliff Swallows with rusty rumps, and Violet-green Swallows. This last species and the Tree Swallow have white undersides; Violet-green Swallows have more white on their heads and a white patch that almost meets at the base of the tail.

The flowering meadow attracted not just our eyes but pollinating insects. A multitude of insects paid the price for pollinating the flowers by becoming food for the fly-catching swallows that patrolled the meadow. On cool days, and even worse, on rainy ones, the swallows would skim closer to the meadow surface than on the warmer drier days when the insects flew higher.

Another champion fly-catching bird is the Common Nighthawk, which, according to our notes for 10–31 July 2000, we heard "peenting" high overhead. These birds are members of the family called Caprimulgidae. The English name for this family is Goat-suckers. Wait! If flycatchers catch and eat flies and other flying insects, do goat-suckers suck goats, then eat them, or what? Are they bloodsuckers or the avian partner to vampire bats? The legend goes that someone thought nighthawks and their relatives prized the milk of goats. Actually, goat-suckers don't suck blood, milk, or have anything to do with goats, except, perhaps, benefit from insects that might fly from a smelly goat.

The Common Nighthawk is one of three species of nighthawks that frequent the United States. Two species breed in southern climes. Our species has a wide range from the Yukon to Middle America and from Pacific to Atlantic seaboards. The last eastern Common Nighthawks we observed were the multitudes swarming around the floodlighted Washington Monument during our last summer on the east coast. Other non-goat sucking goatsuckers include the familiar Eastern Whip-poor-will and Chuck-will's-widow. Those species probably retain their strange English names because the calls they produce may phonetically spell out their name. We call the words that make the same sound a bird might make an onomatopoeia.

Chickadee, Killdeer, and whip-poor-will are examples of onomatopoeia. Still, why isn't the "will's" part of the name capitalized when writing the official name Chuck-will's-Widow? Never mind those pesky hyphens required in the official English name. The question asked here is not the will in reference to his widow, that is, Will's widow? Perhaps the small case will has something to do with what Chuck had in mind. Was Chuck thinking sweet thoughts about his wife before he offed himself? Will that question plague mankind for centures? Probably not. Nonetheless, anyone not familiar, or not, with English might be confused by the renditions of the aforementioned names. Anyone might also be amused by the renditions of those names. The only other caprimulgid that might be found near Morgan Spring country is the Common Poorwill. There are six other species called poorwills that occur south of the border. Incidentally, since poorwills are whipless, the lack thereof may explain why their English name is one word, not hyphenated as are members possessing whips. That may be a poor example, but this is beyond my will. As alluded earlier, delving into the realm of hyphenation according to officially sanctioned species of birds is not a world I want to further explore. Even so, it is worth noting some authors commonly write the call of the poorwill as "poor-will."

Regardless of English monikers, more fly-catching birds were duly noted on 31 August 2001. It was in the low 90s, the sky was cloudless. The warm air was still, making it great weather for flying insects We heard the distinctive call of a fly-catching species, an Acorn Woodpecker, near the edge of the meadow. The call is sometimes rendered *waka*. That doesn't really sound correct, but regardless of the spelling, the call is very loud and unforgettable. When not *waka*-ing it up, this black and white western woodpecker, sporting a patch of yellow on its cheeks and red on the back of its head, goes after acorns and flying insects. It stuffs the acorns in holes it pecks in trees and utility poles for another day. It stuffs the fly-catching spoils into waiting hungry young or feeds its own appetite.

FLYCATCHERS

The third group concerned with flies and catching them was represented by the champion bird that did more than practice fly-catching; it was a flycatcher. This bird was the doctor you hoped will treat you, not just a practicing physician, but one that has already practiced. They are the flycatcher of all doctors.

Flycatchers are birds that are often easy to detect but are sometimes difficult to identify. Flycatchers often perch on a bare limb or wire, which probably helps them see their surroundings in order to catch an unsuspecting flying insect. Some flycatchers are easy to detect and easy to identify. Scissor-tailed Flycatchers are unmistakable, even while a birder is careening by car across the flatlands of south-central United States. This grayish, six-inch long flycatcher, with a forked tail streaming behind another 6 or more inches, is the state bird of Oklahoma.

Our flycatcher *du jour* was a Say's Phoebe that came to Morgan Spring on 29 March 1997. The species could have been called Say's Flycatcher, but not all flycatchers have flycatcher in their name. By definition, a phoebe is a member of the flycatcher family, Tyrannidae, with a grayish-brown or blackish plumage. Never mind that the word phoebe is probably derived from Greek *phoibos*, meaning bright or pure. Vocalization of Eastern Phoebe is often rendered 'fee-be,' but Say's and Black phoebes come close, yet not quite, to announcing their last name. All three North American species are in the genus *Sayornis,* and all three, at least to me, behave more similarly to each other than to other members in the flycatcher family. Eastern Phoebe, a species that frequented our former eastern habitat, rarely visits the far west. One other factoid about Eastern Phoebe: Audubon, in 1804, placed a silver thread on the leg of a nesting Eastern Phoebe and reported the bird returned the next spring - the beginning of a method to study bird migration.

In addition to phoebes, some flycatchers in North America north of Mexico are called pewees and wood-pewees, kiskadees (Texas only), and, of course, king of kings, what else, the kingbirds. These types of flycatchers all belong to the Tyrant Flycatchers, the Tyrannidae, not be confused with the unrelated Old World Flycatchers, the Muscicapidae. Six or more species of Old World Flycatchers have shown up in Alaska, having crossed the frigid Bering Straits to be accurately documented by our friend Dan Gibson of the University of Alaska. Dan has discovered more species of birds, not just Old World Flycatchers, that are new to North America than any living ornithologist.

Our lone New World Say's Phoebe was just one of the species of flycatchers to visit Morgan Spring. This brownish western phoebe is one of about 30 species found in North America north of Mexico. There are about 425 species of assorted elaenias, flatbills, antpipits, spadebills, and more flycatchers with flycatcher in their name than would seem imaginable, tyrannulets, tyrants, and more regal kingbirds, just to name a few. From southern Brazil to Alaska, the Tyrant Flycatchers rule at fly-catching. They put Catching Flies on its head. They have no time to waste. They are fly-catching flycatchers.

Another flycatcher that loves to perch on power lines and fences is the white-bellied Eastern Kingbird, a species found as far west as Oregon. There are four yellow-bellied kingbirds found in the West. Most of them occur in southern Texas and Arizona. The most northern of these species is the Western Kingbird, ruler of the airways. Kingbirds are zealous defenders of their nesting territory and relentless in removing potential trespassers. Even an innocent individual bird, just passing through, minding its own business, may be chased away with violent vigor. Wounding pecks serve to dispatch even a large hawk, a crow, a dog, a cat and humans. It would be interesting to observe sympatric breeding populations of Eastern Kingbirds and Western Kingbirds. What a dangerous place that might be. Our visiting phoebes were usually easy to observe. The shyer wood-peewees sometimes perched on an exposed limb used as a base for fly-catching forays.

Even while perching out in the open for an easy view by birders, many species of flycatchers resemble one another so much that identification is difficult and sometimes impossible. Members in the genus *Empidonax* come to mind. This last group consists of 14 species, many identifiable only by habitat and call note or song alone. The late Ned K. Johnson of Berkeley, University of California, who I had the pleasure of knowing for a couple of decades, wrote several state-of-the-art monographs on *Empidonax* flycatchers. His smart, dry wit and kindness were not revealed in those pages such as the one that detailed and carefully crafted proof that birds known formerly as Western Flycatchers are two separate species, the Pacific-slope and Cordilleran Flycatchers. The breeding ranges of the two overlap in southwestern Oregon. The similarities between the two species often dictated sightings to be reported as "Western" Flycatcher when one or the other species is suspected but not confirmed. The "Western" Flycatchers in Morgan Spring country during summer were Pacific-slope Flycatchers. Silent migrants were considered "Western" Flycatchers, or on the rare day of low optimism and confidence, were considered merely *Empidonax* flycatchers.

One of my last tasks before leaving the museum was curating the flycatchers. I managed to complete perhaps 50 percent of the collection of thousands of valuable specimens. In doing so, I was constantly reminded of the need for more specimens to help answer innumerable questions concerning flycatchers. Over the years, I had rummaged through certain species, sometimes to select specimens of *Empidonax* we loaned to Ned. During my time at the museum I also examined specimens of Eastern and Western Wood-Pewees, Willow Flycatchers, Say's Phoebe, Gray Kingbird, and Caribbean Elaenia for various studies to attempt answering taxonomic questions.

CHAPTER 11

Hunting

Large regions of the West attract those who like to hunt, so, naturally, our thoughts about hunting were with us our first days and beyond, whether watching birds catching flies or juncos twittering at the bird feeders. After all, hunting is a strong subject regardless of time. Certainly, there are legal hunting seasons, but hunting could be almost anytime, especially for certain prey including almost any animal perceived as a predator to ones livestock. Even during the first September at Morgan Spring we hoped the solitude to not be broken by a sudden crack from a fired rifle. During that time, we unpacked as steadily as the rain fell in late September at Morgan Spring. Except for the faint patter of misty drizzle, the air was calm. Wanting to hear at least the out-of-doors, we opened a couple of the double-pane windows to hear more. Steller's Jays calling in the nearby trees thankfully reminded us we were in the mountains. Sound waves travel up, and occasionally we heard the crunch of tires against wet gravel below. We reasoned the vehicles belonged to one of the three families between us and the end of the road about a mile distance. We were only partially correct.

In the meantime, we were out the door and exploring well before hanging the last picture on an unsuspecting wall. We thought it could wait. We also wanted the chores to wait, but we had to face facts. The small supply of groceries we had brought up the hill on our first few maiden days at Morgan Spring was getting low. We were dangerously low on peanut butter. In addition to a list of vittles, we also had a small list of cleaning items, birdseed, and definitely more peanut butter. Perhaps we should have added to our shopping list some sort of brightly colored attire that would signal hunters we were not targets.

Going to the Rogue Valley, the lowlands, was an activity we did usually with reluctance. That was partly because we knew non-residents might be roaming the region for a shot at a deer and it was mostly because we had spent several days and nights alone, without seeing another human, and we loved it. We then had two questions to answer: 1. would Morgan Spring be vulnerable to trespassing hunters and 2. how soon could we return to the muse that is Morgan Spring. Driving home, especially once we turned onto Elk Creek Road, was a pleasure, motoring up our driveway a delight, and the rest I will keep private. Linda wrote about our return: "The groceries and sundries were nearly appropriately placed in record time. I was feeling especially proud of my home-arranging talents and unusually energetic after a very long day to town and back buying supplies and visiting people, or as Ralph put it: 'to hell and back getting grub and dodging rednecks.' He really is a nice person, but paints the picture as he sees it." It is true, I am, or at least try to be, a nice person and not everyone we dodged was a redneck.

Linda also chronicled that "Our reward for the round trip to town was pie and coffee. Ralph would shortly be in from outside when finished putting up and locking down. I opened the refrigerator door, sat the pie on the table and almost turned to the cupboard when something unusual caught my eye. Lying in plain sight at the edge of the table near the last Walmart sack was a brochure that read '1996–1997 Oregon Hunting Regulations.' I nearly gasped and I felt a strange tinge of betrayal as most of the energy drained away. Had my Ralph gone through a secret osmosis from gentle animal lover, scientist, and anti-Safarist to big game hunter while I naively sneaked those forest ferns into the backyard? Turning my head sideways to avoid touching the brochure, I looked closer. 'Bag Limits, Outdoor Adventure, License Changes and HIP Requirements, Permit Zones, Wildlife Regions,' read the front cover. A color picture depicted a beautiful, soft-looking male deer with a disproportionately large set of antlers gazing unassumingly into the heavens as a handsome, clean-cut, perfectly postured man in full camouflage aimed a disproportionately large rifle at the deer."

"Hmmm," wondered Linda. "There had to be a benign reason Ralph had acquired this brochure. I shuffled back to the refrigerator and found myself searching for the six-pack of beer Ralph might have hidden there."

Her concerns were my fault for not earlier mentioning the brochure on hunting. My reasoning for picking up the brochure was safety. We both wanted to believe our home was a sanctuary, but I wanted us to be at least aware that hunters might be in the region this time of year. After all, people hunt in Oregon. Not so many years ago, many people would drive around town, to church, to pick up the kids at school with a rifle or two mounted on the back windshield of a pickup where they used to display their weaponry. More recently, those rifles are better hidden. I formerly hunted and my weapon of choice rested on the car floorboard. My quarry then was Ring-necked Pheasant, a hefty introduced species that used to be relatively common in the valley and delicious on the plate. Hunting deer and elk was familiar since some of our relatives annually took aim and Linda and I gladly accepted cuts for a delicious roast or steak. Hunting was the talk of the town, the valley, and the neighbors. Because of so much habitat loss and alteration, hunting deer is almost a necessity since natural predators of deer such as coyotes and wolves were either scarce or extirpated from southwestern Oregon. Cougars, formidable predators, were a rarity. Deer seemed everywhere, wandered into towns, in front of speeding vehicles, rummaged gardens, and were almost anywhere except during hunting season. That was when people had to actually be at least somewhat stealthy before they pulled the trigger of their rifle.

We would wish most hunters good luck, to have a quick and clean kill, and to bring back all of the meat from their prey. Quick and clean kills were not always the norm and the hunted sometimes died a slow and agonizing death because of a hunter's poor aim and lack of skill or laziness for not tracking down what the hunter shot. We also would wish most hunters not to shoot a cow, horse, or human, something that happens every hunting season. Our concern was that not all deer hunters are alike. A few do not mind trespassing, drinking while hunting, and shooting without a clear shot. Historically, the record shows that hunters occasionally shoot something other than their four-legged prey, including shooting each other and sometimes people who live in the woods. Most hunters do practice their trade carefully and respectfully, but the fact is that an increase of beer cans tossed to the side of the road correlated perfectly with the opening bell for hunting season. That could be a problem. Our confidence in responsible shooting and our safety should not be a topic while occupying our turf. The beer in one hand and a gun in the other should not be an issue.

To avoid experiencing any bad habits some hunters might exhibit, we got busy posting our turf bordering Elk Creek Road and up the slope to the upper fence of the meadow. We hammered signs to trees and wooden fence posts along the road that pleaded no trespassing and no hunting, definitely at our lower gate at the road and other areas along the fence, particularly near game trails that hunters might follow. Because we already had hunters driving up our driveway, we even locked our gate should some illiterate hunter think it was fair game and easy access to the ridges beyond. Knowing the dates of the different seasons, the time for shooting by most everyone, the season for kids, for various categories of hunters to shoot their guns and arrows, was a means of self-protection. That might sound ridiculous, but we were not the only ones who practiced caution during hunting season when hunters sometimes shoot themselves. A forest service biologist and friend told me he hates having to go in the field during hunting season. It is true, hunters are not just competing with each other and any difficulty in locating their prey, their bag limit, they are competing with unarmed biologists studying some aspect of the environment, a birder checking to see if Sooty Fox-Sparrows have arrived in the southern Oregon Cascades, or perhaps people picking edible mushrooms for their next meal or to sell. As a favorite TV police sergeant stated before letting the unit's patrol leave the station, "Let's be careful out there."

The bottom of our driveway, with a dusting of snow and a "No Hunting" sign.

One morning we looked up the silent meadow. The straw-colored grass contrasted with the dark and pale greens of trees in the background. A sprinkling of maples, those pesky plants that aggressively take over a logged forest if forest management does not follow through, splashed the forests with bright to subtle reds and yellows. Two hunters suddenly crossed the fence and emerged from the bordering woods and began coming straight for our house. Fortunately, there were no deer between the hunters and us and it looked as if the two did not need our help. The hunters seemed a little surprised when I leaped outside to wave them away. They recrossed the fence and disappeared. Our binoculars revealed the two were unaware or did not care that they damaged the fence during their thankfully hasty exit from the meadow. It did not take us long to discern the difference between a fence damaged by elk and one abused by people. Even though we did not always see them, hunters crossed the meadow fence from time to time. You would think people could figure out how to cross a fence without committing havoc on the posts and wires.

Although varying from year to year, probably depending on how hot it was, we could make a good guess on how many hunters were traveling up and down Elk Creek Road by the number of beer cans tossed on the road and its ditches. Yes, this is kicking the can down the road again, but the drinking and hunting together appeared to be a chronic problem. Again, not all hunters drink while hunting, but those that did below our house worried us. The more cans we found, the more "No hunting" signs went up on the property bordering the road.

One fall day, I was away. Linda was outside gardening. She could hear gravel crunching from the road below and continued with her chores. She probably did not notice the crunching sound suddenly stopped, but it did. Someone had stopped on the main road. It was quiet except for a Red-tailed Hawk crying over the top of the meadow. The peace broke with the crack of a rifle. Someone was shooting from the road immediately below the house, our home. Accompanying the crack, maybe a millisecond later, was the sickening hum of a bullet violating the air mere feet from Linda's head. That was the last time we felt safe on our own property during hunting season.

Surely, someone shot a deer or two in the neighborhood of Morgan Spring, although we did not hear anyone bragging of a kill. What we called our elk herd did not suffer from so much lead flying around. Likewise, we did not hear of anyone shooting a person, at least in the Elk Creek watershed. From the evidence of beer cans, we could see that more than one container was successfully shot. Were those cans surrogates for deer? Soon, the gunfire and road traffic ceased, litter stopped falling, snow covered the ground and then melted, flowers bloomed and birds staked out breeding territories.

After each year's hunting season, we tried to shore up the weak spots of the fence. In time, the situation seemed to improve. Maybe it was our imagination, but it seemed more signs along the road made any intelligent hunter feel the need to point their weapons elsewhere. Were there also fewer hunters? Regardless of the answer, we kept the lower gate secure during hunting season. During each fall, the hunting season, it seemed fewer and fewer hunters were visiting up the last miles of Elk Creek Road. We are not sure why, but are thankful for the outcome. If we heard the tell-tale crunch of gravel on Elk Creek Road suddenly stop, we still thought of ducking for cover. If two vehicles were involved, which sounded different than one vehicle, it might just be a couple of good neighbors stopping to catch up on local news.

CHAPTER 12

Morgan Spring, Its Human History

Linda and I already knew that Morgan Spring, no matter how inviting, how beautiful, was not the Morgan Spring of yesteryear. The relative tranquility before white settlement, before miners and prospectors scraped the hills for gold, before exterminating most of the native people, before hacking down most of the virgin forests, was gone forever.

In the attempt to conjure a Morgan Spring before there was a was, suddenly something appeared across my vision. Just like a TV or movie flashback, words at the bottom of my screen read "Previously, 12,000 to 5,000 years ago." Apparently, the first humans in southwestern Oregon appeared somewhere between 12,000 to 5,000 years ago. It is hard to know for sure when, but giving or taking a few thousand years ago is a long time. Mount Mazama, the mountain that is now the centerpiece of Crater Lake National Park, stood high above until it blew its top about 7,700 years ago. Native people were around then, but the big eruption supposedly occurred 600 years before the earliest natives called the Rogue River region home. Archaeological findings based their estimate on tools for cooking and weapons used for obtaining food, defense, and yes, just as today's humans, war. Although yet to be called American Indians since America had not been named, the natives who lived in Morgan Spring region were known by many, at least by the early nineteenth century, as the Upper or Upland Takelma. Archaeological data indicates native people lived in the lower part of Elk Creek about 4,000 to 5,000 years ago. More accurately, natives that once occupied regions such as Trail to Prospect were Latgawa. Fast forward when, long after Amerigo Vespucci corrected Columbus, maybe in the early

1800s, the Latgawa and other native nations in the region were collectively nicknamed by white interlopers as les Coquins, the Rogues. No one seems to know how many natives there were in the region. The Cow Creek from the Umpqua region to the north are thought to have explored the Elk Creek watershed. Yes, exploration was not limited to white Europeans. Historians do know that innumerable natives were killed by pathogens carried by invading Europeans. That is because natives had not evolved immunity to pathogens common and perhaps only causing the sniffles to a non-North American, but that were deadly to native people. Guns and other violent means used against natives were not the worst weapons employed by those from the Old World. Estimates of the total number of native people are in the hundreds, but the estimates were guesses made mostly decades after white visitors set foot in the region and let their germs go wild. The estimate of natives living along the Rogue River was a tiny number compared to the thousands of miners and early settlers trying to carve out a living in the region beginning in the mid-1800s. Whatever the historical population might have been, miners and settlers absolutely outnumbered native residents. Today's mostly white population in the Rogue Valley is edging toward a quarter of a million and counting. About ten years after Linda and I moved to our abode, the population surrounding Morgan Spring, specifically in our zip code, reported only four natives among Anglo-Saxons, Latinos, and others.

Meanwhile, back in the nineteenth century, the Latgawa lived generally from Jacksonville to what is now Shady Cove, Elk Creek, Prospect, Union Creek, and part of Crater Lake National Park. My ornithological apologies to everyone concerned if the details are wrong. Anyway, the Lowland Takelma (pronounced Dagelma) lived downstream along the lower parts of the Rogue River and Bear Creek, a major tributary of the river. Bear Creek, called Si'kuptpat by the Takelma, means 'dirty water,' which explains why my parents always told me to stay out of Bear Creek. Another tribe, the southern Molalla (sometimes spelled Molala), may have limited their territory to near Elk Creek's headwaters; Molalla occupied the Needle Rock region, just four bird-miles northeast of Morgan Spring. The Molalla, according to our sources, also lived along the Rogue River just north of Prospect to Trail. A stone arrowhead that we found exposed by rain on an abandoned and eroding logging road about a half mile from our house could have been carved by Molalla or Latgawa. Made from agate, we suspected the arrowhead was from the Agate Desert, a flat grassland in part of the Rogue Valley. The arrowhead was not far from other archaeological finds such as large cables and a couple of five-gallon oil cans waiting for rust to empty their oily contents. Some of the reported ranges of the different tribes seem to vary depending on the consulted reference. Probably, there was some overlap of ranges since at least the Latgawa were described as somewhat nomadic. Historians supposed that anadromous fish, Roosevelt elk, mule deer, black bear, marmot, and gray squirrels, as well as quail and grouse, were available for food. More than likely, most bird species were available for food, but obtaining larger birds, such as quail and grouse, made for a more efficient hunt. Acquiring food was no game.

Plants that were eaten by native people included berries, acorns, pine nuts, roots and tubers such as camas, green parts of some plants, and plants we probably could use in our diets today. A popular fast food joint in the Agate Desert probably occupies a formerly choice habitat for camas. We noticed some historians use the term "blackberry." My days struggling through systematic botany are long gone, but it is doubtful the writers meant Himalayan Blackberry, a plant introduced to eastern North America in 1800 as a prospective crop. That invasive plant crept, seed by seed, to western Oregon where it is now a common scourge on the land. Himalayan blackberry and evergreen berry, another introduced species, were likely unknown to southern Oregon until later in the nineteenth century. A museum person has great difficulty throwing anything away, and according to my old college textbook on Oregon plants, there were three or four species of edible berries likely available to the Latgawa.

Long before introduced blackberries wove patchwork quilts across the land, Alexander McLoed, employee of the Hudson Bay Company out of Fort Vancouver, Washington, became the first white person to visit the watershed of the Rogue River. Was his visit the beginning of the end of native occupation of their own land? Did he have a common cold, the mumps? Like all of us, he must have been carrying a measles virus, the one that is the culprit causing shingles. McLoed's visit may have unwittingly began the decimation of the local natives. Later, in January 1827, Peter Skene Ogden, usually credited to be the first white person to trap animals and communicate with local native residents, arrived on the scene. Peter Skene skinned fur-bearing mammals for the British Hudson Bay Company, and remarked in his journal, "It is almost a sin to see the number of small beaver we destroy." Ogden's boss, John McLoughlin, was the chief of the company. He was instrumental to the settlement of southern Oregon and ultimately, Morgan Spring. McLoughlin was host to David Douglas and other early naturalists such as John Kirk Townsend and Thomas Nuttall, the last two people who did not travel far south from their headquarters at Ft. Vancouver. With the establishment of the Applegate Trail in 1846, more and more whites settled in the Rogue Valley and began quenching their thirst by drinking water mixed upstream with Morgan Spring. What is now Oregon became the Territory of Oregon a couple of years later.

In 1850, the US Congress passed the Donation Land Act. In other words, Congress offered 320 acres of land to each adult immigrant, eventually giving away 2.5 million acres. However, surviving natives who had occupied that same land never received compensation, nor were negotiated treaties ratified. Gold, discovered in 1851 at Jacksonville, about 75 miles southwest of Morgan Spring, further changed the environment. Miners hungry for gold, or just plain hungry, swarmed up and down streams and hills of the Rogue Valley. Many of the miners were Chinese men who, according to a nineteenth century publication, made up one-half of the mining population. Most immigrating Chinese were not allowed to bring their wives because of the American fear of them creating families. By 1870, the Chinese contributed to 13 percent of the population in Jackson County, where they were employed in several endeavors. The total population of Jackson County in 1870 was only 4,779 people, contrary to stories that Chinese were over-running the county. Thirteen percent of the total is only 621 Chinese. Mining operations depleted fish populations and often destroyed salmon spawning grounds. The settlers' farming practices began to diminish plants depended on by natives. Loss of land and food, and by and large genocidal attitudes fueled by greed and hatred toward natives, eventually led to more and more violence. Any excuse to violate the natives was the norm, which caused more violence and retaliation. In 1851, the lower Tekelma and possibly others fought army troops near the Table Rocks along the Rogue River; the upper Rogue, including Elk Creek, was not directly affected by the conflict. Caught between the settlers, miners, and military, most all of the Takelma, the Latgawa, and any other natives within the range of a gun were heading for extermination. The few survivors were marched, Trail of Tears fashion, to coastal reservations at Grande Ronde and Siletz. That also included individuals who did not participate in the Rogue River war. Despite a treaty with the Latgawa in 1853, most white settlers attempted to make sure any natives were not part of the landscape by 1856. However, not all members of the Latgawa were killed or captured and some Latgawa today continue to live in southwestern Oregon. However, the US government elected to not recognize many tribes, including the Latgawa, by officially legislating them out of legal existence. Struggle between non-natives and natives continue.

Not all of the local history involved genocide and removal. A group of prospectors led by John Wesley Hillman, wandering up the Rogue River in 1853 on their way to a rumored mine in eastern Oregon, accidentally discovered Crater Lake. Later, in 1859, the bulk of the Territory of Oregon became the state of Oregon. Travelers passed the confluence of the Rogue River and Elk Creek while using a trail that terminated to the south in California and to the north at the John Day River where gold was discovered in 1862.

The trail from California to northern Oregon crossed the Cascades south of Diamond Lake and apparently ran north of what was to become Crater Lake National Park, established in 1902. Merchants in Jacksonville regarded the trail as an important route for distributing products from the Rogue River Valley, and adventuresome sightseers considered the trail important for trekking to Crater Lake. Part of the route built in the mid-1860's branches south of Crater Lake and connected Fort Klamath on the east side of the Cascades to Jacksonville in the Rogue Valley. The route, although occupying one side of the Rogue or the other and subject to considerable streamlining, was what we now know as Oregon State 62, the Crater Lake Highway that runs from Medford to near Ft. Klamath east of the Cascades in northern Klamath County. I like to think of Charles Bendire, Oregon's first ornithologist, passing by the confluence of Elk Creek with the Rogue River when, in the mid-1800s, he traveled between Ft. Klamath and Jacksonville. The creek surely had its present name by then. While at the National Museum of Natural History, I read through most of Bendire's original notes but did not notice any records about Elk Creek. I confess that at the time I was more focused on sapsuckers he collected at Ft. Klamath.

Near the turn onto Elk Creek Road stands the Rogue Elk Inn, built in 1916. It is hard to believe that in its day, the inn was considered one of southern Oregon's finest. Further up Crater Lake Highway, at Prospect, is the Prospect Hotel, established in 1890. For a few years, the hotel dining room was our place of choice for anniversary dinners. Not far north of Prospect, timber interests wanted to cut down the trees along the highway. However, locals in 1934 voiced concern for keeping the forest along the highway in a vertical condition. The forest service bought 8,000 acres of the forest to maintain the scenic route. The average motorist is fooled into believing they are driving through acres and acres of forest. Instead, the route is surrounded by a huge "hedge." Nonetheless, the illusion is calming.

Earlier, in the 1870s and early 1880s to be sort of exact, farmers and their families began homesteading the lower parts of Elk Creek. Linda and I passed some of these old homesteads in the flatter reaches of Elk Creek considerably downstream from the creek's confluence with Button Creek. In 1891, the agricultural community and other settlers established a school on the lower part of Elk Creek. One source wrote that the community consisted of ranchers, but some were farmers. Further upstream, some land in our neighborhood came under the administration of the US government that established the forest reserve of 1893, but management by the Forest Service did not begin until 1906. In 1897, the Elk Creek Fish Hatchery was established. During this time cattle ranchers also began driving their cattle 25 to 30 bird miles up Elk Creek as far as the Umpqua-Rogue Divide. At the same time, shepherds were grazing sheep northeast of Elk Creek. Open range had begun. That means unfenced cattle grazed wherever they wish, something discussed in later chapters of this chronicle. The upper Elk Creek watershed, described by one forest service document, was "very inaccessible" to people, but not sheep or cattle, in the early 1900s. Around the turn of the century, an influx of homesteaders moved up the creek, but many failed in their agricultural endeavors. They sold their property to Big Bend Milling Company. Timber people and cattlemen largely controlled what went on in the mountains at the beginning of the twentieth century. Overgrazing, blamed on sheep, became a problem in 1908, when the upper reaches of Elk Creek watershed became Crater National Forest. Raising sheep declined in the 1930s. By 1955, the forest service considered cattle grazing to be moderate, a term something like a fair amount. It was actually an unfair amount, since Linda and I found thirsty proto-hamburgers commonly soiling streams, damaging riparian vegetation, and compacting surrounding soil.

On several occasions, we chased cattle that broke through fences on their way to Morgan Spring. Of course, the home turf was fenced, but during open season, cattle occasionally found a break in the fence, possibly caused by elk, and would find their way to our spring. We had to keep a watchful eye on the fence and a lookout for cattle mucking the spring. When an interloper did appear, we would give chase. To persuade the bovine to leave, we generally made it feel unwelcome by throwing sticks and yelling unrepeatable salutations. By outflanking its movements, we would drive it off Morgan Spring property.

In addition to cattle and logging issues, local mining had impact to our region including some prospecting that once took place along the Rogue-Umpqua Divide. Significant amounts of gold were discovered in 1897 near the headwaters of Elk Creek. Eventually, a mine opened as the Elk Creek Mine but carried the moniker of the Al Sarena Mine, or the Buzzard Mine. We liked to call it the Buzzard Mine because miners attempted to pick the area clean while managing to produce about $24,000 of mostly gold and some silver and lead from 1900 to 1918. Buzzard Mine reopened during the Depression when gold prices increased. The mine, sitting at almost 3,700 feet elevation, is north of Morgan Spring by 4.5 miles as a Turkey Vulture might fly. This mine employed all kinds of extracting methods, including the use of cyanide. We wonder how the fish and other wildlife, and maybe humans, fared downstream. Bad mining practices are exactly why our wedding rings were recycled rings. Why contribute to the gold trade and their practice of poisoning the land? Meanwhile, back in the 1950s, the Buzzard Mine mining claim was involved in mineral vs. timber rights on national forest lands. The gold in them there hills was not enough. The trees on the claimed land were cut before the 1960s. Forest cover outside of the claim is relatively good as it is southward on Grey Rock Road, but not for the last three miles of the road, which are outside national forest property. The spelling of the word gray, the preferred American spelling, spelled as "grey" possibly means Grey Rock and its road was named for someone named Grey, or perhaps the purveyor of the name was harkening back to their English roots. Private property along Grey Rock Road and elsewhere outside the federal domain would appear to a high-flying buzzard as having been excessively thinned to being clearcut, a forestry term discussed beyond. Fortunately, there are patches of actual forest, which outline land owned by thoughtful stewards.

More and more people came up Elk Creek and onward to Button Creek and the Morgan Spring country. A post office was established in 1902 at the Willet ranch. The post office had the name Persist for the persistence of its first postmaster. Persist, at the end of Elk Creek Road, is about a mile and a half from Morgan Spring. Another post office named Ulvstad existed in 1904 at the mouth of Sugar Pine Creek, about four miles downstream from Morgan Spring. A few more miles down Elk Creek was the Alco post office that opened in 1896. The three post offices, among dozens of such local establishments, were only around 10 miles apart but in those days, that was a longer distance than at present. Even today, the time it takes to drive nearly 15 miles from Persist at the end of Elk Creek Road consumes at least 30 minutes of hard driving, the tires noisily protesting around sharp corners. If you are worried about weather or hitting a deer, elk, or a heavy bovine, as one should, worry that is, or sliding off the road due to fresh cattle manure or ice, the driving time is even greater than half of an hour. The early post offices partially serviced the people who squeezed their own milk from their own cow, baked their own bread, and whose mode of transportation did not involve petroleum products. Every minute counted.

The three post offices also partially serviced people who began homesteading in the region about 1890. According to historian Jeff LeLande, most of the homesteads were barely lived on. Mostly, they were somewhat camped on, the homesteaders enjoying a summer outing under a cheap structure that sufficed to allow them to claim the land under homesteading rules. Many settlers in the late 1800s and early 1900s were what old forest service documents called stump ranchers. These so-called homesteads were part of a scheme for fleecing America because the land was later sold for the timber, usually for a price below what it was worth. Still, both parties were happy and richer. By the 1920s, most of the timber homesteaders had sold their land to large timber interests.

Trees were becoming more and more of an asset. If not owned, they were sometimes stolen. Fire consumed many a tree. Fires in 1910 flared at Bitter Lick Creek and nearby Needle Rock. There were many other fires. A blaze apparently caused by the Buzzard Mine destroyed about 6,000 acres in 1916. That year, over 60 percent of the fires in the Trail Ranger District, the region west of the Elk Creek watershed, were human-set and many such fires were started to either clear land for game or ranching. No bush browsing and self-respecting deer prefer a dense forest. Of course, some must have started from careless stupidity, something that happens all too frequently today.

Some local residents were not accepting of so many fires, and people along Elk Creek had grown tired of fighting fires they might have learned about earlier from a lookout before a fire became larger and far more difficult to control. During the 1900s, the US Forest Service began erecting fire lookouts, one of which was on Whetstone Point on Bald Mountain. The site, a relinquished homestead, started out in 1914 as crow's nest in an 80-foot tree. An actual lookout was constructed in 1924, which was demolished by a fire crew in 1958. Prior to that, lookouts were established on the same mountain ridge at White Point by the Oregon Department of Forestry in 1951 and at Halls Point (Forest Service) in 1958. Elevations of lookouts at Halls Point, Whetstone Point, and White Point are around 5,000 feet, but none allowed for detecting fires within Alder, Button, and parts of Elk Creek watersheds. At least, those lookouts were not visible from Morgan Spring and other regions we visited but were certainly visible from parts of the Elk Creek watershed. Other lookouts were constructed in the region, including Burnt Peak in 1933. A fire caused by a hot bearing from a mechanical saw in 1942 almost put an end to the lookout, but the lookout was maintained another 30 years before it was dismantled. Burnt Peak is five miles southwest of Morgan Spring. Hall Point and White Point are respectively 3.5 and 3.0 miles east of our abode. Only a couple of local lookouts are maintained today; others are gone, but not forgotten. Fires are still detected by existing lookouts, but planes and helicopters partially fill in the gaps of decommissioned lookouts.

The New Deal in the 1930s brought the Civilian Conservation Corps (CCC). They had a camp at the mouth of Sugar Pine Creek. From 1933 to 1942, the CCCs constructed fire lookouts, built a road along much of the Rogue-Umpqua Divide, and strung telephone lines between the newly established lookouts and guard stations. We found some of the old phone lines not far above the meadow that originated from either the CCC or the forest service.

Logging increased during WWII. That would be from 1939 to 1945 for those too young to remember. The rate of logging on both federal and private lands continued to accelerate, especially to supply lumber during the post-war housing boom. Since then, the rate of logging has varied depending on economics and conservation efforts. The methods of logging vary from sustain-yield, leaving seed or so-called wildlife trees (also amusingly christened as leave trees), selecting trees by size, and clearcutting. The forests still owned by the government were under the administration of Crater National Forest until 1932, when the name changed to Rogue River National Forest. It later became the Rogue River-Siskiyou National Forest. Matthews Guard Station, less than a half mile from us, was built sometime, local historian Jeff LeLande related, between 1935 and 1937. Near the station, was a small log pond, and, according to longtime resident, Mose Bush, a tiny sawmill existed. Mose guessed that the mill was once one of many. A little digging revealed that the sawmill was one of 140 counted in Jackson County in 1946. The Button Creek sawmill ceased operations, and Matthews Guard Station, turned over to the Bureau of Land Management in the mid-1990s, is a fallen shell of its former self. In the early 1960s, Button Creek was also the site near logging operations by the Elk Lumber Company. Proof of ownership came from our peregrinations along the fence of the meadow where we discovered some metal signs indicating the forest on the other side of the fence and beyond was owned by Elk Lumber Company. That large consortium probably was the owner of the older littered cables and fuel cans Linda and I found scattered throughout the region. A still larger company bought Elk Lumber Company, much like small farms are purchased by larger farms. Elk Lumber Company was bought by the still larger Boise-Cascade in 1965. Our hikes near Morgan Spring frequently brought us to abandoned large oil and fuel cans, some of which were not empty, heavy cables, and other littered logging paraphernalia.

The big trees were gone in Morgan Spring country; the forest, as far as can be seen, had lost its virginity long ago to the ax and saw. What possible use was second-growth forests? Little to no money could be wrenched from the region. However, the forest service began noticing that in the 1950s and 1960s people were visiting the mountains to camp for the mere pleasure of it all. How strange. They were enjoying the remaining wildness, much of which was visible across tree stumps, hard cow trails with lots of their accompanying insects, and ribbons of roads scraped through the slopes. Eventually, timber companies had removed the more accessible guardian soldiers, the old-growth timber, and realized there was money in harvesting second-growth, trees that managed to grow decades after the initial harvest.

Leftovers are better than nothing. Logging continues, with the smaller not so grand or rotund tree trunks being fair game. Of course, the sizes of those fallen trees sometimes depends on what forest management does, which is often tied to politics and money and less on science. Who knows, in a couple of generations, with gold prices going up and timber becoming scarce, history might repeat itself, with larger and larger clearcuts and the yell of "timber" in all directions. We hope not. It is true that large tracts of terrain in the region of Morgan Spring are owned or leased by timber companies headquartered hundreds or possibly thousands of miles from the Elk Creek watershed. Do those entities have a vested interest in the future of the local watershed? Some residents along Button and Alder creeks possibly resent the invasion resulting from logging and mining. Others may embrace it.

In comparatively recent time, some ranchers were forced to move from lower Elk Creek. Those folks were evicted to make way for a proposed and eventually failed reservoir in the late twentieth century, almost 150 years since the Latgawa were forced to forfeit their homes and way of life.

The history of Morgan Spring itself is only partly known. We pictured it bubbling out of the ground and flowing all the way to the Pacific. Today, the spring overflows during winter and mixes with rain to form what Linda and I dubbed Morgan Creek. In summer, the little spring marsh of purple camas dries. Still, there is enough water for us to drink and bathe, to clean and water our garden.

Jeff LeLande told me he knows little about documents on water rights relating to the Mathews Guard Station. The name Mathews begs to be spelled Mathew's. Unfortunately, some individuals believe dropping the possessive apostrophe is the way of the future. Such people provide us less grilled in grammar with examples such as Lincoln Township and Disney Channel. Okay. I would not say Jackson's County, but if I had discovered our little spring, I would not want it named Browning Spring. Who would drink water that is becoming brown? Was the spring browner because of too many Morgan horses stomping in the mud? Would that hawk flying from the edge of the forest be a bird named in honor of barrel makers or would it be a Cooper's Hawk named for William Cooper, a New Yorker living near what would become a township named in honor of Lincoln? Being the new kids on the land, we were not ready to change the name Mathew, or Morgan, by adding an apostrophe and its little "s."

Incidentally, LeLande's spelling of the eponym of the guard station was "Matthew." That name belonged to Oliver V. Matthews, a botanist living from the late nineteenth century to 1979. Recent maps use the spelling "Mathew," the same spelling of three former forest service employs. That extra "t" or missing "t" slightly tingled my taxonomy and nomenclature senses until I took a deep breath and told myself the issue has nothing to do with scientific names of birds. The spelling of the eponym did not matter. What might be of concern is that old maps indicated the forest service owned more land than appears on more recent maps. Maps sometimes vary in accuracy and detail, but it appears the forest service sold off some of its holdings. That certainly is true of the small guard station that is surrounded by private property. The culture today seems to be that people want to build a house in the forest and any new opportunities such as the sale of land by anyone, including the forest service, translates to people living not just in the urban sprawl, but almost everywhere. When fire season rolls around, many of those people end up starting fires by ill-advised burning of their refuse, sparks from machines, even lawn mowers, and expect protection from wildfires. To protect so many properties by firefighters is impossible.

Anyway, it is reasonable to believe Morgan Spring was once on federal land, but determining that meant digging beyond bedrock. At any rate, someone did build a cistern to collect the naturally slow flowing spring, and someone had laid a one-inch or so pipe from that cistern for about 500 horizontal yards and 200 vertical feet down to Mose Bush's house near the site of the old sawmill.

Wiry Mose Bush had been in the small wooden house only a few feet from Elk Creek Road for decades, first as a logger and later as a school bus driver. Asked about driving large vehicles, he grinned and said he did not worry so long as he did not hear glass breaking or smell blood. He and his late wife drank water from Morgan Spring long enough for Linda and me to know the crisp liquid was safe. As for our share of Morgan Spring water, a small electric pump assisted the water down some 25 vertical feet to our house.

The human history changed Morgan Spring and every inch of what lay downstream. The little Elk Creek school stands and was active during our Morgan Spring days when we slowed to 20 mph in the school zone. Back in the day, wagons likely never moved that fast. The fish hatchery is gone, as is the local sawmill, and also gone are the original residents, native people and the old-growth trees. By 1900, large game had become scarce. Grizzly bears disappeared by 1900. The last wolf in southern Oregon was reported in the 1920s although today the species is making a come-back. Thirty years after the turn of the century, so-called varmint hunters scoured Elk Creek and Morgan Spring country until Jackson County replaced these unregulated hunters with "regulated" government hunters. Mining has come to a standstill, at least temporarily, but building roads for logging and other uses had produced 100 roads by 1975, and the beat keeps rolling on. Another saga of human history is a movement in 1941 to create a new state known as Jefferson, a region carved from southern Oregon south of Roseburg to northern California south of Redding. The state of Jefferson would have included Morgan Spring. The fat lady, not that there is anything wrong with being fat, has yet to sing concerning the state of Jefferson.

A relatively recent historical event, which I almost forgot, occurred in 1952. I hasten to relate that all of the above, the early history of the region, was not something I remembered but something I gleaned from the hard work of historians and other chroniclers of the past. So, the 1952 event was mostly related to us by an astute neighbor. It involved murder, the kind that goes into history books. It seems a 67-year-old miner roamed the region looking for and stealing food from the few residents. Besides his disregard for others, he apparently also did not care for the presence of certain people encroaching upon his territory and shot what he called warning shots at forest service people building a trail. The long arm of the law of the Fish and Wildlife Service was called in and caught up with the culprit somewhere between Persist and the Buzzard Mine. There was a gunfire in which a state trooper was shot and died.

More recently, and already mentioned, was the late Harvey Morgan of Morgan Spring fame. He and Mose Bush must have known each other. What a missed opportunity to write down the stories they might have told. We never got around to quiz Mose enough. Still later, new kids who moved onto the block, including us, might contribute a sentence or more to chronicle Morgan Spring and its surroundings,   Linda and I discovered that tales about the region provided only some of the answers to some of the puzzles. We recognized our region's history was long and complex, but we hoped to learn more. Conversations with Mose Bush emphasized a history worth telling. Linda and I should have taken notes during those times sitting in the warmth of his wood stove and listening to words of his interesting past. We have good recall, but should have put in writing those stories that are now slowly fading from memory. We heard that a local historian had collected an oral history from Mose. Someday, we would like to hear what our old friend had to say. It would surely be plenty, colorful, amusing and enlightening.

As for our paradise, Linda and I could not help imagining the Latgawa camping nearby and savoring the land that held Morgan Spring. What stories they might tell. Maybe much later, perhaps in a footnote or more, someone will reveal a mark we left behind. In the meantime, Linda and I were just getting started by becoming acquainted with every tree and bush, with the wildlife, the mountains beyond, with whatever Morgan Spring might offer.

Morgan Spring and surroundings would be our Shaolin priest, our teacher. We would be the grasshoppers.

CHAPTER 13

The Dirt on Dirt

Once upon a geologic time, lava flows exuded from the steaming bowels of the mountains near Morgan Spring and volcanic debris crept down valleys while fiery rocks exploded into the sky before raining down on a smoldering landscape. Ash from volcanic eruptions smothered everything, white-hot fiery igneous rocks went flying, and lava flooded the land. It was geology beyond the tachometer's red line. It will happen again, probably. We didn't worry. We'd be cool, so to speak, even though we knew Morgan Spring sits in a landscape produced by red-hot volcanism.

The origin of the soil of Morgan Spring is volcanic rock, dust, and ash. Many eruptions along the long chain of the Cascades have left their mark from exploding debris ranging in size from microscopic dust to boulders that could kill a herd of elephants. Volcanic activity is not over. Signs of volcanic activity range from as far south as near the southern terminus of the Cascade Range at Mt. Lassen in California north to Mt. Hood overlooking the Columbia River, Mt. Rainier in Washington, and all the way to southwestern British Columbia at the northern end of the Cascade Range. Mt. Lassen erupted as late as 1915. I have seen the hot spring a few feet below the summit of snow-covered Mt. Shasta. Linda witnessed Mt. St. Helens blowing its top in 1980. Most all the volcanic debris sailed eastward on the prevailing wind currents, but not all. Sitting on a bookshelf is a small vial of volcanic ash my sister collected south of Mt. St. Helens in Portland. The last eruptions for Mt. Shasta was around 1786 and for Mt. Rainier, 1894. Wafts of hot steam emanating from numerous peaks in the Cascades signal we are close to volcanic activity.

About 17 miles east-northeast of Morgan Spring is Crater Lake, the caldera of Mt. Mazama. A category four+ earthquake at Crater Lake must have caused the hairs of many humans to stand on end in 1920. Morgan Spring probably shook that day. Since then, geologists have detected numerous earthquakes in the Crater Lake region. Most were below magnitude four. Quakes are not usually rated according to the Richter Scale, but use what is dubbed the Modified Mercalli Intensity Scale. For inquiring minds that either want or ought to know, a quake on the scale of three in a populated area might be disastrous, but not as calamitous in an unpopulated rural landscape. In a city or in the country, a scale five is something to avoid. According to the scale, this is what to expect: "Felt outdoors; direction estimated. Sleepers wakened. Liquids disturbed, some spilled. Small unstable objects displaced or upset. Doors swing, close, open. Shutters, pictures move. Pendulum clocks stop, start, change rate." Holy do-do! Who wants their pendulum clock to go from tick-tock to tock-tick? Only a few years before moving to Morgan Spring, tiny seismic activity kept the region shaking more than usual, but more activity focused near Ft. Klamath, where Charles Bendire once worked. Are the quakes a precursor to a pyroclastic event?

Old Mt. Mazama of Crater Lake fame has not erupted since historic time, as most chroniclers write. Historic time of white man is what they mean. Of course, history existed before white man mowed through the west. Native people have been traced back to before the cataclysmic eruption of Mount Mazama, with the discovery of sandals and other artifacts found buried by the eruption 7,700 years ago. Although there is evidence that Mt. Mazama was apparently a temporary camping site, there is no evidence anyone made it a permanent home. Early accounts of Mt. Mazama erupting can be found in stories told by the native Klamath. These stories orally passed from the Makalak, the ancestors of the Klamath that lived southeast of the present park. Slightly different versions were borne from oral histories that involved different but powerful spirits who shaped the future, spirits of other legendary cultures that are given homage today.

Of course, Mt. Mazama actually began erupting about 420,000 years ago, give or take a year or two. That was definitely before there was a was. Even 7,700 years ago, when the last big eruption occurred, the prevailing winds were from west to east. That's probably because the earth spun in the same direction then as it does now, which is a good thing. Some of Mt. Mazama's pyroclastic 12 cubic miles of earthen detritus ended up at what is Morgan Spring, but much of the lighter stuff blew eastward. Actually, a map of the distribution of the pumice blown from Mt. Mazama is nearly egg-shaped; the top and broad part of the egg is in most of southern British Columbia and Alberta and as far south as central Nevada. Wait. Pumice? Pumice is very unusual stuff. It can float on water. Pumice is usually frothy, like hardened foam, which is light in weight because of mostly tiny trapped air bubbles inside a glass-like matrix. Many of the qualities of pumice (absorbency, abrasiveness, and more) make it commercially important, even for mixing with soaps, decoration, and filtering vegetable oil, to name but a few. Easily pulverized pumice and other ingredients produce a product called pozzolan, which was used to cement Roman buildings back in the day of Caesar and his knife-wielding senators. A pit mine for extracting pumice existed some years after the Roman Empire about 15 miles southwest of Morgan Spring near the unincorporated settlement of McLeod. The mine is now engulfed by Lost Creek Reservoir, formed in 1977. Bendire, by horse or wagon, and I, by car, must have unwittingly driven right by the site of the mine while he traveled from Ft. Klamath in the late 1800s and while I drove from Crater Lake in the 1960s.

Pumice from Mt. Mazama fell on parts of what would become known as the Willamette Valley, including Portland, and north to the Puget Sound. Still, the brunt of the burnt rocks and pumice rained down east of the nearby site of Morgan Spring. Our home would definitely be a hard-hat zone, but most pumice must have fallen eastward. We did not find pumice in abundance around Morgan Spring, but did find pockets of it only about 16 miles to the south-southwest near the Rogue River and Big Butte Creek. There was probably pumice closer than 16 miles, but it was presumably buried by more local volcanic activity, for example, 20,000 and 30,000 years ago.

Coming in second among volcanic peaks within the zone of rock and ash fall for Morgan Spring is Mt. McLoughlin. The 9,493-foot peak, once known as Mt. Pitt, but renamed McLoughlin for John McLoughlin of the Hudson Bay Company, is the highest mountain between the Three Sisters in the central Cascades and Mt. Shasta in northern California. Mt. McLoughlin would not have its rank in height had not Mt. Mazama, formerly about 12,000 feet in elevation, blown its top. Mt. McLoughlin also experienced some top blowing behavior when the northeast side, with its summit, joined the ranks of smithereens; its maximum height was about 10,200 feet, 700 feet above its present summit.

From what remains, one can see some of the lava flows and debris from Mt. McLoughlin. The lava flows reached the Butte Falls region but not Morgan Spring. From the summit, according to my memory as an 11-year-old climber who scrambled to the rocky outpost with a scout troop, Crater Lake was visible to the north. Klamath Lake filled a significant part of the eastern horizon. This magnificent body of water is the largest freshwater lake in Oregon, at least for now, as debates about water rights could change shorelines. Westward, in the haze, was the Rogue River Valley. Southward, down the Cascade chain stands mighty Mt. Shasta.

Mt. McLoughlin appears ever so symmetrical when seen from the Rogue River Valley and from Klamath Falls. The mountain is the shape a child might draw, with about 45-degree slopes on either side ending with a sharp apex for the summit. It is almost too perfect, too organized for nature. From the town of Butte Falls 24 miles to our southeast, Mt. McLoughlin appears less symmetrical. There are few ridges near Morgan Spring that affords views of Mt. McLoughlin standing roughly 30 miles to the southeast. From those views, the mountain appears more round, which is the result of part of its slope having been blown away. Eruptions of Mt. McLoughlin have been considerably less messy, to use a non-geologist term, than eruptions by Mt. Mazama. Current soothsayers concluded that an eruption from Mt. McLoughlin today would probably terminate thousands of people, but would produce nominal mortality compared to the destruction of an eruption by Mt. Mazama.

Geologically, the scorched earth from north to south was certainly not limited to the local giants of Mt. Mazama or Mt. McLoughlin. Remnants of eroded volcanic peaks and hills surround us. Volcanic dikes stand hard and black on the side of Bald Mountain near the headwaters of Alder Creek. Of course, Linda and I had to explore Bald Mountain when we drove up Alder Creek and higher to White Point and Hall Point on the difficult way east to Prospect. Up close, the basaltic dikes tower above the steep slope. Broken talus, a testament to thousands of years of erosion, litters the base of the dikes. When at home, we kept an eye on these vertical once molten slabs from our east window. The gray rock and talus of Hibbard Point reach 1,300 feet above and two miles northeast of Morgan Spring, reminding us of looking inside the caldera of Crater Lake. Perhaps, but we are left to wonder if the south side of Hibbard Point and possibly the basaltic dikes of Bald Mountain were part of a larger mountain. I should have paid more attention in geology class.

Volcanic dikes of Bald Mountain fill the horizon.

Some of the various kinds of igneous rocks, be they airy pumice, black basalt such as the dikes on the west face of Bald Mountain, or shiny glass-like obsidian, to name a few, are the foundation of soil. Luckily, all of the fire and ice of volcanic activity and glacial grinding produced soil on the old, weathered slopes of the Cascades that now grows hemlocks, firs, and pines, and further down the slope around Morgan Spring, a mixture of pine and fir, with madrone and oak. What thrives where depends on soil, slope and exposure, moisture, average temperature, elevation. and more ecological factors than our Morgan Spring hearts can enumerate. We do know that pines generally prefer dry regions, which is exactly what decades of logging and fires help produce. The removal of firs that mostly grow in cooler regions exposes soil to the sun, which causes snow to melt too fast and speeds up runoff, thereby automatically causing the water table to drop. That is not so bad for pines, but hard for firs to make a come-back and a small lesson in plant ecology that touches, for example, on climate and water availability. To say it again, replacing hemlocks and firs that shade a landscape with pines that offer a less dense forest exposes soil to the sun that heats and dries the forest floor. Warmer and drier forest habitat is more susceptible to wildfires than cooler and wetter habitat. Forests depleted of their trees by wildfires and logging are today more likely to be replanted with what formerly grew there than using pines. Whether the quality of soil after being burned is taken into account is not always addressed during attempted reforestation. Again, replanting mesic species of trees such as firs may not occur immediately. In the meantime, soil and underlying water tables become better suited for xeric species such as pines.

We were naturally happy with whatever trees that survived cataclysmic volcanic activity. Trees and other plants representing a multitude of species did manage to grow. Some appear to even be thriving. At the edge of the forest, touching the meadow, we thought maybe a garden might produce a good salad or stir fry. There would be plenty of sun from morning to early afternoon, just before the shadows of the ponderosa pines west of the house inched up the meadow. A product of tuffaceous rock, the reddish soil at the edge of the meadow was most reluctant to grow tomatoes, potatoes, or nonnative flowers. In soil lingo, the hard soil was not friable and required considerable help. The soil lacked loam and we suspected it had plenty of acid, although we never gave the reddish dirt the litmus test. A county agent might have helped, but we never invited one for a consult. My ornithologist approach left me more confused than if I found myself in a mixed flock of silent *Empidonax* flycatchers. One reference on soils bandied about such terms as Bly and Royst soils and Donegan and McNull series. A heading for some kind of soil reading "Crater Lake-Alcot-Barhiskey" seemed promising, but I soon became lost in the details. Getting the dirt on our local dirt would have to remain a mystery.

Although the identity of what rocks begot what soil remained unsolved, at least by us, we did learn that rich volcanic soil is not a myth and was good for feeding Greeks, Romans, and other citizens lending their ears. We also learned that fertile volcanic soil giving rise to good vegetables is not everywhere, including Morgan Spring. Luckily, the trees growing in Morgan Spring country seem to thrive on the local volcanic dirt, but growing nonnative plants is not for the faint of heart.

Gardening was not our first rodeo and perhaps we could have used some help, but after all, it was our honeymoon and we were enjoying our solitude together. Homegrown tomatoes are not everything. We quickly realized that the original soil, no matter how classified, needed buckets of sand, which were available from nearby Button Creek. The measured amounts of available sand were largely from deposits created during heavy rains that had eroded clearcuts. A year or two of composting in a pit dug between the pines down the hill from the kitchen window offered some good seasoning. Any poop deposits from an opportunistic raccoon or opossum grazing the compost pit or droppings from horses or mules skimming the succulent grasses in the meadow helped cajole the soil to grow seeds and bulbs. In time, and with Linda's amazing green thumb, we eventually won the battle. Several square feet of flowers and some tasty vegetables added to the habitat of Morgan Spring.

Where there is soil, there is potential for mud and dust. Our driveway and the road below were well graveled and our infrequent and slow travel up and down it kept the narrow lane in good shape. Elk Creek Road was another matter. Gravel on its hard-packed surface had a way of flying off the road. Fortunately, most traffic on Elk Creek Road involved people living in the three residences beyond our driveway. The few travelers on the road were enough to make a mess. The gravel that did not bounce off the road was the optimum agent for vehicular tires to complete a kind of perfect mortar and pestle. The more traffic and the faster the traffic, the more tires pulverized the whitish-gray volcanic soil of the road base to talcum-powder dust. Repeated clouds of dust and lack of summer rain resulted in smothering roadside vegetation and ever-changing populations of wildflowers. Summer and unpaved roads in southern Oregon always produce dust. We had been responsible for sending clouds far and wide during our youthful explorations. Dust would rise in rooster-tail fashion, the dry version of a high plume of water from a speedboat. What we had not experienced was living near a dirt/gravel road. Because Morgan Spring sits above the county road and because the prevailing day-time wind in summer is up, we did experience more dust than we bargained for. Luckily, the oaks and conifers between the house and the county road managed to filter out a large portion of the heavier dust particles. Even so, we often kept the windows closed during the day. At night, when the air drained down the hill, we opened windows. By morning, the trapped, clean and cool, unadulterated mountain breezes stayed inside. It was nearly perfect.

Jackson County took care of the road by occasionally grading it or adding new gravel, which the byway needed by the end of summer. Winter rain meant lack of dust while winter snow meant we were on our own. The county did not add cinders or sand to aid traction as they did for the paved lower portion of Elk Creek Road. After all, the graveled section was covered with gravel, but snow often covered everything. Travel was possible only if one could get a grip. Each winter a few extra slick spots also made themselves available on our driveway. That was when we searched for a few shovels of gravel and even our unidentified dirt to shore up our narrow path up the hill from the road.

CHAPTER 14

Trees and Memories of Trees

Speaking earlier of the geology that grows forests and of juncos coming out of the shadows of trees, most of the trees near our Morgan Spring home are ponderosa pine. Tree people know this common tree by the surprising name *Pinus ponderosa*. It is impossible to think of Morgan Spring and not think of its many trees. Fire-resistant ponderosa pine are tall, pushing more than 150 feet, with straight trunks to the sky. Some of these reddish-barked pines were less than 20 feet from the back of the house. Should we worry that one might fall, crushing our home and us cringing inside? We were aware that conifers are notorious for their shallow root system, but the grove nearest us looked as if they had been standing tall for decades and would continue for years to come. One reason conifers can withstand high winds is that they grow in groups, groves, or forests. Isolated trees readily become horizontal from the forces of wind. It is safety in numbers. Wind often blows down conifers at the edge of a forest, but those trees within the forest survive. Still, the root system is small considering the amount of vegetation above ground and trees do topple. The ratio of roots to above-ground in redwoods is tiny compared to the diminutive ponderosa pine, but when the wind did blow at Morgan Spring our pines stood tall.

Ponderosa pine needles are several inches long and attached to the tree in bunches of three. This streamlining of needles, besides allowing for water conservation, permits wind to sail through the needles with less resistance than in broad-leafed trees. Linda and I reasoned the pines probably will not blow over, at least in our lifetime, and that our duration at Morgan Spring would not be short. We saw the trees as an important part of the environment. We also enjoyed the wind singing through the needles. It is a lulling sound not to miss.

Besides pines north of the house and down the ridge, there were several down the slope from the kitchen window. That was, we decided, a perfect place to put a suet feeder. A what? There must be different types of suet feeders, but the one we selected was made of thick molded wire, square in shape, about 6 X 6 inches square and an inch in depth. Had we lost our minds, the scientific minds we left back east? The suet feeder, in our former and perhaps to an extent, our present state of mind, was 152.4 X 152.4 mm square and 25.4 mm in depth. In other words about the size of two or three slices of bread. The suet feeder was attached to the selected tree about five feet above the ground with nails of considerable girth and length. The heavy-duty nails might prevent some animal from dragging it off the tree. In the recesses of my mind, I made a mental note to remove the nails should we abandon the suet feeder from that tree. Nails hammered into trees, forgotten or by unconditional design, would be hazardous to anyone cutting the tree. Of course, our suet tree, we hoped, would stand guard forever. In any event, a valley butcher at a supermarket supplied free scraps of suet. Part of it was frozen and stored among some of our own vittles, the rest was stuffed into the suet feeder. The suet sat in the clutches of the feeder, unspoiled by the winter temperature while waiting to be discovered by some fat-craving bird. Days passed by. Then, one morning, looking out the kitchen window, we saw that the trunk of the ponderosa pine was bare. The suet feeder was nowhere to be seen.

Filling the suet feeder and checking the nearby compost pit at the ponderosa pine a few yards from the kitchen window.

Checking the tree trunk, we found a couple of scratches in the soft reddish bark near where the suet feeder once was attached. Lack of snow did not help prove what we were certain had happened. One of the nails holding the feeder was bent and the other was gone, probably somewhere in the forest litter below. The feeder was located after searching around the trunk of the tree for 15 or more minutes. The suet was gone and the movable side providing the opening of the feeder was slightly more than out of kilter. The feeder was damaged, but not beyond repair. A service station manager I had worked for years ago was fond of saying "if it doesn't work, get a bigger hammer," so I got a bigger hammer and bigger nails. As luck would have it, my generous father, having a great collection of tools, wire, fasteners such as nuts and bolts, and of course nails of many flavors, supplied us with just what we needed. This time, four longer and sturdier nails pinned the suet feeder to the unsuspecting ponderosa. The feeder was scraped off the tree a few more times and each time more and bigger nails were used to anchor it to the tree. We always reckoned the scratches on the tree belonged to a bear. Maybe it was the same one that once scratched at our back door. Having to periodically replace the feeder on the tree was slightly annoying, but it was pleasurable knowing we had a bear as a neighbor. There came a time when the feeder stayed put. We were a little sad. Had our bear moved on?

That same pine holding up the suet feeder continued to shade the forest floor, and its needles joined the chorus of trees singing in the wind. The feeder hung on and became a favorite to a male Hairy Woodpecker, but usually in my absence. That is when Linda saw the male woodpecker swoop to the feeder as I drove down the driveway. This happened frequently enough for us to draw an analogy: birds cannot count, our house was a blind, and the male reasoned the coast was clear to visit the suet feeder. Researchers and photographers have long depended on two people entering a blind and one leaving since birds seemed to think the blind was empty. Of course, birds can count, but our woodpecker may have been a poor student of basic arithmetic. After years of solitary feeding, the male began to share the suet with a female. Steller's Jays tried their best to raid the feeder while attempting to balance on the vertical tree. We saw our first California Scrub-Jay on the feeder one late summer. The dominating Steller's Jays must have intimidated the scrub-jay back down the slope where the species normally foraged.

Ponderosa pines dominated the drier terrain. Two small ponderosa pines, both at least a foot in diameter, anchored the ends of a very comfortable cloth hammock. Further down the ridge toward Elk Creek Road and along the lower part of our driveway grew oaks, a few madrones, and a couple of sugar pines. The oaks littered the floor with the crinkly, tan, lobbed leaves, leaves that before hitting the ground in late fall and early winter hung on as snow fell. The forest floor also was littered with the broad leathery leaves from the smooth reddish barked trunks of madrone and offered perfect stomping grounds for Ruffed Grouse. We tried not to bother the grouse, but on several occasions saw them scurry away when we walked to the mailbox.

The madrones (aka *Arbutus menziesii* or Pacific madrone), a broadleaf evergreen, grow from the Rogue Valley floor to elevations well above Morgan Spring. Our species has two smaller relatives, one in Arizona and one in Texas and all belong in the Heath family that includes manzanita, a scrubby bush. Pacific madrone is unique because part of its usually twisted trunk and crooked branches are covered with scattered patches of rough gray bark; the remainder of the tree has a skin of rich chestnut smooth to the touch. This smooth bark is shed in paper-thin sheets as the tree grows. Underneath the old bark is the new greenish bark that in time will become chestnut. This tree also produces fist-sized flower heads hosting quarter-inch jug-shaped white blossoms. The blossoms are often favored by spring migrating warblers since the blossoms attract insects. In turn, the warblers, along with hummingbirds, help pollinate the flowers. During the fall, a host of birds dine on the madrones' clusters of round reddish fruits. Because the seed containing berries from festive orbs are too heavy for the wind to carry, birds are important in dispersing them. Madrone grows scattered singly or in small groves in nearby forests. The trees are a bane to people involved with timber harvest who believe madrones take up water that could otherwise be used for commercially valuable conifers. I am no botanist, but some studies show that Douglas fir, for example, do quite well with madrones. Mostly though, the canopy of madrone is regarded as a boon to sun-loving pines, a type of tree that grows well once logging has lowered the water table.

Because fast-growing madrone is much maligned, the trees are sometimes poisoned and cut from potential pine fields, thus it is readily used as firewood. We enjoyed the changing colors of the bark, the white flowers, and clusters of fruit and all the birds that benefited from such a wonderful tree. Perhaps our favorite was one madrone next to the driveway that held up a nest of Cassin's Vireo.

Another unusual tree is a dark green-needled conifer called Pacific yew, aka *Taxus brevifolia*. Botanical references state that yews prefer shady and wet regions, which was exactly where they grow in Morgan Spring country. The species occurs throughout northwestern California to western Oregon and north to Alaska. Its seeds are extremely poisonous, which Linda and I did not know at our first yew encounter. The few trees we found were stubby examples of themselves, perhaps hiding from human poachers that might steal their cancer-fighting bark. Linda and I imagined natives fashioning bows from local yews. We read that the wood of a yew is often used for fence posts.

Having labored on fence lines, I do not recall any posts of yew. In fact, most of the wooden fence posts I had the honor of planting were, to the best of recollections, some kind of cedar. Our cedars, the cedars of Morgan Spring, were incense-cedar. Cedarologists, or dendrologists by any other name, know the species as *Calocedrus decurrens*. Almost everyone has held *Calocedrus decurrens* in their hands while using a pencil to perhaps write the burning question: What is pencil rot? The answer: it is the result of an infestation by a white fungus, a symptom common in cedars. Incidentally, most of the world's wooden pencils once originated in southern Oregon.

We found several cedars with wide girths, that is to say in tree manager lingo, they had a large DBH. Usually given in inches, DBH is diameter at breast height, which, of course, will be different depending on the height of one's breast. Officially, I was told, DBH is defined as 4'8," but the consensus in the US is 4'5"; it may be higher or lower depending on the country of origin of said breast. My breast is four feet and two inches and I am a 6-footer and do not sag. A park ranger who was a roommate at Crater Lake National Park too many decades ago would be obtaining his DBH at least 11 inches above my mark. For those measuring DBH, folks under 21 need not apply. Most of the cedars we found distributed throughout the surrounding forests were much too large in diameter for my reach. That the diameters of those trees were noticeably greater than most other species of conifers growing nearby begged the question: could it be that the local cedars had been spared the saw for several years? Perhaps the larger and therefore older cedars have developed what foresters call heart rot. One thing Linda was sure of is that her father was once in demand for his expertise in splitting cedar rails for fences.

Within view of the madrone hosting the Cassin's Vireo nest stood the stately dark-barked sugar pine, known as *Pinus lambertiana* by your local tree people. Generations of cones lay at the base of the tree trunk. The newer, unweathered cones, those fallen the same year, are something to behold. Compared to the thorny cones of the longer-needled ponderosa pine, sugar pine cones are giants, being much wider in circumference, and may reach up to two feet in length. Being under any pine tree is risky, but standing under a sugar pine might be fatal. We took our chances, gathering some of the cones for decoration in our Morgan Spring abode. One particular sugar pine was favored as a place to sit and contemplate whatever struck our fancy, which was often each other. That tree and most sugar pines are in danger from beetles and fungi. One survey concluded that 84 percent of the sugar pines surveyed were killed by mountain pine beetles. Around thirty years ago, I recall our fire crew at Crater Lake National Park falling lodgepole pines that were infested by some kind of bark beetle. We identified troubled pines by their beetle-caused pock-marked bark. Once on the ground, we sprayed the tree trunks in order to kill beetles under the bark. Most of the trees we felled were less than a foot in diameter. Lodgepole pine does not grow at our low elevation.

Sugar pines can grow for hundreds of years. Confirmed by tree rings, one tree reached its 614th birthday, and several sugar pines are suspected to be close to 800 years of age. During all those years, centuries before Columbus did NOT discover America, sugar pines gained respectable height. The tallest sugar pine in Oregon is 255 feet up there. Its height may be a product of what forest managers call "wind firmness," which means the species does not easily blow over from strong winds. In the old days when small-capacity sawmills operated in the Elk Creek watershed, sugar pines were favored for making wooden shakes. Shakes, I discovered, are thinnish pieces of wood split on both sides whereas its less expensive cousins, shingles, are sawn on both sides and, as the lexicon stated, thinner than a shake at its butt. One of the surprising if not esoteric modern uses of sugar pine is piano keys. Whatever its wide array of uses, by 1900, sugar pines had become rare on the lower slopes of the watershed. The species is presently doing alright but is under threat from diseases such as rust enhanced by drought and climate change. The tree's name was the root for the name of a creek and road, and much later, the name of a wildfire, all within the Elk Creek watershed.

Our favorite sugar pine was not of record height but looked healthy as it stood isolated from taller conifers and oaks below its lowest needle-bound branches. Its southern exposure was at the whim of wind coming up Button Creek Valley, especially from the hotter gales spawned in the concrete heat sinks in the Rogue Valley. From the base of the sugar pine, our view offered a panorama of fire-stricken Burnt Peak. During a lull while looking for nearby birds, it was possible to think of eagles sailing over Button Creek, a forest that might have once grown on Burnt Peak and the mountain land further south, including, beyond view, Lost Creek Reservoir, Crater Lake Highway, and a route taken by pioneering ornithologists.

Growing under our sugar pine and in numerous other locations were small bushes in the genus *Ribes*, which represents gooseberries and currants. Unfortunately, a fungal pathogen uses *Ribes* as part of its life cycle that eventually does damage to pines. There is a lot more to the story, but there are more trees to discuss, not to mention many other aspects of living at Morgan Spring.

Oaks, the most common deciduous trees near our home, would lose their leaves each fall to remind us winter was coming. The oaks of Morgan Spring country were low and mostly stunted, even compared to the so-called scrub-oak groves of the Rogue River and Bear Creek valleys. Those lower elevations contained black and white oak. The white or Oregon oak, the one without the bristly-tipped lobes on their leaves, grows marginally at elevations shared by Morgan Spring. In the event inquiring eyes want to know, the acorn producers in the region are *Quercus garryanna*. These oaks connected us to the valley of our youth and were the only major species that reminded us of seasonal changes in tree foliage. Fortunately, the oaks stood too far from our Morgan Spring home to worry about raking shed leaves or collecting their nuts.

What I did not realize is that although no oak leaves landed near the house, several pounds of long, tan needles from the nearby ponderosa pines fell year-round. Very few fell until autumn. When the needles rained down, they rapidly covered the roof and tenaciously clung to it like thatch. Left without any other choice, we had to sweep and sweep to remove them. It was frustrating, but not so much that the wind singing in the conifers, wind blowing clean and crisp air across their musical needles, went unnoticed and unappreciated.

The last major species of tree growing close to our abode were scatterings of long-living Douglas fir, second only to the redwoods in potential height. Douglas fir is but one of 30 species of coniferous trees found in Oregon. The species grows in a wide variety of habitats, soils, and elevations, which helps explain why the species is the most common conifer in Oregon. Several Douglas fir towered over the understory in the wetter and cooler canyon of Morgan Creek. Why the species was restricted to those specific localities is difficult to know since most of the region has been logged at least once since being settled by man.

Douglas fir is also known as *Pseudotsuga menziesii*. The word "pseudo" is a clue that Douglas fir is not actually a fir, it is a false fir, insofar as concerning the English name, and is not a hemlock insofar as the *tsuga* in its generic name. Go figure. Superficially it has characteristics of hemlock, and, stretching the imagination, a true fir, but I will stop here before I exceed my knowledge base, get out of my lane and go above my pay-grade. The soft feathery boughs of Douglas fir remind us of the Mountain Hemlock of nearby Crater Lake National Park. Douglas fir was discovered by Archibold Menzies in 1792. Lewis and Clark collected specimens of Douglas fir in 1806, but those were unfortunately lost. David Douglas is credited with having rediscovered the tree in 1825 and with having collected specimens that were sent for further examination and proof of Douglas's observations.

1825 was the year a French botanist proposed the scientific name honoring Menzies. There is considerably more hovering around the nomenclatural history of the tree, but I will rein in the story. Suffice to say, Douglas, who was headquartered at Hudson Bay Company facilities in the early 1800s, introduced the tree to England, thus giving the species more notoriety and he becoming the namesake for the English moniker, Douglas fir.

Doug fir, a shorter name for the tall tree, are capable of living past 1,300 years and growing over 300 feet in height. At least one Washington state Douglas fir lived to a ripe old age of 1,400 years before being cut from a long existence. When Linda and I looked at our Douglas firs, we could not imagine how someone might feel ending such a tree.

Douglas fir are fast growing trees reaching three to five feet in five years, maybe sooner. Owing to their appearance and soft texture, young trees have become the nation's favorite for Christmas trees. Although each December at Morgan Spring presented ample opportunity to have one of the many Douglas fir sprouts for our Christmas tree, we opted for a less traditional holiday. After all, we had to have the energy for those over-the-top holiday dinners with relatives down in the Rogue Valley. When at Morgan Spring, no matter the season, we enjoyed the safety and comfort of our home standing tall from lumber carved from Douglas fir.

In addition to rediscovering Douglas fir, David Douglas, the intrepid botanist and explorer, was the first to describe another noble tree found at Morgan Spring. That tree was the sugar pine, a tree that almost got Dave killed, but that is another story. David Douglas collected as far south in Oregon as the Umpqua watershed. During his treks in Oregon, Douglas also collected the first Oregon white oak, which he named for an employee of the Hudson Bay Company who helped him in 1826. David Douglas might have felt at home at Morgan Spring since so many species of trees were already in his wheel-house. David Douglas' discoveries were based on specimens and observations from old-growth forests. At the end of the twentieth century, our nearest old-growth or virgin forests were miles and miles away, save those within the protective boundary of Crater Lake National Park. We would never see the Pacific Northwest as did David Douglas.

Scottish born Douglas collected several species of birds new to science. Sorting out exactly where he was during the time he collected the first specimens of Mountain Quail enticed me to study his itinerary, since the collecting localities of the quail affected their subspecific nomenclature. My research produced a four-page paper published in 1977, which was printed in a journal headquartered in England, a wee bit south of Douglas's home country.

Getting back to trees, David Douglas, pioneer discoverer of trees, left a story of extraordinary accomplishments. Like many good field workers, Douglas kept a journal. It makes for enlightening reading that once you get into the journal you want to turn the page to see what happened next. In addition to his journals, it is definitely worth reading books about his accomplishments during the exploration of Oregon, Washington, and parts of California. Douglas's last adventure was Hawaii, where he mysteriously died, either by the hoofs of a mad bull or the hands of humankind.

Trees help make Morgan Spring, not just by creating a watershed for liquid to bubble from the ground. Trees cover the rough volcanic skin with color and continued life for everything growing under the their crowns and all life living in and above the branches. Morgan Spring trees, from the reddish bark on the scaly trunks of ponderosa pine to the silky smooth madrone, the grays trunks of sugar pine, Douglas fir, gnarly oaks, and the amazing multitude of varying shades of green, mostly covered all but the meadow and beyond. We kept our fingers crossed that future logging would not be clearcuts and that oxygen-giving forests would flourish to give the planet, the surrounding landscape and Morgan Spring a long and healthy future. Were we naive?

Okay, okay. It is time, finally to explain the term clearcut. After all, the method may fall somewhere in the reality of naivety or economic smartness. Regardless, and without further ado, a definition of a clearcut is in order. First, though, it must be said that the word or form thereof, is not in most dictionaries. Oxford, for example, prefers clear-cut. Spell checkers also prefer clear-cut or clear cut, omitting the usually useful hyphen. However, forest managers and the timber industry like the term clearcut. The timber industry especially likes the term clearcut since it is a fast and cheapest means of harvesting timber. By cheapest, I do not mean the most economical for the forest. According to good old Oxford, it is "(an area) from which every tree has been cut down and removed." That is pretty much what Linda and I thought. However, we would later see that although all trees were cut down, not all were removed. According to the Associated Oregon Loggers, Inc, "Professional foresters define "clearcutting" as the harvest of nearly all standing mature trees within a specific area for the purpose of then regenerating a new young even-aged forest." Oh, the trees are cut just to make room to regenerate new trees. Why not also say "and to make money from the harvested trees." Oregon would not have had to pass a law that logged regions must be replanted if every company was voluntarily concerned about reforestation. Of course, there are those looking at a future longer than their own generation, but the rate of cutting (not to mention rate of wildfires) should make everyone nervous.

There was much to learn. When we moved to Morgan Spring in 1996, we were unaware that relatively recent changes had occurred in the Elk Creek watershed. From 1948 to 1993, a report on the watershed stated there was a major increase of hardwoods (oaks?) and 12 to 22-inch DBH Douglas fir, with a huge increase of Douglas fir larger than 22 inches DBH. We also read that logging in the 1980s changed from clear-cutting to the so-called shelterwood cutting method, aka cutting most of the trees, but leaving those needed for sufficient shade to produce a new age class. According to an on-line web article by the US Forest Service, the shelterwood method is more complex than my statement above. It is complicated.

Regardless of what had happened and will happen to the forests surrounding Morgan Spring, we hoped the habitat would be safe from too many changes, especially those so severe that generations would be required to return the habitat to what we enjoy today. The reaction of forests to environmental changes, whether natural or human-induced, will tell part of the story concerning human evolution. Climate change will alter temperature, precipitation and cause increases in fatal insect infestations, which will make or break some forests through drought and susceptibility to fire, natural or otherwise. Although climate change is a natural phenomenon, human-induced climate change is not and is occurring at an unnaturally rapid speed that is much too fast for any evolutionary adjustment. This disaster is already ongoing, its severity more obvious in some regions of the globe than others, but looming at every corner of the planet. At the same time, greater demand for wood products and human-caused wildfires will likewise change the quality of forests by decreasing the number of trees. That is to say, forests cannot be sustained in the face of too much logging and rampant wildfires.

Meanwhile, we admired the thin needles and wide waxy leaves, the glory of conifers, madrones and oaks that yield their many shades of green. Ranging from bright to dull green, from rich and dark hues to a gradually changing green, a green that on a not too distant ridge is greenish-blue, but is bluish-green on the furthermost mountains. From our window, we daily watched the trees. From our vantage, we could observe the first snow march down the slopes, first frosting distant green trees at higher elevations, then descending with flakes dancing across the bird feeders and hanging on the needles of our ponderosa pines and Douglas fir. When the snow melted, the burbling of intermittent creeks competed with the soothing wind bending branches, curling around pine and fir needles. Some of that melted snow and rain quickly ran downhill, too rapidly to soak in and fast enough to erode soil, but nearby the water soaked into the forest floor to quench the thirst of wildlife, including green trees. How could anyone not appreciate trees and the memory of trees?

CHAPTER 15

Mushrooms and Telephones

Mushrooms grew under the trees and trees provided poles for telephone lines. Mushrooms and telephones have a close relationship for us since their kinship began during our first cool and wet fall at Morgan Spring. At that time and later each fall, our explorations on the damp forest litter allowed us to navigate the area with the stealth of our ancestors, or so we told ourselves. The deer, skittish from either being chased by natural predators or shot at by unnatural hunters, were surprised as we rounded a bend on an old path down a ridge above Morgan Spring. So many animals are vulnerable to man.

Animals on our first day of exploring, slogging across the wet leaves shed from summer growth, must have been listening more intently than when it is drier and the forest floor is crunchy. When you are food to anything larger than you, it pays to be extra alert. A Hermit Thrush, intently foraging along the wet and dark ground, was startled by our approach. Were we its predator? Looking past the thrush, our gaze became transfixed downward to the ground. Mushrooms were growing almost everywhere, and every step revealed even more and more mushrooms. In minutes, we realized that not all mushrooms are created equally. There were many kinds of mushrooms. Some of them were colorful, some on stumps, many under trees, and some with large portions of them gone.

Fungi of all shapesk sizes, and colors grew in the fall.

All kinds of mushrooms covered the forest floor. We had purchased several field guides at Smithsonian's store in the Natural History Museum. We had one on flowers, a new one on birds, trees, and fungi. According to our count, we found 20 species of mushrooms during our first walk in the immediate vicinity of the house. At least we think we saw 20 species. We cannot be sure, but we were even more amazed while exploring different slopes beyond the meadow and finding mushrooms that differed from the ones near the house. There was a plethora of the so-called toadstools, the type that has a stem holding up a wide-brimmed cap. We observed a wide variety of caps from bell-shaped to flat, sunken, with surfaces ranging from smooth to scaly. Peeking under the hood of the mushrooms we noticed variation in the spacing of what we think must be their gills. Most of them appeared to grow solitarily, but there were some that grew in groups. Colors were mostly white to grayish brown or shades of browns and tans. Some had white stems with dark tops. Many of the white kinds were so pure white that they nearly glowed in the hushed forest light. A few fungi were gorgeously bright orange. There were more orange-hued fungi growing on sides of trees, some on dead wood, some on live trunks. We were fairly certain that we were looking at shelf fungi. We also found fungi that looked every bit out of water, which we later found to be coral fungi. Although not abundant, stubby brownish mushrooms with cupped tops appeared to contain whitish nodules. The mushroom is a member of bird-nest fungi that make up a whole order appropriately known as Nidulariales. The eggs contain spores.

We were in mushroom city, or so we imagined. Experts are not in total agreement, but there may be anywhere from 1.5 to 5.1 million, yes, million, species of mushrooms worldwide. Numerous mushrooms, like so many other organisms, wait to be discovered, let alone even partly studied. Most mushrooms grow in the tropics, but the number of species in North American is 10,000 and counting. Wow, 10,000. That is about the number of species of birds worldwide. Apparently, there are thousands more of mush-rooms and maybe our foray at Morgan Spring is putting us in touch with undescribed species. Unfortunately, our observations did not contribute to science.

At the time, we did not realize the importance of fungi to the trees that grew above. Of course, fungi breaking down dead plants was something learned in grade school, but it seems that in 1885, someone recognized a widespread association between plant roots and naturally occurring mycor-rhizal fungi. Technically, there are three types of mycorrhizal fungi that live inside the cortex, surface or around the epidermal cells of plant roots. Ar-buscular mycorrhizal fungi are the ones that carry out phenomenal tasks of creating partnerships between the fungi and plants. Mycorrhizal fungi help plants absorb nutrition from the soil and ward off harmful predators, while the plants provide nutrients to the fungi. By the 1970s, 80s and early 90s, people were describing the strange partnership between plants and fungi as occurring from the tropics to arid deserts and arable acres everywhere. The beneficial symbiosis between fungi and plants goes beyond nutrition, and - I am not making this up - it helps plants to communicate. That is correct, research on a highly reputable scale by scientists of good stand-ing working for established organizations, some that we all know and love such as Smithsonian and National Geographic, have proven tree A talks to tree B. Well, not exactly talks, but the trees communicate chemically. Yes, really. More amazing specific examples of scientifically proven mutualism involve insects. Oh no, some might sarcastically scoff that insects are mak-ing sounds which cause the trees to buzz about the bugs. Actually, that is close to the truth. A tree, possibly weakened by drought, might be attacked by a leaf-eating bug. The tree under siege transmits a message to the sur-rounding trees that respond by increasing a chemical causing their leaves to taste bad to the attacking insects. Again, trusted institutions back up their conclusions with reams of data supporting their observations that commu-nications occur between plants and between plants and mycorrhizal fungi.

Arbuscular mycorrhizal fungi were under consideration for agri-culture at least as early as 1991 and are more currently sold to forest tree nurseries, orchardists, commercial farmers and gardeners. Why? It turns out that the teeny tiny fungal roots or filaments, actually the hyphae, that interconnect mycorrhizal fungi with plants help in the survival of about 90 percent of all plants. What might at first seem like a joke about plant communication turns out to be the real thing.

Meanwhile and above ground, Linda and I marveled at the diversity of fungi growing around Morgan Spring. Obviously, neither of us are experts in identifying mushrooms. Neither of us comes close to being a mushroomologist or mycologist, as they would say back at Smithsonian. According to some sources, about 1 percent of mushrooms are deadly. More, perhaps 20 percent, will cause anyone to use up sick days while nursing an alimentary canal in trouble. Those sickening toadstools are said to be expelled from whatever end of the digestive tract that is closest to the offending fungi. About 50 percent are either inedible because of taste or texture while 25 percent are edible although not tasty or are simply tasteless. Only 4 percent taste good, at least to most people. Even so, we wanted to be somewhat expert in our identifications regardless of dreamed-of mushrooms in our salads, in a sauce, or lying on a simmering roasted chicken. We knew it might be possible to hallucinate a good mushroom soup, given the right species. The store was open, but there was no one to tell us which mushrooms would be safe and which ones might ultimately kill us. False morels came to mind, but could we be sure the true morels we thought were in view were telling the truth? Gambling was not in the cards. We knew that something had been munching on certain mushrooms and we did not notice any deer or other animals tripping out on what they had eaten. We decided that learning which mushrooms would be good for our diet might just be our last lesson. The range from edible mushroom to fatal error was just too large for a sure thing. However, a relative down in the valley phoned that some of the mushrooms were likely morels. You could hear him salivate.

Speaking of telephones, having one in remote Morgan Spring country was essential when you needed one. There was a landline connection. Cell phones and their ugly towers seemed hardly beyond on the cusp of science fiction. Anyway, most of the time we could have lived without a phone, but an emergency might require a one. Under normal circumstances, we considered it a pleasure when the phone was not working. It was especially pleasurable when it was not ringing, particularly during mealtime or other times when you did not need it. It was almost pleasurable when the phone company mistakenly cut off our long-distance service to our landline. We never really understood why. We paid our bills on time. All we did, or at least we thought we did, was change from one long-distance company to another. The new long-distance company told us how much they were going to appreciate our business. However, they somehow did not turn the right switch that would actually allow them to enjoy our business. Ordinarily, that would not have been a problem except almost all calls from our remote abode were long-distance, all except calling down the road to our neighbor. He sympathized with our predicament.

So far, the story may seem rather foreign. That might be because phone companies in the days of yore had a local calling area and anything geographically outside the local area was considered long-distance. Each and every long-distance call was attached to a fee, which varied depending on the distance of the long-distance call and the duration of the call. At the time, it was possible to have one company handle your long-distance calls and another for one's local calls. At least that was the way it seemed in the mid-1990s in rural southwestern Oregon. Cell phones with unlimited calling were not in our vocabulary.

Although stuck in a sort of phone limbo, we could access the 800 number of the phone company. Linda and I began a daily campaign to connect to the world beyond Morgan Spring, especially because we had offspring and parents. As strange as it may sound, in the mid-1990s, not everyone, including us, had the benefit of email. Communicating to the outside world took the two of us over a week to reach the correct phone person, who might ultimately flip the correct switch for us. Our task was more difficult than trying to reach the President to ask that the White House Christmas Tree be switched on a day early. Huh? That is another story.

We especially needed our long distance service to call down to the valley. Our flatland relatives worried that we would end up as a meal for a cougar, mauled by a bear, or fallen into quicksand. Not wishing to do harm, we took solace knowing that even if a cougar dined on our bodies, it would at least get steroid-free meat. We saw bears, cougar tracks, and sand that was too slow to be quick. What we feared immediately was the phone company.

Once the phone company finally reconnected us to the world beyond Morgan Spring and vicinity, we could call and fax to our heart's delight. Of course, back in business also meant receiving pesky unwanted calls. Dozens of callers asked us if we wanted to replace our car windshield. They were all from the same company. Begging them to take us off their list did not help. They promised but called back the next day or two, perhaps thinking a windshield breaker was harassing people way up Elk Creek. We began to wonder if our windshield was going to be broken, perhaps by the unwanted callers. We tried screening our calls most of the time. Of course, there are always those friends and relatives that do not like answering machines and will not leave a message no matter the circumstances. They are not leaving information to a machine, which at that time would be a tiny tape recorder.

The same people will let the phone ring just long enough for you to run from outside, slide to the phone just as they hang up. They also ask you, when a connection is actually made, "where were you, I've been calling and calling." My Dad once asked, "Don't you answer the phone?" It is enough to drive one crazy. What was worse is that some businesses are just as bad. We like informality but when a business acts like a relative, the situation has gone too far. Actually, it went too far with the real-live relative, who leaves incessant mystery rings but knows you cannot fire them. Instead, the phone becomes an object of conveying guilt. For example, there are the long conversations about the weather. They are experiencing essentially the same weather as we are because they are only 50 to 60 miles away. Hello! I do have to interject here that the temperatures are cooler and there is more snow at Morgan Spring than in the Rogue Valley. Finally, it would be time to end a conversation. Should we feel guilty for trying to shorten the interminable good-bye? Whoever hangs up first is the guilty one. Linda and I used to have long good-byes during long-distance calls because we genuinely feared that might be the last time we would be able to speak to one another. What if one of us was run over by a truck? Maybe our relatives also worried about wayward trucks, but there were numerous reasons for getting the hell off the line. It could be that I am unable to articulate a proper ending to the conversation at this time, I want you to feel guilty, I am bored and want to make you bored also, talking on the phone is my entertainment, I think I have something important to say even if I know I am repeating myself, I am repeating myself but don't realize it, I don't think you have enough to do so I am going to entertain you, I called to see how you are doing but really want you to ask me how I am doing, and more. There is always that lurking possibility that someone might call to announce they have fallen and cannot get up, oblivious to the fact that calling 911 would bring help faster than it would take us to negotiate our driveway, let alone traveling 50 to 60 miles down a winding mountainous road. In the meantime, we thought of answering relative calls by saying that we would have picked up sooner but had to get the quicksand off our boots and dislodge the cougar's teeth from our favorite body part.

A minority of our relatives did not play the game of making us feel guilty for living in such a wonderful environment as Morgan Spring. However, any worry on anyone's part was unfounded. After all, Linda and I partly moved to Oregon to worry about them, particularly to help our ailing parents live out the remainder of their lives as comfortable and dignified as possible. That was why using a phone from time to time was so important.

We also phoned our parents to discuss visiting with them. It seems impolite just to show up at their door. Surprise! Your wonderful kids are invading your home, again. No, we would call ahead. We expected the same in reverse. Our parents rarely visited, mostly because they were at the stage of being unsafe drivers. However, other, more distant relatives seemed to think we would enjoy unannounced visits since they thought we sat around the house lamenting the absence of kinship. That was far from the truth, and we quickly communicated a kind of polite manifesto that we did not appreciate impromptu rendezvous. Asking for a little decorum elicited misunderstood reactions from a few who were born never to close the barn door behind them. Eventually, most training sessions worked. Knowing guests were on their way gave us time to bake a cake or at least be dressed, or at least dressed for the occasion. Fortunately, most of our time at Morgan Spring had nothing to do with phones and more to do with mushrooms and watching more juncos coming to the feeder.

The behavior of calling ahead was also handy for businesses and us. Because of the distance between Morgan Spring and any commercial enterprise, we did not have the time or inclination to drive all over the countryside to find something we might need at Morgan Spring. We practiced the old practice of letting our fingers do the walking. That is harder to do that now than a few decades ago. Merchants now frequently hire people who, for lack of training or interest, do not know what product or service they are selling. We have often been in stores and gotten more information from customers than from the folks that work in the establishment. Try that on a phone. If the clerk cannot answer the question, ask to speak to a customer.

Late in our Morgan Spring residency, one of the more modern stores where we did business gave the employees cell phones. An outside caller could ask for a department and then be switched to a clerk roaming the floor. That worked well for calling in but once physically in the store, it was impossible to talk in person to an employee because they were on their phone answering questions.

At that point in time, we had not fallen into the open pit representing the technological device that keeps everyone connected, everywhere, constantly, so that there is never silence, never a person left in the darkness of not being in touch with all members of the species. Although we did not arrive at Morgan Spring with cell phones, we eventually and reluctantly succumbed, but our devices were for real emergencies such as I hit a cow, careened into the forest but luckily the trees were cut and the stumps burned and stumbled into a stream where I shared a pool of quicksand with a hungry and ferocious cougar. In other words, I have fallen and can't get up. We never hit a cow or had to dial 911, but had we used our phones while driving, we might have hit a cow, and if we did, we would probably be unable to dial 911.

If we used our cell phones indiscriminately, they would have come in handy when calling the roaming store employee. We could have hidden around the corner from the clerk, called the store and asked for the appropriate department, and waited for the employee to answer. We would say just enough to focus his attention, sneak up behind him, tap his shoulder, and as he spins around to say something important to him like "hang up the phone and give me your full attention so that I can contribute something toward your wages."

We especially appreciated the phone when one of us ran the gauntlet to the stores and the other held down the fort. That's when we called to see if there was something else to go on the list to purchase before coming home, maybe mushrooms, and, most importantly, to say "I love you."

CHAPTER 16

Lists and Lists

Living in Morgan Spring required making lists. We needed lists for our survival, lists for learning, lists of discoveries at Morgan Spring, and lists to help tell its story.

We have always been list makers. We made "to do" lists when we were employed, lists that sometimes became information used in reports, lists of materials we needed to carry out our jobs, lists of people, and all kinds of lists. We kept lists so that our careers would not list. Of course, there were other kinds of lists such as lists of birds seen and people we wanted to see when planning a trip to list birds. We even had a list of our Liszt compositions on CD. That was a long list; he's a favorite and was very prolific. Liszt probably kept lists in order to keep track of all his music. There were also lists of our other stuff, mostly for insurance purposes and for an inventory when we moved from our Arlington apartment to Morgan Spring.

Once at Morgan Spring, we began an important list, a list of species of birds, other animals and plants we saw. For example, one of the species we saw during our first day at Morgan Spring was a Hairy Woodpecker. That bird, or one just like it, soon became a regular at one of the feeders. Before the month of September was over, we recorded a rare Northern Goshawk chasing some unlucky Yellow-rumped Warblers. Migrant Savannah Sparrows and Violet-green Swallows on their way south and a list of birds coming to our bird feeders were recorded. By October, we listed a covey of eight Mountain Quail and wintering Golden-crowned Sparrows.

Listed mammals included a species of ground squirrel locally called gray digger. A few reside in the meadow, which probably attracted coyotes seen loping across the meadow. We entered onto our list the black bear during our first night at Morgan Spring. Thoughts of making lists for flowers and mushrooms we identified were abandoned because of the difficulty in identifying them correctly. A lister should not list the wrong species. Besides, too many lists could make life cumbersome if not eventually listless. Not everything needs listing, but sometimes priorities change. I wish I had made more and better lists.

My work at Smithsonian helped train some listing qualifications. Museum work was one list after another, starting with when a given specimen arrived to what is its correct name, right down to the subspecies. The museum catalog contained well over 600,000 different specimens of birds. That is a long list. It is second nature for some humans to make lists and first nature for a retired museum bird persons.

Maintaining some lists, whether they are permanent or temporary, may be important. The museum catalog is a very important list. By some standards, it is a golden list.

There have been plenty of other times when permanent lists have been important. Teachers often said that some particular behavior was going to be listed on the permanent record. Fortunately, that so-called permanent record was not the eternal document we believed it to be. Whatever ink used to record the permanent record turned out to be as ephemeral as our memories of what provoked the warning that it would go on the list. Of course, the scribes were not using acid-free paper and carbon-based ink used in catalogs and specimen labels as was common practice at Smithsonian.

Besides listing birds in a catalog, listing them on life lists, field trips, and bird feeding stations, I had also started a list of music compositions. The pieces were not a list of works by Liszt, but by this very scribe. In the old days, I recorded on a simple tape recorder iterations of my improvisations I played on my upright piano. So much imagined music was trying to escape and I needed to catalog it, to make a list and someday go back to the tapes and transcribe the recordings to paper. More on that process elsewhere. Anyway, my first entry, one of hundreds, was opus one "Four Scherzos," with the first piece with the autumn date of October 1977. Fall is a good season, Linda's favorite, a time when I began composing and fall was when Linda and I moved to Morgan Spring. We could make a list of good thing that happened in the fall.

There are plenty of other things, happenings, memories, that are important for keeping safe. Some of those things might go on your permanent record. Probably the note slipped to a fellow fourth grader that might have led to giggles, embarrassment and general disruption of the class might go on the permanent record. Later partnering with the person receiving that note would definitely go on the permanent record. Other than lists of things of a legal nature such as birth certificates, there are those insidious warranty slips that ask you to answer about 500 questions ranging from your sex (usually restricted to identification of gender), what you eat and how do you chew it, brand of preferred toilet paper and number of squares used, mode and distance of travel, number of children and other pets, and many, many more. "Required" information also includes full name, address, phone number, email address, and the same for friends and relatives so the company can sell more of their product. There might be the promise of extra points for turning in your friends and relatives, who, afterward will probably no longer be friends and the relatives will claim you were adopted. That kind of permanent record is definitely one to avoid. Once you submit to the list of questions you might think your guarantee is assured. Just maybe it is, but sending in your memoirs to a company is not worth it. The information not only becomes part of your permanent records, but the company receiving the information makes a list, sells that list that contains your name and information to other companies who sell your name and information. It is an opposite version of the trickle-down theory in economics. It is the trickle-up theory.

Being on everyone's list or permanent record means the post office will be very busy delivering tons of advertisements to your personal doorstep or mailbox. Junk mail will come forever. Moving or changing your name will not help. The post office is very efficient, we think. We still receive mail for a, let's say, May Jones, even though we have moved several times over the years. A uniform company sent us their catalogs for years. We had never ordered anything from them but the glossy pages kept coming. Even informing the company that the addressee had died and that seeing the catalog caused much grief in remembering the horrible demise had no effect. Maybe a death certificate or crime photo would have helped. We tried marking the catalog "return to sender," but it was business as usual. Nothing worked, and the glossy pages just kept coming. Years later, the catalogs suddenly stopped arriving. Maybe the company died. Maybe they should have given us a warning. They could have first written that the cat was up on the roof. A week later they might have said we could not get it down, that it appeared sick and for a final notice told us the cat died. We thought about sending a sympathy card, repeatedly, one each month, and forever.

Linda and I did maintain some lists that we considered permanent. The status of our permanent lists will naturally change after we are gone. It is relative. Our lists of employment have a status of some permanence in that there is a paper trail of records kept somewhere, at least for a while. Things like military records, employment files, and social security data are important permanent records. Our medical files are permanent but probably only as long as you are able to maintain them for yourself. Some medical facilities maintain paper files only so long, and some keep their records on computers only. Being on the computer, as they say, is no guarantee that records will be maintained. Even medical clinics and hospitals are not virus-free; in fact, those places are great places to shop for viruses and other bugs.

Some lists will not cause floods of junk mail and are fun to make. One example of keeping a permanent list was during the compilation of bird observations along with other information. That list helped produce the first publication on the birds of Jackson County by Ira N. Gabrielson in the 1930s and the second such publication by yours truly in the 1970s. Of course, most lists are temporary in nature, such as the to-do lists and food lists. Some lists might have a longer half-life than food lists, and most are not candidates for a time vault or take up space at Smithsonian. Of course, one person's list may be a treasure trove to someone else. Biographers love to pick over lists.

Possibly the most important list was one we maintained daily. It was the food list. After all, if we didn't eat we could not make other lists. The food list was sometimes referred to as the grub list. The food/grub list also listed other non-grub (note that our spell checker, although liking grub, hates the word non-grub) items. Anything was fair game. Whatever we needed, assuming affordability, went on the list. Items that we thought we might need also went on the food list. It was too far to a store to pick up a few light bulbs, and it was too far to forget something that we needed. Actually, we rarely ran out of anything. To completely deplete something we needed meant that we hadn't planned well. Nonetheless, whatever it was, it had to be on the list. Once in a while, a recipe might call for something missing from our cupboard and we either could not whip up the dish or we had to re-purpose something for the missing ingredient. Linda was good at that. She was especially proficient at creating grocery lists that would produce not just tasty meals but ones that were well-balanced and nutritious. Sometimes we returned home with items not on our list, such as fresh vegetables picked from a garden or home-made jam. We always tried to reciprocate such generosity.

The list was completed whatever day we decided to make the long trip to civilization. Even then, we had plenty of groceries to get us through several days. Whatever the day of the trip, the time had to be a day the weather would permit our return home. The only season that was a problem was winter. We had no fear of being snowed in, but the idea of being snowed out was dreadful. The idea gave us the shivers. Being snowed out was unacceptable. A Morgan Spring morning could be sunny but by night, there might be several inches of snow on the upper part of the road and coating our very steep driveway. Whatever the season, the day we descended to the stores, our grub day, started early in the morning and ended usually well after sundown.

The list of grub and other needed items included things to do while in the valley. We might, time permitting, check a reference at the library, drop mail off at the post office or pack and mail a package, and offer help to some of our ailing relatives. One of the principal reasons for moving west was to be closer to our relatives if and when they needed our help. Since we ultimately ended up an hour or more by car from them, we attempted to follow through by checking in on them when we went to the valley. There were other stops to make, such as doctors' appointments for our folks and possibly for us. Often, there were trips to have something photocopied or music to be bound, the usual visit to the hardware and garden store for some tool, paint, caulk, board, or some other fix-it-thing-a-ma-bob. All those stops meant we had to have a list of where we were going and when we hoped to be there. An itinerary was required.

The grocery store was the last stop. Even though we had a large ice-chest, the rush home was a race against the thawing rate of our favorite low-fat frozen yogurt. There were always many items to buy, plenty of produce for salads and lots of fruit, staples such as dry beans, rice, nuts, dry fruit, flour, very few canned items but there were a few items such as chicken broth and condensed milk that were common staples.

Once in a while, we would encounter an item on the grocery shelf labeled "America's Favorite," or some such hyperbole scrawled in large letters on the product's container. Was it our favorite? Maybe, maybe not, it depended on our taste, not our nationality. If the product was high in fat content, large amounts of salt, or contained chocolate, it was not our favorite. Should we feel un-American because we didn't want to embrace chocolate as the flavor of a lifetime, or were we trying to keep our fat and sodium intake low? We do not make a habit of buying hot dogs, those rolled up symbols of baseball that look like some other kind of symbol, albeit small, but we cannot help to give attention to packaging and advertisements. One brand of these rolled butcher scraps, an old but here unstated brand, touts that the makers of the salty dogs answers to an authority well beyond governmental inspections. That really isn't saying much, and we won't provide a direct quote of the tout of touts for fear of starting another crusade. We did wonder if nondenominational hot dogs should carry a warning from the Surgeon General. Maybe the message could read, "Hot dogs should not be masticated in public," or "Hot dogs should not be in a car driven by a drunk pregnant woman," or "Do not take internally." Scratch the word "masticate" and replace it with eat; some people avoid the use of mastication for fear of going blind. In all fairness though, we have been known to eat an occasional hot dog.

Continuing on down grocery store lane, we tried to group all the frozen and "requires refrigeration" items together. These are the last items to go in the basket. On hot summer afternoons or evenings, depending on how many earlier stops we had to make, required bringing the icebox, which was chilled by ice and that blue stuff that is supposed to be better than ice. Sometime between the checkout and trundling the shopping cart to the car was when we quickly made a mental list, a triage, for what was most critical to keep cold. Frozen yogurt, wrapped with the large packages of frozen vegetables for good measure, garnered the coldest spot in the ice chest. Milk and other dairy products were followed by whatever else might fit.

The drive home usually took about an hour, but that depended on what might be on the road. Sometimes there was construction, an extremely slow driver, or some other animal. It's a long list.

CHAPTER 17

Whose Odor is that Odor?

Habits often develop with repetition and become more habitual with time. Individuals habitually dress the same way, style their hair the same way, and make a habit of making a habit. People lucky enough to have been in a coniferous forest habitually expect it to have a certain odor. That odor is commonly sold in your finer warehouse super-stores as cardboard trees impregnated with a myriad of chemicals pretending to be real pines and firs. We have developed a habit for good smells and some noses habitually look for memorable odors. For those experienced noses, the same forest will smell different depending on the season. The odor of a Pacific Northwest forest in a wet winter smell quite different than the same forest on a dry summer day. Although describing those differences is something beyond the present scope, many recall smells that may have wafted across of nostrils decades ago. Older individuals may remember the odor of an endearing grandparent when they gave an unconditional hug. I remember that and odors I want to avoid such as rotting potatoes and odors I would not mind reliving. One such nice memory is that of being in the middle of a nesting colony of Leach's Storm-Petrel, a small dark seabird that nests in burrows on offshore soil-covered islands. The petrels produce an unusual odor that I translate as pleasantly musky and maybe a little sweet. Others have different takes on the odor of storm-petrels. The odor may function as a means for individual birds to locate their nesting burrow among thousands of other burrows, all of which takes place in the dark. The reason for the cover of darkness rests on the fact that diurnal gulls like to snack on most anything, including Leach's Storm-Petrels. As it happened, my first exposure to the odor of the nocturnal petrels was at night among tens of thousands of birds so close I could touch them. They were all around me and their odor filled the air and stamped a memory in my nostrils. Years later, my office at the museum was close to the specimen cases of storm-petrels. When some researcher opened one of those cases, a mass of air carrying the odor of petrels would waft my way. Even in death, the hapless specimens reminded me of an unforgettable odor. Every now and then, as the habit allowed, I would sneak a whiff of the specimens of storm-petrels all the while never admitting I inhaled.

Although I never want to forget the odor of storm-petrels, some people become so accustomed to particular odor or to other components of their environment that they no longer register what was initially recognized. We tend to get used to the same old thing and begin to not notice what might have once been something significant. One such component of the environment at Morgan Spring was something so horrendous that it was impossible to turn a blind eye. Rather, we could not turn a blind nose to what opened our sinuses. What was causing the stink? Whose odor is that odor? We hoped the experience was not habit-forming.

The idea of habits goes beyond what might be perceived as smelling good, bad or an odor that becomes a chore to smell such as smoke from a fire or exhaust from too many vehicles. I do not mean habits that are actually chores. Unlike most previous residences, including the apartment on its traffic-infested street, our Morgan Spring kitchen did not have a dishwasher. So, we got in a habit of the chore of hand washing our dishes. We did not mind. The lawn had to be habitually mowed at least once a week until late summer, when its growth naturally slowed. House cleaning and laundry were regular habits, but really they were chores. Topping off the bird feeders should be classified as a habit. It certainly did not feel like a chore.

By now, a few habits had developed from living at Morgan Spring, and the longer our time there, the more certain habits became second nature, ensconced in the brain, habits carried out without requisite thinking. The habits were not chores since we essentially enjoyed them. One such habit on cold mornings was to slip on a trusty insulated flannel shirt. Yes, how and what we wear are habits. A fastidious employee at Smithsonian habitually wore khaki pants and polo shirts. Other associates never wore that get-up. For awhile, I wore loud neck-ties, a habit I eventually broke. Anyway, Linda and I love flannel. It certainly beats the winter wool of my earlier Donald Duck outfit while in the Navy at the Pentagon. Those were the itchy-scratchy years. Anyway, I often wore flannel shirts while working at the Division of Birds. So did several of my colleagues at Smithsonian. Falling into non-GQ heaven, my insulated flannel shirt was not only toasty warm, but it was also fashionable in our neck of the woods.

As habit dictated, the lower part of my real-estate was covered by blue-jeans, followed, depending on the weather and destination, by anything from boots to sandals. In summer, it felt good to walk bare-footed on our lawn, which was covered, much to our encouragement, with cool green clover. Meanwhile, back to winter, a jacket, or if really blustery, a coat did the trick. I am not so sure jeans and footwear are habits, but for a while, there was the habit of wearing cowboy boots when we went to town. The boots were part of my wardrobe since 1963. They had a sunburst design, which, at the time not part of my knowledge base, was remarkably similar to Smithsonian's logo. The boots were clunking down college hallways and occasionally worn to my bird job. I finally retired the habit of wearing cowboy boots to town when feeling foolish set in.

There were some non-wearable habits that came into being by learning the hard way. A good example was priming the pump, which was needed when the electricity failed. Water was needed to prime the pump. Arriving at the pump house without water was a wasted trip, which meant going back to the house where we kept bottled water for such emergencies. The trip back to the pump house was full of mumbled reprimands. After a couple of trips from home to the tiny pump house without water to do the priming, it became obvious I should have carried up at least a quart or two of water. The next time the electricity failed, I was ready. Oh, luckily the electricity rarely went off at night, but when it did, we waited for daylight.

One reason for not ranging far from the home hearth at night was something in the air. Most of the time, it was pleasant to inhale the outside environment. Sure, we usually could detect the pissy odor of elk, but the odor that got our attention was beyond awful. It is difficult to describe odors, but what we infrequently smelled was almost suffocating, it was acrid and beyond pungent, something worse than a dead animal or a rotten potato, a smell that you hoped to never experience again so long as you lived. To paraphrase the title of a recent best-selling book, we wondered: Whose odor is this odor?

We were too far north for a hoatzin, a stinky bird of South America, and the closest patch of skunk cabbage was too distant from the house. Mammal visitors, mostly at night, included skunks, an occasional raccoon, and opossum, but past experience or past sniffs allowed us to rule them out. We did see a coyote from time to time, but they do not smell as bad as the absolutely horrifying odor wafting across our innocent nostrils. So, whose odor is that odor?

Perhaps a bobcat was the culprit. Felines are known to signal their kind with squirts of odoriferous material. Wait, could Cat, our adorable indoor pet, be the perpetrator of the odor gone wild? No, the smell was not emanating from our beloved Cat. Following the scientific method of process of elimination, we were getting closer to the animal discharging its reeking odor. We had a reasonably good idea, a working theory, that the smelly cat was a cougar. Although we never saw a cougar near the house, we saw cougar tracks in the winter snow not far from the front door. Could a cougar have sent its messenging fluid onto an unsuspecting tree, the garage, or even the house? After all, we were living in their territory. The odor's ground zero was somewhere not far from our little brown house. We knew this since the further we were from the house, the weaker the odor and the closer we got to the house, the stronger the odor and the weaker we became. Could it definitively be stated that a cougar or cougars periodically marked territory by tagging our house with their odor? No, not for certain, but we were reasonably sure. We were also reasonably sure Cat was probably one lucky cat.

Alert Cat, our trusty and nonsmelly cat of many years, rolling in a bed of buttercups.

Long periods of time when our air was free of probable cougar odor, of course, did not mean a time when a cougar was not around. At least, maybe our noses were safe until next time. Cougars have a home range, the territory where they live, ranging from 30 to 124 square miles. Of course, one might be in our square mile at any moment. During periods of snow, tracking a cougar was not particularly difficult, and, based on retracing our steps, at least one cougar had no difficulty tracking us. Witnessing cougar tracks over your fresh tracks makes a person think.

Linda and I went to great lengths to avoid tracking up the snow cover. We frequently retraced our own steps so that as much snow as possible did not hold our tracks. The more undisturbed snow surface, the more animal tracks we might study. And, we did find tracks that ranged from tiny steps made by rodents to large foot prints and well-defined trails stomped by bear and cougar. There were plenty of bird tracks, especially near the feeders that ranged from diminutive tracks made by juncos to well-defined tracks from Wild Turkeys. We also located bobcat, skunk, and raccoon tracks. Close to Elk Creek Road, we might run across a rare human track and, of course, dog tracks. When possible, we sometimes packed a lunch and cranked up the beater, our old but reliable Subaru Brat. Being parents of a brat, the compact-sized four-wheel pickup, kept us safe and took us up snow-covered Grey Rock Road. Increasing elevation meant increasing snow depth, and once the front bumper began plowing snow, we had to turn around. Such trackless turning points were more remote than regions adjacent to Elk Creek Road where the greater abundance of winter tracks appeared to reveal the effects of humans and their dogs on wildlife populations.

Following tracks on Skunk Road.

When not looking down for tracks or out for birds and friends, we looked up. Observing the sky, no matter the season, became a comforting habit. On a clear night, as were most, the stars were bright beyond belief. The Milky Way appeared so close in the celestial panorama above that it seemed to draw us upward into the sky. This view cannot be seen in the city. Astronomy 101 came in handy, but a visit by Linda's brother helped far more. He was a keen fan of Carl Sagan and the art of finding planets and stars. It was a treat to identify such far away orbs, but our view was limited to the northern part of the sky; our pines obscured a southward view. We could have walked up into the meadow, but elected to avoid a possible roving and smelly cougar or tripping over a muffin left by one of the meadow horses.

From our yard, we had a good view of the North Star. It is not as big and bright as many other stars, but it always is north of a viewer. Many following nights opened to a crisp clear view of the Milky Way, and, of course, the North Star. We got in the habit of watching the moon, knowing what phase it displayed, where it was in relation to the horizon, and where and what phase would appear in the future. Many people today barely look at the lunar satellite, perhaps only knowing when it is full, but otherwise paying the moon shamefully little attention.

Daylight offered a different view of the sky above Morgan Spring, and we quickly developed the habit of watching for any changes that ranged from a clear blue and cloudless sky to one full of dark and menacing clouds. We also sniffed the air for meteorological changes. Would the odor of dry forest soon caress our olfactory senses with the welcome smell of rain? In summer, most days were cloudless, which is typical in the Pacific Northwest. Once in a while a wispy cirrus cloud might give a hint there is moisture up there, maybe thousands of feet above us. Linda and I often hoped for what some call a buttermilk sky, which technically consists of cirrocumulus clouds. For some reason, these high-flying clouds bring childhood memories of good weather. Also, a sky with clouds is far more interesting than what might become the boring blue of summer days. What we did not want to see, and I am not making this up, were cumulus congestus clouds, which seem one step from the dragon cloud known by cloudologists or meteorologists as cumulonimbus clouds. Those dangerous clouds are dark and boil to great heights, topping off with a flat anvil-shaped summit that towers ominously overhead. Cumulonimbus clouds produce wind, rain, and dreadful lightning that frequently causes wildfires, especially in the dry west. We made it a habit to keep an eye on the sky and nostrils to monitor the air for dreadful wildfire smoke.

Even at our relatively low elevation, clouds frequently clung to the ridges, especially in winter when we drove through and above them along Elk Creek Road. Clouds low enough to obstruct our view during summer months were rare if not worrisome. If the clouds were so close we could not see up the meadow or the ridges beyond, we were too close to accurately identify clouds. It was impossible then to know if a cumulonimbus cloud was about to spill its massive power. It was during those times that we might have been safe sitting on wooden stools with legs implanted in large glass insulators. That would be the plan for a fire lookout, but we were positioned down a slope, not on the summit of a mountain waiting for the white heat of the lightning bolt.

We remained safe, but our surroundings did not always similarly fare. Once the boiling clouds lifted, we expended considerable effort to scanning the slopes for smoke. Having worked lookouts in a couple of national parks, I knew our efforts should be continued for days to follow. Experience by now also taught us that certain parts of our terrain were not visible to nearby lookouts. That was especially true for much of the Alder Creek watershed. We also noticed spotter planes, airborne vehicles sent by various forest agencies to search for possible fires. Unfortunately, the frequency of overflying the region seemed inadequate. Most of the time, thankfully, smoke was never detected, but on a couple of occasions, it was necessary for us to phone the proper authorities that something was smoldering.

After fire season, the clouds hid the North Star most nights and favored our time with rain or snow and not lightening. Rain might loosen up the quicksand wrongfully perceived by one of our lowland relatives, but that was not our main worry. As average temperatures fell we began to become concerned. It was then, without warning, that we could expect an olfactory attack of such magnitude it made us hold our breath, pinch our nose, and laugh a little about the strange if not promising smell. Was a cougar marking its territory and would we actually see the big cat in action? Perhaps. Just whose odor is that odor was on our minds. One thing for certain, whose odor was that odor sure did stink.

CHAPTER 18

Snow White

Most people these days experience a good snow cover by driving to one, maybe up into the mountains or traveling north. However, there is something very special about waking up surprised that snow is all around, snow that is deep and covers the car, plants, and clings onto surrounding trees. Snow that will not melt in the foreseeable future and certainly will not be removed by plow or other mechanical devices. There is a very special feeling of being safely marooned by clean white snow. There is a strong notion of, for lack of a better word, coziness. That all is alright in the world, that the blanket of snow was clean, protective and beautiful.

By our first November, we realized that the meteorologist reporting from the Rogue Valley often did not predict the weather observed at Morgan Spring. That was more or less acceptable to us since unpredictability is often the spice of life. We knew 45 to 50 inches of precipitation would land on us sometime from fall to spring, and a good portion of that would be white. We began looking forward to snow. November was when the temperature began dropping, the mushrooms were disappearing as the nights became too frigid for their soft tissues, and snow occasionally fell. The white flakes at first only warned of what was approaching. The higher ridges, often white for days until a warm air brought in rain, told us that white snow would soon dominate Morgan Spring. We were a little surprised since our elevation was only 2,500 feet. Based on our youthful days living in the Rogue Valley, most winter snow fell more commonly above our 1,500-foot elevation. On the other hand, we were well aware that a couple of passes on Interstate 5 north of Grants Pass, a town 30 to 40 minutes northwest of Medford, were often snarled by snow falling at around 2,000 feet. Exposure, prevailing winds, and other non-ornithological facts must create the anomaly of more snow at certain locations. Perhaps Morgan Spring is a snow zone usually reserved for more rarefied air.

If it snowed at Morgan Spring, would we be prepared? We believed we would. The pantry held enough food for weeks and our water supply, Morgan Spring, was very unlikely to freeze. Should the electricity go off, which it very likely might, water from the spring was gravity fed. There would not be enough water pressure for showers or the clothes washer, but we could manage. Weather, especially in the form of snow, was not our biggest concern.

What we began to worry about was the fulfillment of holiday duties. Could we be holiday guests and be home by dark? Mercifully, the day of gorging, what many dub Thanksgiving Day, came on a day of drizzling mist, precipitation too warm to classify as snow. Armed with homemade pies Linda baked in our Morgan Spring kitchen, we rolled down the narrow driveway, drove the gravel road paralleling Button Creek, then, on pavement, followed Elk Creek and the Rogue River to Trail, a town occupied by our post office. Stamped on our license plate were the words "Oregon Trail," which, in our minds, we reversed for Trail, Oregon. Also on the license plate is a painted tree. It is standing tall. Owing to the pace of logging, we wondered if that tree on our proud license plate should be prostrate, perhaps on a logging truck or sitting on a high pile of logs waiting to be milled.

After passing Trail, we drove a few more miles along the Rogue River to Shady Cove, where we sometimes bought groceries. We had stopped there back in September, before our first night at Morgan Spring. Accustomed to the cost of groceries in Arlington, Virginia, we were floored by the considerably lower prices. They were lower than those at the small grocery and gas station at Trail, the only public business in town other than our post office. However, the best deals for grub are in Medford.

We would soon be in the Medford region. Our first stop, if my stomach serves me correctly, was at the house of Linda's mom. There was turkey and ham, the usual trimmings, and of course, an assortment of pies. There were relatives ranging from brother and sister to spouses and their progeny, after which I lost track. People asked us about our home in the mountains. Some at the gathering would make the journey up Button Creek to Morgan Spring, but most would not. For now, the group seemed almost puzzled why someone would live so far away from their beloved relatives. Maybe we should have stayed 3,000 miles away in Arlington. Others asked questions, some warned us of cougars and quicksand. In addition, speaking earlier of Button Creek, by the end of the sumptuous meal, the button on my pants was straining.

The day was not over. Being new at being together on such a prestigious holiday, Linda and I had decided, at least this one time, we would also have Thanksgiving dinner at my folks. So, we toddled to the car, drove a few miles south up Bear Creek to my parents. My generous father was anxious to feed us. My sister and her husband were also there. If there was anyone else, the pressure on my brain from my stomach blocked out any other mouths shoveling in the usual turkey day affair. We did not tell them we had already spoiled our appetites with a multiple-course dinner a couple of hours earlier. We sat, enjoyed and ate some more. Linda and I vowed to never again suffer eating two big holiday meals.

The drive back up the river and two creeks was uneventful, if not gastronomically painful. In fact, we were almost sullen from the heavy food coursing through bodies accustomed to health and healthy eating. In fact, it took a few years before we could find humor in our escapade of visiting relatives on holidays. Maybe the day will go on our permanent record. Our alimentary canal was hard at work, and no lumbering cows in the road, no deer in the headlights, even the tiny beads of cool mist and growling stomachs would dampen our anticipation of being almost home. Our greatest fear was not the cougars and quicksand we so often heard warnings about, or our punishing indigestion. Our greatest fear was not being snowed in, but being snowed out. Our front-wheel sedan should suffice if the snow was not too deep. That was our hope. Somehow, we would make it home. The ground was bare, but what if it had been under snow? The thought of being relatively marooned at our relatives, eating another big meal and listening to the same stories did not whet our appetites.

A few weeks before Christmas, snowfall became the norm. We were ready, with a fully stocked pantry and plenty of blankets in case the electricity failed. We even had a single burner propane hot plate we could cook meals on if needed. We also had a good supply of film and got busy taking pictures right and left. Using a mail-order photo developer, we sent in a few rolls. Luckily the mail, delivered only on Monday, Wednesday and Friday, kept coming, thanks to the husband-and-wife team driving their over-used jeep from the post office in Trail. We selected one of the better photographs and Linda, with my help, produced a Christmas card. Linda's creative eye resulted in a card that friends back east relished as a collectible. The card was our way of showing off a bit and flashing our pride that we found Morgan Spring. Anyone seeing the card could hardly ignore what looked to be a place that only could exist in fiction. However, our picture was proof that Morgan Spring was real, it was beautiful and it was home.

There was a downside to Christmas. That is, beside the commercialization of the holiday. Linda and I once again had to pay homage to our former homes. After all, the prevailing thought of the lowland relatives was that Linda and I are only a few easy miles away. Those miles were not easy, which was the way we liked it. Nonetheless, how could we not want to come down off our mountain? We knew how, but did not know how to say no. Before retirement, we had visited our parents over the past years, traveling at great expense of money and time from the east. Usually, we made the pilgrimages during the summer, not wishing to experience snow delays in a Denver storm or wondering if the de-icer sprayed on the plane's wings will actually de-ice. We did not want to end up in the Potomac River, where one winter sent a passenger plane. Now at Morgan Spring, there was no excuse, we had to be there this Christmas.

We loaded the car with our contribution of food and Christmas gifts, blankets, water, and a little food in case we got stuck going down to the valley. We knew we would have plenty of leftovers, as we did Thanksgiving Day, if we were stuck coming home. Coming home. We were thinking that comforting phrase as we slowly made white tracks down the driveway. Stopping completely at the top of the driveway, we looked down the steepest part of the lane, then eased off the brake and ever so slowly managed to get to the road without going sideways. Deep furrows made by other vehicles marked Elk Creek Road. The low carriage of our car rasping along, plowing the snow between the ruts, somehow got us to the pavement a little over a mile from our driveway where there was less snow. Dropping nearly 400 feet in elevation seemed to make a big difference in either snowfall or temperature, or both. In about a half-mile we passed the waterfall of Button Creek and drove down to Elk Creek. With another 100 feet toward sea-level, there was even less snow, driving was easier, and gradually the snow disappeared.

Linda and I performed our due diligence and were happy that everyone else was happy with what the day brought. Again, we wondered if we should try to please everyone by spreading ourselves so thin. Repeating our two-dinners-in-one-day ordeal, we might be spreading ourselves too thick. More importantly, it was late, temperatures had fallen and snow might have filled the ruts on the higher reaches of Elk Creek Road. What kind of Christmas present awaited our vehicle?

Some snow had melted during the day. Had it refrozen, producing an even more hazardous drive? Would we be home tonight? Luckily, the snow had not refrozen, but the slush was definitely slippery. Slightly before the last sharp turn on the snow-covered, graveled Elk Creek Road, at the turn where Morgan Creek flows under the road, the slush disappeared. Now, we traveled on regular snow. A rear-wheel drive would have been trouble if not impossible, but our front-wheel sedan kept us steady. It was necessary to slow at the open gate of our driveway. Could we make it? We first had to negotiate the steep part. In about 100 feet, we had to go up 25 feet in elevation. Not being good with story problems, I consulted an expert who said that was about a 14-degree climb. That is about twice the grade of the steepest part of most public roads. The steady and straight climb went well, but would turning cause us to lose traction? It did not, and we carefully made our way between the trees overlooking a drop down into Morgan Creek. Just as we came to the edge of the meadow, we had to make a sharp turn requiring the wheel to be turned all the way to the right. Of course, we could not get traction. Backing up just right, which means very carefully lest we slip down the embankment behind us, we finally had a straight shot to the front door. The front tires gripped, then slipped and spun, then gripped again. Home at last!

Snow sometimes covered our newly installed satellite dish. Thankfully, the round antenna was not one of those six-foot monsters. The small, maybe a foot-and-a-half diameter gray dish had to be set away from the house since the signal would not transmit through our ponderosa pines. The dish stood on a small metal pipe cemented in the ground next to the fence. The cable from the dish ran several yards along the bottom of the fence before diving into the house. The company allowed us to pick individual channels. Only one problem: local stations were not available. We phoned one Medford station, which told us local channels would never be available. Of course, things changed, but that would be much later when local channels became available and when customers unfortunately were not allowed to pick and choose individual channels. At least, we could watch the weather channel and CNN to keep up with the world, since even the local newspaper was not delivered in our neck of the woods. If the meteorologist predicted snow at 3,500 feet, we would certainly have plenty of snow at Morgan Spring and sometimes I had to trudge several yards from the house to sweep away accumulating snow. Linda then kept watch, protecting me from the possible odor of a visiting cougar.

Four years after our first winter, my sister called one morning. All she said was turn on the TV. Our little dish at the side of the meadow collected the satellite signal and sent the signal through the long cable to the house where Linda and I watched what happened on the frightful day of September 11, 2001. Had the horrible event occurred in winter, snow might have covered the dish, hiding, at least for a while, those awful images we wish no one ever saw.

Snow covered Morgan Spring most winters. A white Christmas was normal. By February 1997, Linda and I decided to slightly alter the state of our partnership and travel in the snow as a married couple. It was about time. Knowing someone since you were nine, being sweet on them, holding them in esteem, dreaming about them and finally coming together after years of mistaken marriages begged for a forever. Of course, as far as we were concerned, forever was always our mantra. Our date was Valentine's Day at the Medford Courthouse. It was just the two of us and a few witnesses. Now, we had a real holiday to celebrate, and snow or lack thereof was not important.

Snow might decorate winter sometime in November that periodically lasted into February. There is no sharp delineation for the seasons, but winter seemed to begin with cooler days shortened by the earth's tilt. That's when to expect mist gathering on the trees to succumb to gravity and fall to the leaf littered forest floor. At first the falling misty droplets rattle the leaves, but soon even the leaves become wet and lose their power to rustle warnings as some predator hunts its prey. Quietly as possible, an alpha predator finds its meal and quieter still, beta predators hunt and eventually find their meal. Prey that was once predator fill in the cycle of life from smallest to largest. The eerie-sounding Varied Thrush, a harbinger of November in certain parts of the country, had to worry that it would not be prey, to not be eaten before it could eat, to be a predator to a variety of insects.

Cooler temperatures and snow would make insect hunting difficult and Varied Thrushes would soon concentrate their diet on seeds and berries. We observed one Varied Thrush eating birdseed, the common fare we offered our winter birds. Snow and winter brought us more and more to see at the feeders and beyond. Staring northeast out our window, our frequent gaze caught uncommon sights of both Bald and Golden Eagles flying over the meadow. Other birds of prey were arriving as the kinglets, juncos and Steller's Jays coming to our feeders increased in number. The hawks were in the genus *Accipiter* and are known for their ability to catch and kill small birds whether they might be the Pacific Wren skulking between the house and Morgan Creek, one of the many Chestnut-backed Chickadees, and juncos, or even one of the few coveys of Mountain Quail coming to the yard. Feisty Steller's Jays were less likely to be candidates for hawk fodder.

One of our first observations of the *Accipiter* hawks occurred by scanning the meadow. What caught our eye was something perched on the boundary tree at the far edge of the meadow. A boundary tree marks the border of the property. According to all sorts of legalese, the trunk of a boundary tree might be on one property owner's land, but the roots and overhanging branches might encroach on the property owned by a different person. In this instance, at least one of the historical owners was the old Elk Lumber Company. There is more than the legalese of a boundary tree than meets the eye, which, from our remote rural perspective, comes down to a great place for a bird to perch. It was. It was a favored place for a Sharp-shinned Hawk, the smallest species of North American *Accipiter*. A few days later, the Sharp-shinned was replaced by a slightly larger Cooper's Hawk. In a day or two later, the Cooper's Hawk disappeared. Taking over the same perch, and I am not making this up, was a Northern Goshawk, the largest North American *Accipiter*. Goshawks are nearly the size of a Common Raven; Sharp-shinned Hawks vie for the size of a pigeon, whereas Cooper's are crow-sized. In a couple of days, the perch on the boundary tree was vacant and the two smaller species also vacated the tree. We did observe Sharp-shinned and Cooper's Hawks near the house and occasionally at the feeders. Once a Cooper's Hawk flushed a Song Sparrow that flew to the bottom edge of the sliding door off the kitchen where it huddled until the hawk departed. The Song Sparrow's beautiful plumage against the snowy background allowed identification of its subspecies. One of my last projects before retiring from the museum was the taxonomy of northwestern Song Sparrows. Preliminary results would eventually appear in the new Birds of Oregon.

The Song Sparrow that missed becoming a hors d'oeuvre was soon joined by a couple dozen juncos hidden nearby, waiting for the outcome and possibly just worrying that the Song Sparrow would eat all their birdseed. Purple Finches, Steller's Jays, nuthatches, and falling snowflakes added to the fray. The fresh snow allowed us to indirectly glimpse wildlife when we identified their tracks. Occasionally, we found tracks made by Ruffed Grouse. We also found tracks from a small mammal that suddenly stopped at the end of their trail where snow had been lightly brushed by the two wings of an owl or perhaps a hawk. We learned from snow, had fun with it, brushed it off the satellite dish some nights with a broom, hiked in it till our feet were cold and wet, watched elk play in it, and drove in it. Even with our Brat, we worried as we drove down the road to the valley. Could we return home and check the boundary tree for hawks? Would we suffer being snowed out and unable to enjoy being snowed in together?

CHAPTER 19

Spring with Swallows

Spring is the beginning of the birthing seasons at Morgan Spring. It is the time for all the elements of reproduction to pass through their sequences from bud, bulb and egg, from flower to fledgling, and all between. It is when the soil thaws, territories are established and defended, when bird song dominates the ear and blossoms overpower the eye. Spring is when tree frogs, amphibious peepers, fill the air with croaks and chirps in all directions. Their sound was almost constant until some unseen animal startled them into silence, but they were back to filling in the audible background with their calls once the perceived danger had passed. Spring is when the duration of night becomes shorter and days become longer. The mornings are crisp and clear but not frigid and damp with rain or whitened by snow. Green becomes the color of the hour, gray clouds of winter disappear to unveil blue skies open to swallows by day and revealing sparkling gold stars that invite a Western Screech-Owl's trill by night. The meadow was greener than we thought possible and attracted grazing elk, grew a plethora of wildflowers that would invite pollinating insects and swallows to catch them.

The temperature gauge hanging on the east side of a ponderosa pine about 20 feet from the house registers higher and higher numbers each spring. As the season progresses from late winter to spring, as the northern half of the earth tilts more southward, the shadow of the house no longer shields the thermometer from the warming sun-glow. The big 18-inch diameter temperature gauge, shadowed from the west by the tree trunk, requires relocating to a tree a few feet to the north in spring. There the gauge will stay until the fall, when the tilting earth causes the sun's rays once again to raise the thermometer beyond the temperature in the shade. Then we will reattach the thermometer to the "winter" tree. No matter the season or which tree the trusty thermometer is attached, its large face is visible from our bedroom window. We frequently checked it each morning and sometimes at night with a flashlight shining from our room. Knowing the temperature, the sky and its clouds, the wind, all this seemed important for living at Morgan Spring.

Since our arrival last September, we had been looking forward to spring, when the light and warmth of the sun nourishes flowers and trees to bud and bloom. We were anxious to explore the new season. Grass in the meadow, tender and pale green, began reaching out of the cool spring soil to take in the sun. Dogwoods showed their white petals before other deciduous trees species grew their leaves that would hide the dogwood's spring contribution.

Plant and animal behavior in spring, their preparation and business of rejuvenating and reproducing, is in response to a change in the photoperiod, a time when the duration of light from the sun changes. Just how much change depends on numerous variables. Two of those variables include elevation, slope and pollution. The intensity of the sun is greater at higher elevations, and air pollution acts as a filter that could lower the intensity of the sun. North slopes are generally cooler than southern slopes and eastern slopes do not get the brunt of the sun heating a western slope. Higher elevations are cooler than lower elevations and the higher up a slope, the brighter the sun appears. Cancer-causing UV rays from the sun have less air to penetrate. Pollution tends to bend and reflect light and filters UV rays. For about every 3,300 feet rise in elevation, the number of UV rays increases by 10 to 12 percent. The gently sloping Rogue Valley, compared to Morgan Spring, receives less UV because of air pollution and its elevation, which is roughly 2,000 to 1,300 feet. Of course, all that depends on global climate change, which, at the time, was not yet the talk of the town.

Naturally, spring brings warmth as a response to daylight length and ever so slightly warmer and warmer days surrounded by nights shedding their cold winter to more comfortable coolness. Normally, the climate is forever changing, albeit slower than molasses, in fact, so slowly it is difficult to notice by most average citizens. Those natural changes of the climate and biological responses to it take place over thousands of years. The process is so slow that many animals and plants produce enough generations to go through the gradual steps of evolution. However, spring is now coming noticeably earlier each year because of climate change. Unfortunately, climate change in our present time easily out-runs evolution. How did this predicament happen? Humans simply burned too much fossil fuel, which, in itself wreaked havoc with the chemistry of the atmosphere that, in turn, caused global temperature to rise. And, we humans, with all the technology of the world, are not keeping pace with climate change for several reasons. One, there are political and economic contingents that refuse to believe climate change exists, or if they do believe it is real, they do not believe it is economically feasible to do anything about it. Other reasons are bureaucratic log jams and stagnation that prevent any positive action. Politicians paying homage to the wishes of the energy industry contribute greatly to not doing anything about climate change. Even though scientist have known about climate change at least since the late 1950s, and have gathered ever increasing and compelling evidence, the concept of climate change has been woefully denied, dismissed and ignored by too many politicians. Science, even the local weatherman, know that global temperatures began to sharply increase in the 1980s. That helped raise the issue of the danger or rapid climate change, but some argued, and continue to do so, that increasingly severe winter storms disprove climate change. However, warming oceans, a result of climate change, are the instigators of those pesky slippery winter storms. Beginning in the 1990s, improved computer data crunching added to the dreadful insight that, yes, we are in deep, deep trouble. Climate change is absolutely real. There is so much to discuss, so much more action to take, and potentially so little time before climate change may make history that will not be recorded. We hope for the best.

Meanwhile, with hope that someone will always be around to chronicle the hems and haws, the ups and downs and sensible paths of civilization, one wonders what else might go wrong. Concerns about nearby Mt. Mazama clearing its throat have already been evoked. Volcanoes are nothing to blow smoke about. When Mt. St. Helens blew in 1980, the sun, for some, became quite dim to such a degree that one could stare at the dim red ball that would, on a clear day, poke out your eyes. Similar to a volcano belching into the sky, human-created smoke from the large percent of wildfires, and other particulates we so successfully stir up into otherwise breathable air will affect the amount of sunlight reaching us.

The intensity of the sun, sans volcanic eruptions, may also seem different depending on the ambient temperature and relative humidity. Drinking sodas and beer is no help, since they can raise body temperature and both are diuretic. Beer or sodas were not on our drinking schedule, since we preferred to imbibe the clear cool water from our spring. As the sun set the tone for life at Morgan Spring, we drank more water and enjoyed the opportunity to wear fewer clothes and more sunscreen.

Although birds were my game, whether at the museum or checking around our home, Linda and I quickly became aware that spring and summer was when the insects also go through their breeding activities. Insect activity at Morgan Spring was different from that found back on the

Potomac River. That is not to say our former citified habitat did not have insects. There were bugs of many varieties, some thriving in the uncomfortably humid summers, but, like most locations of dense humanification, a plethora of insecticides were mixed in the air like a primordial soup. Morgan Spring, on the contrary, was chemical-free. Well, almost. We used mosquito-be-gone occasionally. We mostly left the insects alone, allowed them to do their thing, including becoming important fodder for our birds. Even the seed-eating juncos fed their offspring insects. Most insects are not long-lived, and some are even less long-lived when they become prey for our summer birds. Without insects, the world as we know it could not exist. I am not just thinking of honey bees that pollinate our food, but all insects, even those pesky, sometimes disease-carrying, mosquitoes, feed the world's fauna, including what we call *Homo sapiens*.

Admittedly, we did have on major problem with insects. It began when we heard noises emanating from the attic. It was a buzzing sound, a sound arousing fear, since I had developed a definite allergy to stinging insects. Could the sound actually be from bees? There didn't seem to be anywhere that bees could enter the attic, but whatever they were, they wanted out. We could barely see something buzzing at the screened vents under the eaves. Were they some kind of fly, hatched from a maggot-infested colony of mice? Mice, what mice? As far as we knew, nothing lived in the attic, nothing until now. Linda and I are not afraid of nature, but the unknown was unnerving. We finally discovered that the outside door accessing the attic, a small 2 X 4 foot affair, was slightly open. With arms and legs covered, I crept up a ladder to the door. I thankfully could not hear or see anything as propped open the door before beating a hasty retreat 10 or so feet down the ladder. If the winged creatures really wanted out, they had the opportunity.

We quickly dismissed the idea of spraying anything into the attic that might kill, or at least enrage, whatever was lurking there. Perhaps we could coax the flock of flying critters out with the perfume of a flower or an old piece of meat. Being short on both items, as appetizing as they might have been, we opted to wait. It worked. Whatever the flying invaders were, they disappeared and no new interlopers entered in the meantime. The buzzing noises stopped. Nothing was bumping against the vent screens, no horrid smells of food were left behind by yellowjackets, and no honey bee honey was oozing down our walls. Our Morgan Spring was back at peace and we returned to watching for more signs of spring.

In many parts of the country, people regard the American Robin as the harbinger of spring. Harbinger, according to my kid memory, was spelled harbringer because the first spring bird brought the season. Never mind that I had no clue to define "har." It was one of those times when aged by but one digit, one might hear the familiar hymn refrain "bringing in the sheets." At age 9, I had committed something like a mondegreen. American Robins did make their appearance, but as a resident species to most everywhere in Oregon, the harbinger of spring at Morgan Spring would have to be some other species of bird. That place of honor has to go to the Rufous Hummingbird that arrived at our nectar feeder anywhere from 25 March to mid-April. The smaller and greenish Calliope Hummingbird was usually detected by the third week of April, about the time we began expecting Chipping Sparrows and Black-headed Grosbeaks. Gray-hooded Nashville Warblers sometimes arrived in April, but usually were detected in early May along with yellow-hooded Hermit Warblers. Yellow Warblers, a personal favorite and constant study subject for perhaps too long a duration before my retirement, kept a close time table by arriving most years during the third week of May. April and May brought Western Tanagers that lit the dark green conifers with their startling yellow, black and fiery red plumage. Spring anywhere, and especially at Morgan Spring, was always exciting.

Not all of the species of spring migrants actually nested in and around Morgan Spring, at least as far as we knew. Townsend's Warblers ordinarily nest north of the local county. Yellow Warbler and Black-headed Grosbeak may have only been passing through, although such species breed not far from Morgan Spring. MacGillivray's Warbler, a species giving us the slip at Morgan Spring, except for a sighting of two there in early September, bred in an unnamed canyon above the meadow. While on the subject of warblers, Morgan Spring was habitat for wintering Myrtle Warbler and for resident Audubon's Warbler. Yes, I know, Myrtle and Audubon's are accused of loving each other in British Columbia and, by some standards, are lumped as one species, the Yellow-rumped Warbler. The affair suggesting a marriage of Myrtle and Audubon's warblers is challengeable, and don't get me started.

Life beyond warblers included several neotropical migrants, among them Lazuli Bunting. That species apparently nests from low valley elevations up to near timberline. Buntings arriving in May probably bred in our specific region. Cassin's Vireos raised a brood a few feet from the driveway and not far from a Western Tanager nest in a limb of madrone hanging over our private road. We observed House Wrens in May with young and once suspected a second brood in mid-August. Townsend's Solitaires, one of several members of the thrush family, probably were on their way to higher ground when individuals stopped by in mid-May. We heard them singing at White Point in early June.

Before leaving the subject of neotropical migrants heralding the arrival of spring, one other species deserves at least honorable mention for reminding us of a different season. By now, the idea that Dark-eyed Juncos were around Morgan Spring most times of the day and most days of the year should join common thought. It is true. Juncos were ubiquitous. However, their numbers were seasonal. In spring, our usual winter flock abruptly increased sometime in late April or May. Suddenly, the greening meadow was crawling with juncos. Luckily for the wintering juncos, the new arrivals confined their foraging to the meadow. The newcomers and our feeder flock would eventually disperse into the surroundings to nest. By summer, juncos became almost a rarity at our smorgasbord.

Aside from the omnipresent Steller's Jays, Tree Swallows were one of the most detectable species breeding at Morgan Spring. These white-bellied, metallic dark greenish-blue backed swallows are diurnal migrants, although a handful of Tree Swallows sometimes winter in the Rogue River Valley. Most Tree Swallows migrate and travel in flocks numbering in the thousands. As a young Danny McSkunk living in the lowlands, I witnessed huge spring flocks flying down Bear Creek, a route for the swallows running north and south from the foot of the Siskiyou Mountains to the Rogue River. Only a few individual Tree Swallows reach the upper elevations of southwestern Oregon. Unlike other fly-catching species foraging from perches, swallows catch flying insects while on the wing, and above the valleys, the kind of flying performed by Tree Swallows is impeded by too many trees. I never thought I would ever even think the phrase "too many trees," but the meadow at Morgan Spring offered the swallows an unobstructed location to hunt insects. This species, along with other species of swallows, is an expert at fly-catching. Variation in the ambient temperature is a factor that dictates the height above the ground where insects might fly, and, likewise, the height swallows will likely forage. Cooler days keep insects closer to the ground, and hotter days mean that more insects will be flying high, sometimes above the treetops. The weather in early spring at Morgan Spring could change abruptly. One day could be warm; the next could be cool and wet. Drenching rains and even snow were possible, and on those days the Tree Swallows we had seen the day before were nowhere to be found.

Tree Swallows arriving at Morgan Spring were usually in pairs or, coincidentally, the individuals were in even numbers indicating the sex ratio was probably 50:50. Whether paired before or after arriving, a point I should have ascertained, birds quickly recognized the two nest boxes attached to wooden fence posts. Although the houses were built to specifications for bluebirds, the boxes satisfied the house-hunting criteria of Tree Swallows. Establishing ownership required an individual to perch on the house or hang from the entrance hole while another bird flew nearby. Both individuals defended the area around the nest box, whether from other Tree Swallows or more timid Western Bluebirds. All the while, the liquid warble of the Tree Swallows dominated distant songs of all but the loud strains of a nearby Cassin's Vireo.

The two nest boxes near our home were originally occupied by Western Bluebirds during our first nesting season. The next year, 26 April 1998 to be exact, the bluebirds had competition for the nest boxes. Tree Swallows, which are one of 74 or more species of swallows world-wide and one of 12 species of swallows breeding in North America, inspected the boxes. In July 1999, one box contained young bluebirds a few days from fledging and another box contained five Tree Swallow eggs abandoned a week ago. The eggs did not contain embryos. In order to possibly relieve the pressure on our two cavity nesters, I hit my thumb a couple of times as a prerequisite for constructing a new bird house. It was of the same design and dimension as the other two houses. The new nest box was attached to a fence post on the other side of the meadow far from the original two boxes. Trees grew just feet away. The setting seemed perfect for Western Bluebirds, the less aggressive species that probably needed the most help. Unfortunately, neither bluebird nor Tree Swallow took up residence and what became an annual conflict, a boxing match, between the two species continued.

Although Tree Swallows did not use the house on the far side of the meadow, they did nest in a house closely surrounded by trees. The discovery was on a cold December day when I opened the screech-owl house to clean it. Inside were five very dead and nearly mummified Tree Swallows, which were somewhere between 14 to 20 days old. The owl house was on a secluded slope outside of view from the house and surrounded by ponderosa pine. The pair of Tree Swallows almost raised a brood, but the loss of their young was likely the result of the adults having to dodge trees. There could be several reasons for the mortality, but the selection of the nest box by the swallows strongly suggests there are more Tree Swallows and other hole-nesting species, including their local nemesis, the Western Bluebird, than there are natural cavities or birdhouses. Housing shortages are a chronic problem facing at least 85 hole-nesting species of North American birds, ranging from Buffleheads and Wood Ducks to owls, kestrels, woodpeckers, chickadees, nuthatches, bluebirds and Tree Swallows. Forest managers often manage away trees that have cavities. In fact, it is difficult for a cavity to exist in today's world spinning around money and horticulture without unsightly holes. That is partially why I risked uttering four-letter words and cruelty to my thumb while assisting some of our local hole-nesting birds.

A pair of non-hole-nesting Barn Swallows rested on the fence wire before swooping over the meadow one late day in May. These birds have steely blue backs, rusty breasts, and deeply forked tails. This species brought fond memories of when Linda and I, at the ripe old age of 10, were students of our fifth-grade teacher, who, mostly unsuccessfully, tried to teach us fidgety tykes something about birds. The class even went on birdwatching treks around town with our teacher, who was barely taller than a fifth grader. Later, back in the stuffy classroom, the teacher instructed us in the art of wood burning, a process involving scorching wood with a very hot electric device that had a small, very hot end. No doubt, there are now tools much more sophisticated than in 1955. The reason, the teacher announced, was that we will illustrate a bird by burning its image into the wood. We pressed our hot brands on the wood, all the while following a pattern we had drawn on the pithy canvas. Linda's pattern was of an American Robin, mine was of a Barn Swallow.

Two score and four years beyond our youthful wood-burning days, we watched the Barn Swallows at Morgan Spring as they flew low, skimming about two to six feet above blooming flowers. It rained that day but the Barn Swallows kept trying. We had seen a pair regularly at the Elk Creek Bridge, just down Button Creek. They apparently built their mud nest under the bridge. Whether our Morgan Spring visitors were from the bridge is unknown. The weather remained cold for the next several days and new snow fell on the slopes just 1000 feet above Morgan Spring. The Barn Swallows disappeared. Even the Tree Swallows, two of which showed interest in occupying one of the birdhouses, were gone.

In early May the next year, Barn Swallows once again were seen skimming the meadow for insects. The two birds, acting as a bonded pair, inspected under the overhanging porch of our front door. Several forays under the six-foot structure and our knowledge that mud was available from seeping Morgan Spring added up to a nesting site for our fork-tailed swallows. Additionally, one of the Barn Swallows attempted to pick up and fly with a Wild Turkey feather measuring 15 inches long and about one inch wide. That is approximately 380 X 25 mm for those so inclined. I used to be so disposed, but I am getting off the subject. Anyway, the swallow kept dropping the turkey feather. That feather was definitely larger than the small soft feathers Barn Swallows use to line their adobe nests. Besides, that swallow was getting the feather ahead of the normal sequence in Barn Swallow nest building. Despite our avoidance of the front door, the porch, and any reasoned flight paths around it, the swallows' interest faded and the birds left, probably for habitat in the valley below.

Cliff Swallows at Morgan Spring were not observed until fourth spring when one coursed over the meadow. About one thousand feet down in elevation is the habitat for this colonial nesting species that favors barn eaves and under bridges, where they plaster mud to form it into a nest. Cliff Swallows are generally pale rusty below and dark bluish above but, unlike the

Barn Swallow, Cliff Swallows have a squared tail, rusty rump, and usually have a pale forehead. Some individuals of Cliff Swallow have nearly white foreheads, leading some to believe these birds constituted a subspecies different from western breeding populations. However, our single visiting Cliff Swallow and the alleged subspecies of northern populations from western North America are all one subspecies.

Being a taxonomist and mostly of sound mind, the nomenclature related to Cliff Swallows attracted my attention. There is a story that must be told. The scientific name used for the species has included the names *lunifrons*, *albifrons*, and *pyrrhonota*. The name proposed and published first is the name taxonomists traditionally use for a given taxon. In 1817, Frenchman Vieillot proposed the name *pyrrhonota* for a bird he described that was wintering in Paraguay. However, there was some doubt as to whether Vieillot's description adequately characterized a Cliff Swallow (there was no verifiable specimen associated with the original description; the name rested on the description alone). That is why the names *lunifrons* and *albifrons* were bandied about. Vieillot's salient points in the original French description of this bird from Paraguay were at least partly based on an earlier Spanish publication. Somewhere along the line, or so some thought, something was lost in translation. At least some American ornithologists were confused and for some time, no one, with certainty, knew what scientific name to use for this common species. The cliffhanger was finally settled 178 years after Vieillot took up his pen. Ornithologists should have taken the Frenchman more seriously.

Was the name of the Greek philosopher, that skeptic of all skeptics, perhaps Father of Skepticism, Pyrrho, the root for Vieillot's specific epithet for the Cliff Swallow? Would Pyrrho have thought the Cliff Swallow was named in his honor? Most definitely, he would not. He would not have cared. This guy, Pyrrho of Elis, who lived some time from 360 to 270 BC, believed nothing could be known. People who follow Pyrrho, aptly called Phyrrhonists, are able to attain happiness by not knowing and caring less. You know the dumb and not so happy attitude. Or, maybe they were happy because ignorance is bliss. (Maybe being ignorant and happy is a different ism, but I do not know and do not care). Nonetheless, there seem to be a number of people who believed in Pyrrhonism, including some world leaders. We wonder if they know that their philosophy is anchored in Ancient Greece. If they were true believers, the answer would be most definitely not.

The second half of pyrrhonota is "noto." An "a" ending in Latin denotes gender, which in the case of the name for the Cliff Swallow is feminine. Was Vieillot thinking Latin? Maybe branded was what he was thinking. Was it that a bird had received a brand, which still smarted reddish orange on its rump, and marked it for life as a swallow that did not care? Vieillot surely meant 'noto' to be from the Greek 'noton', literally the back, and, not so literally, the dorsal side. That leaves a bird carrying on its back the weight or lack thereof of being dumb and happy. Of course, it is difficult to survive if you are dumb. Birds, on the other hand, might not have much knowledge, but they do seem happy. At least that is what many think upon hearing birds singing. Of course, we all know that singing is primarily a way of marking and defending territory and attracting a mate. All those are serious undertakings; they are life and death to the species.

Was Vieillot thinking of pyrrhotite, a bronze-colored magnetic material? Pyrrhotite. That is a good word from nineteenth century Greek. Lose the tite and add nota and one has a bird with a bronze color on its back. According to Brown's wonderful book, Composition of Scientific Words, "pyrrho-" is from the Greek 'pyrrhos', "flame-colored, red, yellowish-red, tawny," and 'nota' is Latin for mark. The Latin 'nota' agrees with the color of the plumage of Cliff Swallows more than does the Greek 'nota'. The word 'pyro', or fire, is from the Greek 'pyros', according to several dictionaries. In fact, in post-ancient Greece, a drug company adopted "pyr" for the trade name of their product Pyridium; the drug is an analgesic that turns one's pee the color red or orange. Apparently adding the extra 'r', assuming Vieillot did not hold the key down too long and have it inadvertently repeat, caused the word to become a term for a color. Several names of birds from Middle and North America have 'pyrr' as part of their scientific name. Some part of the plumage is reddish, or some hue that contains red, orange, rust, bronze, and related colors.

Apologies to anyone feeling ambushed by this, but nomenclature is a serious business, at least to a museum guy. Even if not signed up for nomenclature 101, it is fun to contemplate Mr. Pyrrho of Elis, the person mentioned at the beginning of this fiery discussion, who may have had a flaming temperament. That is unknown. Maybe, while pontificating during some torch-lighted evening seminar on Pyrrhonism, his himation or chiton (Greek outerwear) caught fire. Thus, could the legend of the word 'pyrrho' have for its basis the man's red face from a tempered high blood pressure matching the oranges and reds of his blazing clothes? For now, I am relatively certain the taxonomy of Cliff Swallows is, for the time being, reasonably correct and that the scientific name of the species is equally accurate. After all, science is never complete.

Speaking of cliffs, Linda and I counted eight Violet-green Swallows foraging over the meadow. The species often nests in cliffs. New birders sometimes have difficulty discriminating Violet-green and Tree Swallows. The two species are similar, but the Violet-greens have a white face that partially encircles the eye and white patches that nearly merge over the base of their tail. Nesting Tree Swallows did not seem to confuse the white-bellied Violet-green Swallows foraging in their meadow but were aggressive toward conspecifics. We searched for nesting sites of the Violet-greens. Possibly, they colonized some of the volcanic dikes and cliffs near Bald Mountain or Hibbard Point. Unfortunately, we never found where they were breeding.

Other species of swallows never made it up to Morgan Spring. We did see brown-backed Bank and Rough-winged swallows near the confluence of Elk Creek and the Rogue River. More than once, we glimpsed birds at Morgan Spring darting through the sky and behind trees that we thought were Purple Martins. We were never sure. This species nests in so-called apartment birdhouses in the East and uses natural cavities, usually in trees, in the West. Still, every now and then we have seen apartment birdhouses in Oregon; usually, these houses are crammed full of House Sparrows or Starlings. Too bad. A well-placed single-family bird dwelling, with a smaller (1.5 inches in diameter) entrance hole, might, at least, bring the gurgling sound of fly-catching Tree Swallows.

Spring was always anticipated with curiosity and surprise. Each season might bring a different species of swallow or a new warbler or something we had not imagined. Perhaps the most notable surprise was lack of migrant and potentially breeding species of flycatchers. Aside from non-breeding Say's Phoebes and infrequently visiting Western Kingbirds, Morgan Spring hosted very few flycatchers. Our only regular spring and summer flycatcher was Western Wood-Pewee. We fully expected to be challenged by a species or two representing the pesky genus *Empidonax*. At the very least, Pacific-slope Flycatchers should have been detected as migrants to our space.

CHAPTER 20

Do You Have an Altimeter?

Regardless of season, when you live in the mountains, locations of animals, whether they are jays, warblers or swallows and elk or bobcat, and whereabouts of trees, mushrooms, the arrowhead we found, the place where winter snow was deepest, how far on a slope did certain spring plants bloom and more, are important. Part of knowing where things are located is, how high are you? No, I do not mean emotionally or a chemically induced high. I mean the altitude or the elevation above sea level. Morgan Spring, we determined after much squinting through a magnifying glass aimed toward a topographical map, sits at about 2,500 feet above sea level. At least we are reasonably sure that is correct. The symbol indication Morgan Spring on the map practically touches one of the faint brown contour lines that snaked across the green paper of the topo map. Green is supposed to be forest but anyone who uses topo maps knows that the green may mean what was once forest.

Regardless of our map, we always had a shadow of doubt about the actual elevation of Morgan Spring. We did not so much agree that we lived at 2,500 feet but we did agree to settle for 2,500 feet. That is to say, 2,500 feet was an okay answer, but it was not necessarily correct. Sometimes wanting to know something exactly can be counter-productive. We decided not to let our height get us down. Still, there were other elevations that claimed our curiosity.

How tall is Cat Peak where we lost our cat? Our cat, the one earlier and momentarily accused of a dreadfully gagging odor, followed us, dog-like if that is not an insult to cat people or cats, as we ascended an unnamed peak on one of our early exploratory excursions. It must be stated that our cat was otherwise strictly confined to inside the house during the day and let out at night for a short visit with the local skunk that befriended her. So, returning to our story on the hike, Linda and our cat, aka Cat, and I walked to the top of what we would eventually dub Cat Peak. At the time, the green shading on our topo map indicated we were traversing forest habitat. We struggled toward the top, Linda, Cat and I. We marveled how short-legged Cat negotiated the forest floor, which was littered with small trees, dead limbs from above long since felled by the elements and waiting for fungi to feed the forest. Additional debris from past logging made for a difficult trek for the three of us, but we periodically waited for Cat to catch up with our longer strides. Summiting was a team effort. As the afternoon sun began to touch the western ridges, we decided it was best to head down and get home before dark. At the same time, Cat apparently decided to go missing. Maybe she was nearby but our calling was to no avail. Possibly, she was uncontrollably answering her ancestry although we had not noticed any interest in anything but keeping up with us. Nonetheless, possibly instinct of the wild had kicked in beyond Cat's inner power, and she would shed herself from her adoption. We gave her plenty of time to come. We called and called. The sunlight began to dim.

We had no flashlights as we had planned to be home well before dark. Cat or no cat, we had to get down the peak and home while we could see all those dead limbs and rocks poised to trip us, not to mention, as relatives had warned, lurking cougars and dangerous quicksand that would put an end to our fun. Because most of the forest came under the ax decades ago, maybe only 50 years ago, the majority of trees in our route were less than 12 inches in diameter. Many even smaller trees, those that might grow to tall forest, meant many dead limbs jutting horizontally from their small trunks. You could easily poke your eye out, just like Mom or Dad constantly reminded us that almost anything could poke your eye out. What a thought. Just exactly what does that mean? Poked out could mean something like lights out. Certainly, a stick in the eye would mean not seeing light. Nevertheless, it might mean the stick pokes your eye and then removes it, or pokes it out of its socket. We weren't sure and kept heading home. Our major concern was falling and not being able to get up. Walking through a trail-less forest is tricky. You have to step and climb over fallen trees and limbs and around old hardened magma jutting out of the bed of decades of used pine and fir needles. Possibly worse is dodging the dead gray limbs sticking out of the trees. Maybe our elders were correct about loosing an eye. Our concern was not so much about the possibility of Linda and me being attacked by some wild animal, unstable sand or pokey eye gougers, but the possibility of Cat becoming cat food to a bigger cat or some other predator. We also did not want Cat to surprise some unsuspecting skunk, something Linda and I just might do on our way down the mountain. We called our cat all the way down. It was dark when we got to the house. The outline of the peak was black against the paler clouded sky and stars beginning to show. At the time, we wondered if our hike was the high point in cat's life. Our destination that day, we decided, should forever be known as Cat Peak. We wondered just how high Cat Peak was.

There were many elevations to determine while exploring territory near Morgan Spring. Bald Mountain, about a mile from the house, rose above Alder Creek to our southeast. It and the ridge to our east were dressed in conifers except for an old clear-cut on Bald Mountain. In winter, we could watch the snow descend from the summit and down the slopes to Morgan Spring. We determined the elevations of Bald Mountain and the peaks on the ridge to our east from our topo maps. We compared the snow line with what the local meteorologist predicted. The predicted elevation for the snow line was often reasonably accurate, but not for Morgan Spring. If the prediction of the snow line was at 3,000 feet, we always had snow at our 2,500 feet. This was not because we had made a 500-foot error in reading our trusty maps. It was because Morgan Spring country was more boreal or colder than the rest of the weather person's territory. In fact, when the predicted snow line was at 3,500 feet, we often had white ground. Our observations and conclusions about elevations based on those brown squiggles on the trusty topo maps were more or less confirmed by a neighbor or two. Those folks had been around for decades and knew every valley and peak, even those that had no name, even the peak we christened Cat Peak. More importantly, they had additional knowledge, the knowledge obtained only from an altimeter.

The quest was on. Find and purchase an altimeter so that we are better equipped to determine our elevation and further pinpoint our locations. Pinpoint may not be the most accurate term. The modern marvels of technology were not our complete cup of tea or within our reach financially. We did not have a GPS to provide us with latitude and longitude, not to mention elevation, and replete with a picture of a map showing us exactly where we stood. Technology, we knew, would eventually make the GPS smaller and more affordable, and hopefully more user-friendly. From my museum days, I had held an altimeter possibly used by the likes of Alexander Wetmore and ornithological pioneers before him. It was a simple device, about the size of a large pocket watch. Right now, in our Morgan Spring days, all we wanted was to look at a device that had a hand pointing to a single number, the elevation. We did not want buttons to push or programs to enter, we just wanted to know how far up we were from the ocean beach.

One day we descended to the valley for grub, to give care to relatives, and amuse ourselves by trying to find an altimeter. The first establishment we tried shall remain nameless in order to avoid a civil action by the store or personally by the clerk who failed to help us. Probably everyone knows the name of the store and experienced an ill-equipped clerk. Upon finding the likely section where this nationally known department store might sell altimeters, we found what we thought might be an intelligent clerk. We at least hoped for a modicum of smartness. After all, this is the Pacific Northwest where people hunt, fish, hike, camp, and drive to the wild mountains and byways. Wouldn't such endeavors beg for knowledge about elevation? Would not most outdoor people want an altimeter?

We asked. "Do you have altimeters?" At last, we thought we were going to be able to measure the elevation of Cat Peak. We waited with needless anticipation.

"What. What's a alti what?"

"An altimeter. Do you have any?"

The clerk looked askance. "What is an altimeter?" The question was delivered in a tone that suggested we were really stupid for asking something so bizarre. Maybe we should be in the small appliance department or the department for accessorizing your computer.

The person behind the counter must have thought they had a reply that would get them off the hook, remove them from the drudgery of having to think, and to dismiss us altogether. "No one ever asked me that before." Never mind that "before" at the end of a sentence was an all too common grammatical error. The jest of the retort, so thought the clerk, might send us running out of the store for asking a question no one had ever dared to ask. "Do you have an altimeter?" sent Linda and me into some category of freakishness, weirdness, and all too demanding of the clerk's skills. Beginning to feel we had stepped into the twilight zone and possibly in danger of having security sicced on us, we wondered if we should head, altimeter-less, out the door. However, we stood our ground.

Although we did not have an altimeter, we did have a meter for registering our feeling about ignorance. Linda most often keeps her appraisals to herself but I am not so mannered. However, in my kindest voice, I said, "Altimeter, as in altitude."

The clerks face twisted, nearly making a perfect question mark that was dotted on each side with blank eyes. "Altitude?"

Becoming my old algebra teacher, the one who did not like stupid students regardless of where the x and y were located on your chromosomes, I spoke unsmiling and slowly. "Elevation," I said with deliberation, "elevation, to measure altitude!" Unfortunately, I added more than I should, which came out a bit condescending. "We need a meter that measures altitude or elevation. Do you have one?" I wanted to say what I thought, which was I do not like your stupid attitude about us determining altitude.

The clerk, trying to hold some semblance of knowledge, had a question for us. "Are you looking to have a meter for elevation or for altitude?"

Straining every fiber to maintain civility, I answered, "elevation." I was not about how to attempt explaining, again, that elevation and altitude are synonyms of height. Sometimes it is best to avoid causing a head to explode.

Then there was this look of vacancy, with a twist of oh hell, why cannot someone ask me about socks, toilet paper, anything but whatever this is. Who are these crazy people asking me about something of which I am clueless? Actually, the clerk was probably thinking, how can I get away from these annoying people because all I care about is my next break?

Regardless of the employee's shortcomings, I realized that the conversation had reached its lowest point. Linda and I did not need an altimeter to measure the height of intelligence that we encountered. Still, we had hopes for this clerk. Maybe we should try again to get across what an altimeter does, the clerk might remember if the store carried such a device or at least determine if the store included altimeters in their catalog. I repeated, "We are looking for an altimeter. It is a meter that measures altitude." I emphasized the alti part of altitude, but the clerk probably thought I had some foreign accent. I added, carefully enunciating that "Altitude is elevation." That was about the time the question mark-shaped face twisted to a hint of disgust. On the other hand, was that my face? As luck would have it, another clerk overheard our query. He said he knows what we are talking about and that the store did not carry altimeters.

The other clerk was in his 50s. The first clerk was in their late 20s or early 30s. Over time, we attempted to find an altimeter at other stores. At first, we thought that maybe our first clerk was, as an individual, and let us say, to be frank, stupid. After many other youngish clerks, who were likewise clueless, we believe that altimeter is just not in the curricula of our finer schools. The education system had reached a new low. In fact, we wondered if school curricula included such esoteric terms as elevation or even meter. Forget about latitude and longitude. We are hopeful that we just had some bad luck and that almost all the clerks out there clerking are smart, caring people, who will go the extra mile to help their customers so that the store will make a sale that will help pay their wages. Of course, we all know the accuracy of our belief.

Our search for the elusive altimeter finally took us to a couple of sporting goods stores. One said they were out of stock. We could check again in two or three weeks. Check again and maybe they would or would not have altimeters. Moreover, was it two weeks or three weeks? Even when you are retired, you have things to do. Besides hating to shop, we did not have lots of time for shopping. We were too busy squinting at the little brown contour lines on our topo maps. In the meantime, we did revisit the store that was out of stock. That was at least six weeks later. There were no altimeters. None had arrived at the store in two weeks or even three weeks. Or had they? Who would know? We wondered if altimeters were so popular; why not stock more of them. This time we bypassed the clerk and found the empty shelf where altimeters, if they had any, would rest. That is when we saw the price, which was somewhat steep. In fact, the elevation of the price approached that of one of the lower functioning GPS models we thought was simple enough for us to operate. At another sporty store, a clerk at first was clue-less, but not about whether they had any altimeters, but what the heck is an altimeter. Finally, we were speaking the same language. "No, none in stock. Try an auto store."

There is no road to the top of Cat Peak or many of the other places we frequented, a fact that we thank goodness for. Squinting at our topographic map, we estimated that Cat Peak stands about 3,300 feet in elevation.

Years later, we purchased an altimeter for our vehicle. About the same time, fortune would have it that we bought a GPS. By now, our cave-dwell-ing abilities had modernized us above the category of troglodyte, but only by a little. At least we could now determine our elevation, which offers some solace. As for the topographic maps, we still squint at the contour lines just for practice.

The highs and lows of the Cat Peak expedition and searching for an altimeter and losing Cat ultimately ascended to favorable heights. First, for two days, Linda and I revisited the slopes of our newly named Cat Peak and expended considerable wind calling her. She had always been reason-able about her vocalizations. That is, she was not one to utter whining and annoying utterances and answered when spoken to. However, Cat did not answer. Cat was not to be found. Reluctantly, Linda and I decided that Cat was not coming, that she was probably a meal from some larger animal. Two days later, a faint noise at the back door got our attention. It was Cat, who, none the worse for wear, looked up and answered our delight with a little meow.

That was just one of Cat's more memorable adventures. One afternoon, after checking the nesting efforts of a pair of Western Bluebirds, Linda and I noticed the three horses and two mules that sometimes frequented the meadow were checking our efforts. The five craned their necks over the fence near what we call the upper gate, the one we can see from our living room window. We, Linda and I, that is, strolled up to the herd to rub their noses and heads and talk to them. Cat was not far behind, but instead of joining us, she decided to walk on the other side of the fence as if to join the horses and mules. Much to the surprise of everyone, including the three horses that looked embarrassed by the event, Fred, the larger mule quickly advanced toward Cat. Red, the reddish mule, looked on with interest, or was it also embarrassment. Fred's front legs were stiff and unbent as he came down with his two hoofs just inches from Cat, who quickly turned toward the house. Fred kept stomping the ground and each time, Cat narrowly missed expending one of her lives. Linda and I did not know she could move so fast. Like a blurry streak, she zipped past the house and part way down the hill toward the main road. Cat found a hole in the ground where a stump might have been and despite coaxing, would not come out of her perceived mule-proof hiding place. A couple of hours passed before we heard her pawing at the back door. Cat never entered the domain of the mules again and was reluctant to follow Linda and me on hikes around Morgan Spring, especially up Cat Peak, a location measured with our altimeter.

CHAPTER 21

Summer Days

We rejoiced during our first winter, the snow white of Morgan Spring. By now, we had scratched the surface of the history and geology of Morgan Spring, enjoyed a white Christmas, and even found an altimeter. We welcomed a spring that arrived weeks after the first leaves on valley trees. Little by little, spring blossomed from melting snow, budding leaves and wildflowers. Summer, our first summer, was around the corner, a few steps away.

The exact date of summer at Morgan Spring is indeterminate. It might have been the first day we shed our clothes for the naked fun of living free, somewhere where prying eyes won't report us for flashing our winter white skin at some puritanical onlooker. Perhaps it was, concurrently, the first mosquito bite. Prying eyes and insect bites are risks that one takes when exposing what is underneath sleeves and pants. Maybe summer was when certain species of plants bloomed or when fruits, infants of their reproductive effort, began to grow before autumn's time. It was hard to say. Spring was but the prelude of what was to come. Any given species at any given time might bloom in full glory on a warm southern slope and just be peeking from the colder soil of a northern slope. We knew, from our trips to the valley, that spring had marched up the slopes. Summer was only steps behind. Putting a date, other than an astronomical date, on the time when our first summer, or those to follow, began at Morgan Springs is elusive.

Being a student of birds most of my life, it might seem prudent to measure the first day of summer by something birds did. By now, a pair of Western Bluebirds had taken over the birdhouse on the fence post house I cobbled together sometime in late winter. The bluebird pair did not wait for summer to begin and were already feeding young. Spring arrival of Tree

Swallows was long past. Warblers and vireos, migrating from the tropics arrived in what we call spring. Western Tanagers that settled around Morgan Spring country were singing behind the house, and others chorused up the slope beyond the ever-greening meadow. Summer arrived sometime on the sliding scale of nature, sometime after the last snowflake and before the deep purple of camas blooming just down the gentle slope from Morgan Spring faded and dried in the wind. About the same time, days began and ended with fewer and fewer clouds. Finally, there were no clouds. For Morgan Spring country, the rainy season was definitely over. Dryer and warmer days became the norm, the expected weather for what would be our first summer.

Early summer arrived weeks after the last snow melted, sometime after spring when the meadow presented a myriad of wildflowers. The abundance of flowers in the meadow changed from one species to another with the progression of seasons. One morning we might wake to a meadow so full of tiny pink flowers that the petals created a sea of color that dominated our eyes. Another time, we might view large patches of white from the combined total of thousands of tiny white flowers hugging the ground. In time, tall grasses turned the meadow into a sea of green that appeared to ebb and flow during a breezy afternoon. The progression of spring to summer, the changing of seasons, demonstrated by the changes in the dominance of flowers mirrored changes in temperature, length of daylight, and moisture in the soil. Knowing the exact date for different seasons was not possible, but summer was almost here, if not already present. The meadow and all around was warming from the increase in day length, and soil was drying as spring rains stopped. We happily reveled in witnessing some of the undeniable facets of plant ecology. That biological process would continue as the grass grew taller and denser, protecting the soil from the arid sun. Eventually foraging elk visiting the meadow would eat some of the grass, but plant would leave seeds for rodents that might eat them while they the rodents would be meals for coyotes, which in turn will help weed out deer populations.

Many of the flowers were tiny and unidentifiable, with almost microscopic petals, but a few larger and much taller hound' tongue made the meadow a smorgasbord of floral wonder. We could not keep up with identifying the flowers we found on daily walks around the house, the meadow, and the secondary forests on the surrounding ridges. We should have had better field guides. I should have paid more attention to systematic botany. We did the best we could and we enjoyed the flowers whether or not we knew their names. The grasses were a mystery of species, mostly and regrettably introduced species, as were probably some of the wildflowers. We ignored where they came from and were delighted that the meadow was a major attraction to an animal we had only glimpsed since our arrival.

One fateful day, while staring up at the meadow and the ridges beyond from our living room, something surprised us. An elk was standing at the edge of the meadow. Soon, another followed. Both stood tall and watchful. Maybe a minute passed as we held our breaths and two more elk emerged from the woods. Although a fence surrounded the meadow, we could not be sure whether the elk were jumping over the fence or were going through the fence. That puzzle would wait for later discovery. In the meantime, more and more elk entered the meadow until there were close to forty individuals. They cautiously grazed down the meadow from several yards above the spring where we first saw them to around 200 feet from the house. Unbelievable. We whispered our mutual delight and were careful not to make any sudden movements. The black refrigerator and cooking range behind, we hoped, would make any human movements in the house harder to see. At least that was our reasoning for buying black appliances in the first place.

Elk occupied the meadow on numerous occasions.

A couple of hours passed. Gradually, the herd moved back up the meadow. The last to leave the meadow was probably a cow; one of the ones that appeared to watch over the herd should an excited human in the house make a foolish movement. Owing to the slowness of the herd's departure, I think we were successful in not causing the elk to leave prematurely. Thankfully, the phone did not ring.

We never knew when the elk might next appear. Linda and I were relatively hushed most of the time except when playing a Prokofiev symphony or a jazz quartet. Not having a dog increased the number of visits by elk to the meadow. A dog would most certainly scare away wildlife, whether the dog was barking from fright or a warning, or just to hear its head rattle. Cat, our trusty cat, joined us as we watched the herd, the herd that became our elk.

One day, before the meadow dried from summer sun, we returned from a walk that started by traversing the meadow, picking up an old logging road, now mostly overgrown with spindly foot-high trees and forbs, and then to another long abandoned road down a north slope, a trail up to the side of another ridge where we caught another decade-old logging road that circled back to our house. A surprise was waiting in the meadow.

We heard them, the elk were returning. About the same time, we smelled them. We were fortunately downwind from the herd that collectively smelled like elk pee. Unlike humans who have not enjoyed ever hearing the phrase "piss on you," elk apparently do not mind to have a little pee on their gorgeous fur. The elk did not see or hear Linda or me as we slowly emerged from the woods and crept to a dead madrone. We then crawled on our bellies through the weeds as we inched dangerously close of the edge of the herd. We were within bow and arrow range. The closest individual breathed evenly. We could hear the exhale. All of this was taking our breath away. We could hear the closest elk's teeth grinding. I crept foolishly closer, stopping within a yard on an unaware elk that would have bolted or attacked if it detected me. More cautious Linda, staying a little farther away, communicated with sign language we had earlier practiced for such an occasion as this. Daring not to get closer, we waited until the herd gathered up and left the meadow, disappearing into the forest of trees and brush. Getting some unidentifiable dirt smeared on our shirts and jeans was well worth being able to stalk so closely to such a magnificent mammal. We remained speechless, hugging in triumph for being able to experience the remoteness and wild of Morgan Spring. Part of our delight was mixed with a measure of fear since we knew getting so close was something no one should try at home, or any other place, for that matter.

Perhaps the elk sometimes visited at night. We did see them on a few occasions when we beamed our heavy-duty flashlight from the house. Eyes reflected our light, but we refrained from further disturbing the herd. We wanted them to travel without fear of predatory humans. We wanted the elk to feel the freedom that we were experiencing at Morgan Spring. Just how the herd entered the meadow that first day we saw them was not over but through the fence. Elk, we were soon to learn, hardly notice fences, and breaking wires and knocking down fences was nothing to slow the brute strength of such powerful animals.

On more than one occasion, elk and deer concurrently occupied the meadow. Adults of each species kept their distance, usually not getting closer to each other than maybe 40 feet. That comfort zone did not apply to youngsters. Usually, the instigators were deer, just old enough to be beyond their bambi spots, the deer fawn would run toward a young elk. One would run and the other would then follow in hot, playful pursuit. Parental adult deer looked on, seemingly with only slight interest. On the other hand, adult cow elk appeared to disapprove and sometimes would walk quickly toward a playful deer fawn. Often, this menacing had little effect. Kids, whether they are deer, elk or humans, frequently ignore adults.

Concerning the term bambi, it is realized that bambi is a word with various meanings. Bambi was probably first used, if not popularized, as the name of a young male spotted deer around the second decade of the 1900s. Bambi was derived from the Italian bambino for an infant. Surely the "o" ending places the gender as male since banbina ending with an "a" defines a baby girl. Bambi, according to urban dictionaries, can also mean a lavishly cute or beautiful female that gives those attracted to her a good dose of heart palpitations. Perhaps those attracted to a bambi also see spots since spots are abundant on juvenile deer and many other subadult mammals and, yes, young birds. Are junior bluebirds bambis? Maybe.

Rarely, actually too infrequently for our taste, a coyote would amble across the meadow. They usually took a straight path from one side of the open to the opposite side. Their route was about 220 yards from the house. Occasionally, a coyote would stop and look our way. If we were outside, Linda and I would freeze and stop breathing as long we possibly could. Was the coyote also holding its breath?

Like most animals seen in the meadow, the coyote recognized us as human and likely categorized us along with our few neighbors who mostly did not hesitate to shoot at coyotes. The fluffy-tailed canines would surely, according to local thought, increase the mortality of newborn calves. And, of course, small kids and pets must beware of the perilous dangers of coyotes. My guess, and I mean guess, as it seems too obvious to waste time researching, is that domestic dogs take down more livestock and bite more people in just a few years than all the coyotes might have done throughout their history with humans.

Summer was definitely present at Morgan Spring by July. Coyotes panted to cool from the hot temperature. A resident Red-tailed Hawk hunted the meadow for small mammals or a bird and a pair of Dark-eyed Juncos visited the feeder daily. Where were the dozens of juncos coming to the yard during winter? Rufous Hummingbirds, our smallest birds, liked the hummingbird feeder, and our largest birds, the Turkey Vultures, ferried across the meadow and ridges beyond, buoyed by thermals of warm air from the hot Rogue Valley several miles away. In the evenings, we were introduced to another large bird that produced an almost scary thrashing ruckus not so far from our front door. The racket caught us off guard. Dozens of Wild Turkeys were not so graceful in the air or during crash landings into their roosting trees on the west side of Morgan Creek each night.

When not attempting to perch in trees, Wild Turkeys were busy foraging and breeding. They had chicks on 4 July, only a few days after we disturbed a Ruffed Grouse with seven flying chicks as we walked down the driveway to the mailbox. House Wrens, Yellow-rumped Warblers, and Lazuli Buntings sang less as summer progressed. Even the noisy Cassin's Vireo was becoming quieter.

Although officially in the yoke of summer, signs of fall began to appear. Migrant raptors - kestrel, Golden Eagle, Cooper's and Sharp-shinned Hawks - signaled the beginning of migration. These birds, along with shorebirds, or at least some species, begin migrating early. Chances of identifying any shorebirds were slim to none, but we began to notice changes in our local avifauna suggesting summer was soon to end. One sign was an increase in sightings of birds in immature plumage. Chipping Sparrows, bluebirds, juncos, and more had offspring in tow, often begging adults for food. Young Black-headed Grosbeaks and hungry juvenile vireos, Western Tanagers, Lazuli Buntings were all around.

Finches and Evening Grosbeaks put in an appearance, probably to check the feeders for the winter ahead. They disappeared, but Pine Siskins stayed to ravish the thistle feeder. The one or three, we were never sure, Western Screech-Owls stopped screeching. Actually, their vocalizations were pleasant and inviting during our summer nights. The forest was becoming ever so silent as birds wound up their musical business of maintaining territories, attracting mates, and feeding their offspring. The elk and deer visited the meadow less and less as the meadow itself stopped growing and turned to straw. Perhaps in anticipation of hunting season, the hoofed animals avoided the openness of the meadow. Although that might be giving elk and deer too much credit, it is reasonable that most individuals have some memory of humans and particularly avoid the sound of a rifle tearing at the natural pulse of their habitats.

A few clouds appeared in the August sky. Thankfully, they were not the summer cumulus, those dangerous mammoths that most people dislike seeing over a mountain range. Those fire starters gave way to very wispy brush strokes as a sign of summer passing. Nights became cooler. Normally, we opened every window at night so the cooler upper air would flush and cool the house. Early in the morning, we would close the windows, trapping inside the crispness that kept the house cool most of the hot summer. Being opportunistic, we took advantage of the weather in many ways, and obscuring a tan line was a pleasurable one. Now, in late August, we opened only a few windows and sometimes closed them well before morning. A flannel shirt was now required for the early morning restocking of the bird feeders. Compared to the middle of summer when temperatures were nearly 90 degrees, the mornings in late August felt cold. Even the mid-day temperatures were cool, almost too cool for activities around the yard sans pesky attire.

Neotropical migrants began departing. Western Tanagers and Rufous Hummingbirds were becoming scarce. Turkey Vultures rarely cruised the thermals looking for some hapless meal. Most vultures were heading south, following the vireos and warblers, Lazuli Buntings, parasitic Brown-headed Cowbirds and difficult to identify flycatchers. More and more mornings were cloudy until the sun drove their mist to invisibility. The nights became still cooler and cooler. A few spiders and insects attempted to move to our indoors, but we would capture them, returning the creatures outside to fend for themselves. Ponderosa pine needles began falling, raining down on the roof, our car and gravel driveway. Fall was coming. Just as the beginning of summer is elusive, so is its end. When does summer end and fall begin? Again, the birds were telling the story, at least this time, the end of our first summer. One hint was the absence of flocks of juncos at the feeder. As far as juncos were concerned, it was still summertime at Morgan Spring. On the other hand, Pine Siskins, those stripped relatives of goldfinches, were gathering in larger and larger flocks and spending more time in the trees near the house. They had given up costing us a fortune in thistle seeds that they ate earlier.

13 September, the anniversary of our first year of being lucky residents at Morgan Spring, marked the disappearance of the last Western Bluebird fledgling from the birdhouse. What were they thinking? We wondered if it and its siblings would survive the coming rain, cold nights, and scarcity of insects. Our first summer and that of those fledglings was ending. Chestnut-backed Chickadees and Golden-crowned Kinglets, common species last winter and scarce during summer were becoming more numerous, perhaps some of them moving downslope, an attitudinal migration practiced by juncos, jays, deer, and elk.

The end of summer, what we call autumn, was a gradual occurrence, but not for all species. Yes, the birds wintering in Middle and South America departed one day, not looking back, intent on beating their small wings until they reached their destination. For us, the changing seasons, that period of climatic evolution, was inspiring, wondrous, and educational and left us with some answers and many questions. Living at Morgan Spring, being outdoors daily, observing nature constantly, allowed us to tune into life, to feel the pulse of change and observe the small entities that contribute to the core of Morgan Spring if not the core of our own being. Living, as we once did, in mostly large metropolitan arenas, primarily east of the Mississippi, we had missed the subtle changes in nature, the gradual transfer of life from one season to another. Having lived at Morgan Spring during that busy initial fall and winter when learning our place, we stepped back and breathed in a spring that would build the summer and that jolted our psyche with its full beautiful force. We were not prepared for the rush, and it was not until summer that we gathered ourselves together to more thoughtfully ponder the season, our first summer at Morgan Spring.

From the beginning, which is not exactly known, watching the meadow, with its denizens of elk, deer, at least one brave coyote, a swooping Red-tailed Hawk, even watching the grass grow, we were never bored; seeing, smelling, hearing nature that first summer was our minds' treasure. At the end of summer, whenever precisely that was, we knew we could hardly wait for the next.

CHAPTER 22

The Blues and Other Hues

As an expatriate from Smithsonian's Division of Birds, I naturally could not ignore the local avifauna no matter the season or almost anywhere I might be located, and definitely could not dismiss one species common to Morgan Spring. Steller's Jays, or as it is called in the old language, *Cyanocitta stelleri,* were prominent daily fare. They are vocal beyond anything Linda and I had experienced or expected. Surely their complex language is under study. The jay's striking plumage consists of a dark blue body topped off with a black head and upper breast. The back may range individually from nearly black to brownish in color, depending on age, sex, and season. The crest is geographically variable in markings, length, and color, with blue-crested birds in Mexico and Middle America and black-crested birds in the remaining range, including our local birds. I knew this since an unfinished museum study of geographic variation rested as notes in a file in our spare bedroom. Our Morgan Spring jays appear to exude an attitude of flamboyant brashness. Steller's Jays visited the feeders with apparent enthusiasm and tried to eat almost everything in sight all the while demonstrating to other species that they were the alpha birds.

The Steller's Jay is a close relative of the mostly eastern Blue Jay. The two species share generic names. *Cyanocitta cristata,* the Blue Jay, resembles Steller's Jay by also having a crest, and both species are similar in size, Steller's being maybe a half-inch bigger. Blue Jays are paler, with the blue color approaching a purplish blue, compared to the darker-hued Steller's, with its blues ranging from near royal blue to almost a silvery turquoise. Measurements and color vary geographically, which is a good stopping place as I know an old taxonomist cannot help from going too deep. I will leave that, at least momentarily, for someone else. Suffice to say, Blue and Steller's jays are members of Corvidae, the crow family that includes 126 species world-wide. Depending on whose taxonomy you follow, there are about 21 species of corvids in North America. Among those are jays, crows, ravens, magpies, and one species of nutcracker. The family consists of several species of jays, including California Scrub-Jays and Canada Jays. Morgan Spring was just a little too high in elevation for scrub-jays to breed, although individuals rarely visited in late summer. We found Gray Jays at 4,500 feet on the ridge above Morgan Spring. We thought Gray Jays would visit Morgan Spring during winter when snow might drive them to lower elevations, but we never saw them around our home. Another member of the crow family found at even higher elevations at Crater Lake National Park is the Clark's Nutcracker. The closest nutcrackers we observed to Morgan Spring were at Rim Village at Crater Lake.

Magpies are also representatives of the crow family. In Oregon, we have encountered Black-billed Magpies mostly east of the Cascades. The species sometimes visits the Cascades and Rogue Valley. Morgan Spring, as far as we know, was not a host to magpies although I suspect an individual or two might be interested in foraging around some of the ranches not far from our new home. Morgan Spring played host to the Common Raven and the American Crow. The former was a regular and entertaining species that we saw almost daily. American Crows were less common than ravens and apparently breed at elevations lower than Morgan Spring.

Members of Corvidae are opportunistic feeders, and all eat carrion. What a smelly place we would live in if not for species of corvids cleaning up road-pancaked frogs, smashed snakes, unidentifiable bloating carcasses, you name it, even skunks hit and ran over by motor vehicles. They also help clean up the dead animals in the woods and meadows. Corvids compete primarily with each other and sometimes with vultures for the road kills of America.

Visitors, human ones that is, coming to Morgan Spring usually looked at our resident corvids, our Steller's Jays and called them Blue Jays. They repeated this nomenclatural transgression even after being informed of the correct name. Old habits are difficult to break. Other than the crest and relatively similar size, these jays are different as night and day. Even after exhibiting a picture, the same people frequently continued to call Steller's Jays Blue Jays. Is this a case of applying a colloquial name in disuse? Are all crested jays, but not all are Blue Jays? We also heard people identifying the scrub-jay as a blue jay. This species, which we will talk more about, is crestless, and the blue parts of its plumage resemble the pale blue of the eastern Blue Jay more than the darker Steller's Jay. Still, by what stretch of the imagination could Steller's Jay, Blue Jay or scrub-jay be known under the same moniker? Do some people mean blue jay for any jay that is blue? Are those crow-like dull bluish birds we know from central Oregon and the high deserts of the west as Pinon Jays also Blue Jays? Good grief. That would mean lots of species of jays might fall under the umbrella term, blue jay. Even during the days of Linnaeus in the mid-1700s and Gmelin in the later 1700s, when scientific names (those nettlesome Greek and Latin words) were attached in an orderly fashion to plants and animals, the difference between closely related birds was sometimes realized. For example, Linnaeus proposed the name *Corvus cristata* for the Blue Jay in 1758. Thirty years later Gmelin, continuing Linnaeus' pioneering work, proposed the name *Corvus stelleri*. These two guys even knew the difference between three different species presently in the genus *Corvus*, the Jackdaw of the Old World, the Jamaican Crow from where else, and the Common Raven of North America. All are black in plumage. No field guides, no nature shows on TV, actually, no TV or even electricity, no binoculars were available to Linnaeus or Gmelin to help these scholars know the differences between the species they described. Nonetheless, our taxonomic forefathers could tell the difference between a Steller's Jay and a Blue Jay, so why cannot modern man? Thankfully, many can. After all, many people that are jay handicapped have no trouble differentiating a chevy from a ford right down to the model. For those that cannot separate Steller's and Blue jays, perhaps they should be using scientific names so that they and others are on the same page. Of course, good luck with that.

Undiscerning people who perceive all jays with blue feathers as one big globular species they call blue jay might appreciate knowing that some Canada Jays, known as Gray Jays in recent history, may appear somewhat brownish when worn and soiled. And, yes, there are brown Brown Jays from Middle America that are casual in certain locations on the Rio Grande in Texas. The green Green Jay, also from Middle America, is common in southeastern Texas and is mostly green, but sports a shade of blue on its head. Surely, no one would call Brown, Green jays or formerly Gray Jays, blue jays, but anything is possible.

The use of color as part of a common name for birds sharing blue is not limited to jays. Continuing with blue, there are two species of bluebirds that have chestnut breasts, the Eastern Bluebird and the Western Bluebird, both distinct species that differ in several ways including plumage pattern and voice. Male Western Bluebirds have a chestnut patch on the middle of their backs; Eastern Bluebirds have blue backs. Most people refer to the two species simply as bluebirds. Using the term bluebird could, of course, mean both species; the term does not mean a misidentification in the sense of blue jay. There is another species of bluebird in the west that lacks a chestnut breast. That is the all blue Mountain Bluebird. Regardless of season and weather, the beautiful pale turquoise blue males, with paler whitish breasts or the dull brownish female, with a bluish rump, tail, and wings never revealed themselves. We hoped to see this species at Morgan Spring. Some locals thought they might have seen Mountain Bluebirds at our elevation but they never provided the field marks that would distinguish their birds from the Western Bluebird. Of course, some of these people were the very same that called Steller's Jays Blue Jays (or did they just mean blue-colored jays?).

What about red birds? Would Summer and Hepatic Tanagers and cardinals have but one name? Red Bird. What about the drab females of those species? Not much red on them. Locals on a West Indian island I studied used the name Brown Bird and Black Bird for the female and male, respectively for the same species. Luckily, most jays are not sexually dimorphic; they have similar plumages in both sexes. Otherwise, we might have Scarlet Tanagers and some-other-color tanager, both of which would actually be the same species. The term blue, when applied to jays (or other animals that sometimes are blue) is not terribly accurate unless assigned to a particular species. Again, not all blue jays are Blue Jays. Birders, ornithologists, and others who want to communicate correctly, know that the Blue Jay is most often found in eastern North America. Applying the term blue to many species of jays reduces jays to a monomorphic mass of merged species and tells us ground dwelling humans nothing about the many species of jays. Biodiversity of jays be damned to the dark ages. Fortunately, there are people out there that use proper nomenclature along with correct identifications. Such people often belong to informed citizen scientist groups; they are naturalists, birders, and ornithologists.

Maybe we are touchy about our blue Steller's Jays. They are unique after all. Within North America, some populations differ morphologically from one another. Such groups belong to subspecies and some subspecies groups might prove to be different at the species level. As we bird people often say, more study is required. As mentioned, vocalizations of Steller's Jays are amazingly varied. We were missing an opportunity by not at least attempting to record and catalog some of the sounds ranging from whispering high and low-pitched utterances to loud raspy alarms calls and possible conversations among individuals. More study is definitely required.

Concerning the other blue jay, California Scrub-Jays are common in the scrub and oak below 2,000 feet elevation in southern Oregon. They are crestless, but not crestfallen as they act with confidence when confronting other species or one another. It is a jay thing.

Some people we met who referred to our *Aphelocoma californica* as scrub jays, unlike those using the term blue jay, were correct but not precise.

There is only one jay with the name Blue Jay. There are now four species of scrub jays.

An actual blue jay in the form of a Blue Jay might occur at Morgan Spring someday. Blue Jays are expanding their range and a pair began a failed nest in northeastern Oregon in 1991. Wait long enough and almost any species might show up almost anywhere. Of course, that is an exaggeration, but the day is coming for another Xantus's Hummingbird to make its way north of Baja, a South American Swallow-tailed Gull to revisit North America, an Intermediate Egret (aka Goldilocks Egret) to fly across the Bering Sea, or for any number of Old World warblers, thrushes or flycatchers to perform a pioneering visit to the New World.. Perhaps a Mexican Jay, a bluish jay of the southwest US and southward will come to excite not just birders but jays of various colors.

Assigning English names to all those many and variously colored jays and other birds is often based on some characteristic of a given species is complicated. Size, such as Greater or Lesser Yellowlegs, and color, again back to the jays, and is often problematic. Thankfully, few if any birds are named for the way they smell. Some species are identifiable by the way they smell. Storm-petrels and fishy smelling osprey reputations related to how they smell does not extend to their English names. Perhaps that is because odor is difficult to describe. Stinky Starling is not a species listed in checklists and we are mostly left with color for names of birds. Blue is a regularly occurring color that is in use for English names of birds. It is a good thing ornithologists have a baseline for defining the names of colors. That would be a rare 1912 publication by Robert Ridgway, who, while working at Smithsonian and practicing as a world-class ornithologist, wrote the book of color standards. If a bird demonstrated a color, that color, any color imaginable for any species of bird, was depicted as one of 1,115 colors in Ridgway's invaluable tome that included color swathes and names affixed to each color. Other standards for color have been devised since Ridgway's go-to publication. None of them have the acclaim possessed by the man, as some of us at the National Museum of Natural History called Robert Ridgway. Incidentally, several of Ridgway's 52 plates of colors depict shades of blue. Some of them are attributed to various taxa of scrub-jays and Blue Jays. In 1921, Harry C. Oberholser, while characterizing a new subspecies of Blue Jay, referred to at least six shades of blue from Ridgway's standards. Some say Oberholser's special talent at discerning small difference in color of birds originated from his early employment selling ribbons. Oberholser may have noticed there are even more shades of blue found in the plumages of scrub-jays. Were any of the scrub-jays Linda and I saw in the lowlands sporting cornflower blue, a color in Ridgway's standards and the color of bachelor buttons growing along the highway? Maybe, but, again, those local jays were not Blue Jays.

Although some people called all or maybe some groups of jays blue jays, they may have had proficiency in naming mushrooms or at least knew the differences between those that contributed to a good meal and those that contributed to a last meal. They might know the names of many things there were unknown or barely suspected by those who could identity and name a bunch of jays. Even so, the jay namers and those less astute in jays 101 could learn from one another and thereby increase their appreciation towards one another and jays regardless of blueness or other hues.

CHAPTER 23

Building

Friends at Smithsonian's Division of Birds could not believe I had a cat. That even surprised me, but it was a good thing. One thing Cat was missing was a nice warm place to sleep other than the foot of our bed or the garage at night. She needed, heck, us humans, needed a little more space. Could we make that happen? Friends back on the banks of the Potomac also could not believe we were thinking of building an addition. My lack of carpentry skills was legendary. Still, our need for a skosh more space for us, including Cat, was somewhere in the back of thought, especially when it was time for sleep. Cat had to leave our side, a place she stayed most of the time. At bedtime, Linda or I would say to her "Time to go to bed." Mind you, most of the time we said that phrase without any special cat emphasis. We would say the phrase as if talking to another human.

Luckily, Cat had a place to go to perform her sleep. Initially, she slept behind closed doors in the utility room and eventually her place was in the newly built garage. Cat would be escorted to our front door, which opened toward a side door of the garage. Actually, she led the way. Like holding the door for anyone, Cat glided past the doorways without hesitation although sometimes she would look up as if appreciating holding the door open. After all, she was too short to reach the doorknob and naturally lacked thumbs to turn the handles. Cat also sometimes looked up toward our faces as if to say, "Are you sure it is time to go to bed?" It was, and she went to her corner in the garage where a soft pile of clean rags in a cardboard box waited for her to spend the night. In case she needed it, fresh water and a few cat morsels were provided. The next morning, she was waiting to enter the house. If it was a cold night, she slept in the utility room.

Cat would soon have a new place to sleep once the garage was built. For a while after our arrival from the far east, the garage was a mere shadow of itself. The wooden frame, sprouting from the cold gray concrete slab rather suddenly, was quickly covered from top to sides with a pale green metal sheeting of an unexpected if not serviceable color. For the main entrance, a dark-brown roll-up door was wide enough for our car. Along the interior sides was ample space for acquired tools, including the small but adequate chain saw and all of its entourage, the can of gas, oil, files to sharpen the cutting doohickey, the chain. Fortunately, work at Crater Lake over three decades ago had taught me how to operate and sharpen a chain saw. That training included how not to cut wayward limbs and not have wood chips poke out an eye. A dry space on one side of the garage's interior was set aside to store evidence of me splitting wood for the dreamed-about wood stove. Besides the car and other paraphernalia, the garage soon contained a refrigerator we more or less inherited from a friend, a large ice-chest for transporting frozen and refrigerated food from the grocery store to Morgan Spring, and too many other objects. Near the lockable side door and refrigerator was a metal shelf stacked with nonperishable groceries, including a bag of potatoes and other edibles not requiring more care afforded from the indoor pantry. Anything on the shelves that might freeze during winter had to be stored inside the house.

The garage eased much of our anxiety about storing our stuff, but there was little to no space for prose or filling staves with so many musical notes, for creating of any kind and almost as important, we needed a place to have the wood stove, the one I prematurely referred to when discussing the garage. The original floor plan only allowed for heating from the small in-wall heat pump. Besides, a wood stove needed space from the walls and that meant losing valuable floor space in the living room area. A wood stove would not work with the present floor plan. We had been able to maintain a livable temperature during the winter, but the electricity did occasionally fail. Yes, we were not in Kansas City anymore, we were at the edge of the grid, and if something happened to those wires along Elk Creek Road, we would likely be the last to have the lights back on. As for our electricity from the road to the house, it was all underground should one of the magnificent ponderosa pines succumb to heavy snow or wind.

As divulged, it did not take long before Linda and I realized that Morgan Spring is home, not just for the moment, but forever. So, why not build an addition to the existing house to make our home even happier? How much would the endeavor cost? Could we afford it? Could we afford the extra room, a wood stove, and wood to stoke it and not go in debt? Could became would. Our answer was yes. We would like to build an addition and give a wood stove a happy home, but could we?

My carpentry skills were akin to accidentally constructing birdhouses, but Linda's sister could supply us her husband, who had built more houses than he could count. Besides, he loved visiting us when possible and by building our addition, he would have the opportunity to spend more time at Morgan Spring. With labor taken into account, material had to be acquired. In order to do that, a plan, a very detailed plan, had to be drawn by us and approved by the county. There would be no flying buttresses or southern mansion-styled columns, just a simple room. My few months of high school wood shop merged with a cartography college class taken decades ago were somehow scrambled together to produce passable drawings that included the ups and downs for the foundation, pitch of the roof, depth, width, and length of every section, including an outside door, space for windows, door and windows themselves, height of a vaulted ceiling, and so many other details I have forgotten.

Once the plans were approved by the county, we called the organization that locates buried wires and pipes. It took a while before anyone came out. As usual, people complained about the travel time and gas expenditure from the crowded Rogue Valley. It never failed that those same travelers told us how much they liked being at Morgan Spring while forcing a conversation to increase their departure time. We had to hire a couple of guys to dig the foundation. Of course, that is a novice's way of describing the process, but that is the base of my recollection. One of those strange trucks with a rotating bubble lumbered up the driveway and backed up as far as possible to spill out its gray contents into the wooden forms that were the molds for the foundation. Routing the slush from the rear of the truck to the back of the house was a feat we worried might be impossible. Of course, it was not impossible and eventually, the hardened foundation stood at the ready.

From the building plans, the amount of lumber needed was ordered and soon unloaded on the narrow lawn struggling to stay green from the abuse of extra foot traffic and the cement truck. Thankfully, a row of gladiolus somehow escaped destruction. I could not visualize that pile of lumber would become the addition we planned, but the building began to take shape. At that same time, summer was getting organized with increasing temperatures that created hot working conditions. Yes, I was working, too. My job was to follow instructions from our head carpenter, which required me to act as a gofer, the person that goes for this or for that. Actually, I fetched tools, nails, you name it, and lifted and held building parts in position while the expert made those plans drawn up so much earlier become reality. The process was a learning experience. One of the first lessons was "measure twice and cut once." An important second lesson learned was to not hit your phalanges, especially your thumb, with a hammer.

After the subfloor was finished, we, my brother-in-law and I, started framing the walls, which also involved anchoring the addition to the suet tree side of the main house. At the time, all this seemed to consume a lot of time, but it actually did not. Hard work, keeping hydrated at the urging from Linda, and pride in getting the job done sent the clock spinning. Luckily, the climate in southwestern Oregon affords rainless days during summer months, which kept any weather-borne interruptions at bay. Therefore, the framing of the walls was not interrupted. Eventually, I graduated to the use of the mighty nail gun. About that time, extra people, including our brother-in-law's son and grandson, Linda's nephew and great-nephew, were called to help since, as our brother-in-law said, they owed him. Installation of a sturdy and heavy ridge beam required most hands on deck, especially those owned by the younger guys. The heavy beam had to be lifted upward, anchored to the main house and to the far end of the addition. This was a tense situation as the crew barked instructions to each other and grunted the ridge beam into its final resting place. I may be missing a step or two, but soon thereafter, insulation was in place and the outer shell for the walls and roof covered the skeletal frame.

Measuring twice and cutting once.

Healthy-sized windows were placed on three sides of the addition. What was left was fewer square feet of sheet-rocked walls and more window, which was all the better to see the surroundings. Windows in one direction allowed us to see a portion of the driveway and Burnt Peak, and 90 degrees to that view, we could see the suet tree and one more hard turn, we could see parts of the back yard bird feeders and the glorious meadow. The back door of the main original house became the doorway beyond the utility room and the new back door opened to the outside toward the meadow. Some of the 4 x 6 scraps from our addition came in handy when I later fashioned sturdy steps outside the new back door.

After painting the ceiling and walls, Linda and I selected a laminate floor design that mimicked a hardwood pattern more pleasing than any we have seen before or since. We calculated we needed around 200 square feet of flooring, you know, measure twice and cut once. Neither of us had ever installed such a floor, but we could read instructions and, with a little glue, a hammer, an electric saw, patience and delegating back and knee pain to be on hold, we tapped and glued countless planks into place. Planks ending near the walls had to be cut, but somehow we managed to cover the subfloor from wall to wall. It was sometimes frustrating, boring, frequently painful, especially when regaining an upright pose, a point of pride upon completion, and it was beautiful.

The next step was to find a suitable wood stove. Size was a consideration as was the stove being certified for safety and meeting standards concerning the prevention of air pollution. Imagine every household in the county heating with a wood-burning stove. The high density of an ever-increasing population cries for some sort of regulations. Sure, we were almost at the end of the grid. Why should we be concerned about the air quality from our stove? The only six scattered residences along Button Creek surely would not pollute the local air? Actually, yes, any one of us might pollute. We sometimes, thankfully only rarely, could detect the stink of garbage burning, either smoldering in a wood stove or an outside burn barrel. Once in a while, we could smell burning madrone emanating from a wood stove or fireplace. It all depended on the direction of the wind.

We found the object of our dreams, a wood stove that complied with the latest achievements made by expert wood stove builders, namely a stove that burned wood safely and emitted as few pollutants as possible. Thanks to recommendations from a neighbor, we hired a man adept in installing wood-burning stoves. He brought it in his pickup, which looked to be straining almost as much as we did when carrying the heavy metal object up back steps I built a few days earlier. Although the steps creaked under the strain, we managed the job of getting the stove through the back door without any smashed or broken body parts or abusing the door frame with only whispered cuss words. Finally, the stove sat on the heavy fireproof hearth pad that would protect the flooring Linda and I had painstakingly installed.

The wood stove of our dreams.

Careful calculations determined the distance between the stove and the wall, the wall near the back door. Since the stove sat not far from the entrance to the utility room, the configuration ought to allow heat from it to travel through the utility room and on into the remainder of the house. This, we reasoned would work, with or without the assistance of an electric fan pulling the air from the stove and pushing heat into the living room and hallway. Heat even made it to the bedroom. No need for unsafe space heaters or the clamorous in-wall heat pump.

There were two other reasons for the stove's resting place. We wanted it in proximity to the back door so that the removing of built-up ash would occur close the outside, and, second, if the stove became too hot, we would simply open the back door to quickly cool down the room. Linda and I had earlier traded wood stove tales involving over-heated rooms. Our fathers often independently came home from a day of working in cold, often rainy or foggy conditions, with little more on their minds than stoking the fire in the family wood stove to the biggest roaring conflagration that they could imagine. It did not take long before parts of their heavy metal stove began glowing red and causing the whole house to be so hot paint might blister.

The air was so dry your tongue stuck to your lips, but no, no way at all was it permissible to open an outside door to try for a reasonable inside temperature. We missed our fathers and looked forward to using our wood stove.

After the stove was positioned, a hole had to be cut in the vaulted ceiling and the roof. All went as planned, and we soon had a working wood stove keeping our electric bill down and ourselves safe, warm and cozy, with or without a fan. Linda's attractive white teapot full of water perching on top of the black iron stove would help us avoid desert-like air and an electric ceiling fan would assist in circulating the heat. We were advised that a good mixture of fir, which at the time could be had for free at most finer lumber mills, and dry madrone, which could be had for a price, was the start of a good fire. Once embers resided in the belly of the stove, pieces of madrone kept the fire burning, and after trial and error, adjustment of the dampers, one on the stove, the other on the flue pipe, the stove could maintain heat for hours and hours. Although the stove sat on a special stove pad, once in a while a pesky red-hot ember would jump out the stove's door during refueling. Of course, any burning fragments were quickly scooped up, but flooring of many kinds, including wooden, would have resulting scorch marks. To our amazement, our flooring resisted the searing abuse and maintained its allure.

Time and practice helped us move toward fewer embers escaping from the wide side door of the stove, which, thanks to the all-seeing window of the stove, was an easy means for knowing when to add wooden fuel. The muted glow from the embers also was comforting. Admittedly, fire building was at first not so hot. Part of that was from years of simply turning on a switch, a push of a button or adjustment of a thermostat to acquire heat. Another problem was the wood. We had ordered a dump truck load of unsplit madrone, enough wood for the season, but it was too green, much too fresh to split. Stubbornness finally produced blisters, sore muscles and a pile of madrone split for the winter. However, in the following years, we got our dump truck load in late spring or early in the summer. Day after day, the sun dried the wood to near perfection for splitting and burning.

A dump truck delivered a load of madrone, wood already cut to a length that would fit in our stove, was the amount of fuel needed for the cold and snowy season. Learning to split wood, especially sometimes gnarly-shaped pieces of madrone, put my back, legs, arms, and mind to task. Picking the spot where to pound the wedge or place the blade of a heavy ax took time to realize. I often missed my target, which was frustrating, and always missed my foot or other body parts, which was encouraging. Splitting wood became a routine when it cooled enough to keep the sweat from dripping off my nose. The pile of unsplit wood dwindled to nothing just before the first rain. The driest and smaller pieces helped get the fire going, the slightly larger chunks would keep the fire hot as the wood sizzled inside the stove. The slow and hot flame of madrone provided cozy warmer mornings, whether the electricity was on or not. Ashes periodically went into a metal bucket before being placed outside until definitely cold. From there, they were ferried down a gentle slope near the base of one of the hundreds of tall ponderosa pines and then poured into a pit suspiciously shaped like a grave. Any garbage of the organic variety and a few leaves from oaks went into this final resting place. The resultant mulch, stirred, not shaken, eventually was ferried back up the slope and added to the soil of the garden or flowers.

The stove was large but did not overpower the look or feel of the room. Curtains that might block even a smidgen of our view from the addition were not allowed, but the room needed something. We moved a few items out of the small bedroom, which had become a storage room, or as most call such a place, the junk room. Linda located and had delivered a set of beautiful and utilitarian cabinets that hugged one wall and fit nicely in our new space. Their classic cherry finish lent even more appeal to the new room. The stereo unit, with the tall cabinet holding the electronics and the tall ribbon speakers were trundled from the living room to reveal the room was acoustically sound. The addition needed tables for space to create, which meant space for our tower computer. If only a laptop would have been available.

The computer, along with its musical instrument digital interface (MIDI) and enough interconnecting wires to weave a spider web for the arachnid version of Architectural Digest was something I needed for composing music. That activity began back in the 1980s when I penned a few compositions the old fashion way, with a good writing instrument and music manuscript paper. One of those compositions was publicly performed in Alexandria, Virginia. Fast forward to 1994 when the affordability and technology of computers, software and a MIDI made it possible to produce a facsimile of music recorded in a document. At last, I could hear my mistakes. With retirement, a new way of life, thanks to free time and my computer-based tools, I could really go to town in the country beginning with editing all of the compositions created the old-fashion way, the ones by writer-cramping pen and paper. New compositions created by clicking note after note, thousands of them, on a computer screen became new chamber works, a third symphony subtitled "Cascadia," and other orchestral works, but all this may someday be another story.

The new addition was not just for a new musical opus or a taxonomic stamp on the manuscript on birds of Oregon. Linda dusted off several of her short stories, essays and poems filed away since before retirement and created her story about motherhood and her son that appeared in "Chocolate for a Mother's Heart." It was part of a bestselling series and was later reprinted.

Linda also created three-dimensional art using plant material such as flowers, ferns, and leaves. One of many creations were scenes created with tiny strands of moss, lichen, feathers, even teeny-tiny pebbles she painstakingly arranged and glued as outdoor scenes inside a crystal clear glass ball no larger than three-inche in diameter. How? Through the very small opening of the glass ball fortified with a steady hand and considerable patience. These objects of art put a ship in a bottle to shame. On a much larger scale, Linda arranged feathers into breathtaking bouquets. Naturally, she was careful to use the plumes from species of birds not protected by the law. Feathers of meadowlarks, robins, bluebirds, and others were missing from her artful creations. This seems the place to briefly mention the law enforcement division of the US Fish and Wildlife Service once attempted to cause me considerable trouble. Individuals of the organization would rather have gone after an innocent museum person instead of a smuggler, an actual criminal that might actually be dangerous to wildlife and, incidentally, to law enforcement staff. Wrongly accused, my name was quickly cleared, which allowed me to enjoy the perfectly legal plumes from peacocks, guinea fowl and other domestic and semi-domestic stock adorning several of Linda's feather bouquets, many of which took up court in Medford offices.

One of many of Linda's feather bouquets.

Besides the permanent addition, we added a temporary structure, which we parked next to the garage. It was for Sam, Linda's adult son, who was injured at birth by a negligent doctor in a hurry to get to his golf game. To this day, Sam suffers from multiple disabilities, both physical and intellectual. His conditions mostly require 24–7 care. We decided he might enjoy a summer with us while we searched for a new and suitable group home that might qualify to fit his needs. In the meantime, we bought a small used trailer, which would be his place should he want to get away from us old folks. He did appreciate some time in his own space as well as time with us, talking to the horses, of course, and searching Button Creek for frogs, his favorite animal.

As that summer came to a close, we found Sam a place in the Rogue Valley. Linda and I sold the trailer back to the previous owner and continued to relish our time in our enlarged home. At the same time, we recalled our words and thoughts about the value of trees, their shade to cool the water table for fish, fowl and vegetation such as the camas growing from the overflow of Morgan Spring, and the value of trees for the beauty of the landscape and for lumber. Yes, we may have crossed into hypocrite-land since we had purchased lumber for the addition and firewood for the wood stove warming. Could we find a balance while enjoying the lumber from former trees protecting and nourishing our time to create and enjoy the view? We would try.

CHAPTER 24

Unwelcome Visitors

We reasoned that the peace of our home could only be interrupted by a few phenomena. Although one might be fire, we considered the two most troubling ones were volcanic activity and certain humans. Perhaps that is rather extreme. Volcanic activity was highly unlikely, at least we thought so since the odes of anything happening was not mathematically going to happen. Still, it could. We were constantly reminded of the possibility of hot rocks flying everywhere and of smoldering magma oozing down from Bald Mountain. The arrival to our doorstep of certain humans, number two on our least desirable phenomena, was more likely than the flow or explosion of igneous rocks, but we had been informed that uninvited humans sometime visit and speak of fire and brimstone. Were the visitors warning everyone about volcanic activity? Was there a connection?

What ever the visitor, we did not particularly appreciate unexpected ones. We definitely like people, but company without warning was not especially welcome. We also were not particularly hospitable to man-made situations such as feral cats, out of control pets, and wildfires caused by humans.

Plant or animal other than human and environmental influences such as most weather events were usually welcomed visitors. Even if unwelcomed, natural phenomena were beyond our control. We would not welcome a geologic event although a minor earthquake might be okay, assuming the shaking did not cause damage. We would not welcome volcanic activity, although such a magnificent phenomenon would be fascinating. Even though the surrounding igneous mountains were once smoldering rocks set aglow from deep within the bowels of the earth, the chances of more pyrotechnics were slim to none. Even volcanic activity that might create a muffled steam vent in the next few years, or more, was unlikely. Geothermal activity under

Klamath Falls, slightly over 50 miles southeast of Morgan Spring, furnishes energy for heating and hot water for numerous establishments. Utilities have proposed horizontal pipes to access geothermal energy from under Crater Lake. Who knows what kind of unexpected visitor that might bring. Thankfully, the proposal was rejected, at least for a time.

Our closest encounters of the igneous kind were miles behind us where we made our quick tour of part of Yellowstone National Park. We had also visited Mt. St. Helens in southern Washington just a few miles from ground zero where the land was gray and burned, where the trunks of the forest trees not buried by volcanic ash and others lay on the gray land, arranged in neat rows, pointing like compass needles in the direction of the megaton blast. One wonders if other peaks would follow with fire and brimstone. Talk about a wildfire!

We have no control over volcanic activity and little control of a raging forest fire, at least not individually. Even the armies that it takes to control a forest fire cannot begin to match a geologic event, once unleashed. Firefighters, even geologists were welcome, but we did try to provide constraints, in a sense, in avoiding unwelcome humans. For example, we let the answering machine screen our incoming calls. We could either pick up or later tell a caller we were too busy for company or at least set up an appointed day and time that would fit our schedule. After all, we might be out watching birds, looking for the first spring trillium, or listening to elk bugle. And, just because we were over 50 did not mean we were dead. We were even accused of being uppity for insisting on calling ahead. No one liked our policy of if you do not call ahead, do not knock. Unfortunately, some people just liked to drop by, unannounced. Using the telephone to call ahead, although an option, was not part of their thinking. There was at least one visit that occurred when we were trekking and happened to see and recognize the visitors, but were too far away or did not wish to dash back to the house, screaming to the visitors to wait, wait. How crazy would that make us?

Of course, the people who wouldn't call ahead to warn us, to see if we had time, or to check that we were even home, were not always someone we knew. Those that we did not know were even more troubling. There were three major types of humans that we did not know, who arrived unannounced. The two most common visitors that were unwelcome were hunters and proselytizers. We had set up devices less polite than a phone and an answering machine to deal with the hunters and the proselytizers who intruded. We had positioned well-placed signs that had bold fluorescent reddish-orange letters on a black background. These signs stated "No Trespassing" and others read "No Hunting." We also placed bright yellow signs with bold black letters clearly stating that the land was posted (apparently a legal term, at least most hunters think so) meaning no trespassing and no hunting. Another device was a heavy metal gate that we kept closed and locked during most hunting seasons.

Our signs, along with the closed gate were more effective to hunters than to some others. We would have kept the gate locked during the deer/elk hunting season but a lock would have also meant no one else, such large package or mail delivery, could access our driveway and our house. We did not especially want to lock out the company that reads our electric meter, the UPS, FedEx, or whatever transport making a similar delivery and, more importantly, we did not want to keep out any emergency vehicles that might be coming to save our lives. Consequently, we had a few unwelcome visitors.

Hunters, we felt, could endanger us physically. Discussion of human hunters appears elsewhere. The other category of interloper was a group that, at least as they presented themselves, were not drinking or swerving in the road, and apparently not armed. These were the proselytizers. We regard ourselves, as do our friends, as latitudinarians, we are broad-minded and tolerant about different religions. However, we do not appreciate proselytizing from anyone about anything. In fact, according to a word coined by Charles Harrington Elster, author of "There's a Word for It," we suffer from parousiamaniaphobia. That, to quote author Elster, is "a morbid dread of proselytizers who come to your door every week to remind you that the Second Coming is at hand and ask for a handout." We are not the only people who share this dread and also share the black humor found in literature, TV, and movies, which is at the expense of such obsessed and unwelcome visitors. The first time we met Mose Bush, he stepped out of his pickup and before saying his name, he quickly announced that he was not a member of a religion. Perhaps there would not be a problem if these proselytizers did not yield to the temptation of trying to change people and while doing so trespassed upon them.

Unknown visitors visited us within weeks after beginning our residence at Morgan Spring. We heard a vehicle driving up our driveway. It remained unseen, the driveway hidden by the steep slope and conifers until the vehicle cleared the last few feet of the driveway and turned abruptly uphill to our house. It was a sedan containing what looked to be three to four adults and a small child. The passengers were dressed in suits. The little girl with them was positioned so that she was highly visible. One of the occupants got out. By then we were standing in the doorway wondering what was going on. Who were these people and the unhappy-looking little girl? Surely, they were lost.

We quickly determined that these people were not lost but that we were, according to them, lost. We politely informed the spokesperson that we knew where we were and where we were going and that we were happy about where we were and where we were going. We informed them that we were not interested. They drove away. The following visits were similar, with suited adults and a small paraded child. Each time we were less and less polite.

On another day, a bright sunny one, we were collecting vitamin D on our bodies au naturel when we heard a vehicle lumbering up the driveway. We were near the upper gate. We were prepared. We had clothes at the ready, and by the time the vehicle could clear the last corner we were ready to greet our visitor in full attire. We should have presented them in full regalia had we known who was arriving. Of course, that might have been traumatic for the token child accompanying the pious fold about to unfold from their van.

Just as the van had passed the last turn around the slope, a small dead tree fell across the driveway. The tree fell about 50 feet from where we were standing and about 15 feet in front of the approaching vehicle. The little pine snag, about 6 inches in diameter, its roots long dead and decayed, fell more perfectly across the driveway than anyone could have directed. The occupants of the vehicle acted as if Linda and I had directed what was a perfectly natural occurrence, but we were actually pointing to save those who wanted to save us. The van stopped and two people stepped out. One was carrying a briefcase. That was a first. Perhaps a new ploy, but we knew their identity after one of the visitors uttered only two words.

Our parousiamaniaphobia kicked in big time. At the same time, from the blanched looks of the unwelcome, something had touched a thought that maybe we had caused the tree to fall. We firmly suggested that they get back into their van and that we would remove the tree in order that they could turn around and get back to the main road. In addition, we shared a hope that on their way out, our gate would not hit the van in the rear. It was a heavenly moment for us as we laughed and skipped back to the way we were. Our visitors were down the driveway and down the dusty road. Neither they nor their brethren's ilk ever dulled our door or our driveway again. The word got out and we were blessed to enjoy our privacy.

Rarely did someone drive up to the house who was actually lost. Possibly the lost visited other residents whose houses were in view from the main road. It just is not good manners to drive up some driveway and then suddenly find oneself at some previously unseen house. No one appreciates those kinds of surprises.

On still another day, we were visited by several lost souls of a different variety. First, we heard a large truck laboring up the driveway. It soon appeared but was much too large to turn the hairpin to get to the flatter gravel in front of the house. The truck was also pulling a trailer that was bigger than most cars. Two men got out, scratching their, well, let us say, heads. They were employees of a group under contract with the electric company to trim trees along the right-of-way of the electric line, part of which was on the property but just inside the fence along the main road. We were curious. Why did they bring such a large truck up the hill and well beyond the right-of-way where they should be dutifully trimming? They did not seem to know, or at least could not come up with polysyllables.

These two poor boys in men's bodies were troubled by either their error or that we were there and we were asking them what they were doing. Maybe they were scouting for a hunting trip, were curious, or maybe they were clueless. Had they not acted as if they owned the property on which they parked, we would have been more cordial in our directing them back to the main road. We suggested that there was nothing for them at Morgan Spring and that they should return to their duty station, wherever that might be, just not here. They said they would have to turn around by going through the upper gate and making a circle in an open area just west of the woods that surround Morgan Spring. However, that area was wet from water seeping to the surface; it would not be dry for at least another month. They did not seem to realize the concept of water producing mud that would sink their vehicle up to its axle. I pointed out to the employees that the meadow was wet and that their huge truck would leave eternal ruts deeper than a goat stands. We flatly refused their request. By then, the tree guys were getting a little annoyed by our efforts to protect the wet meadow, and we were becoming wearier of them.

In the meantime, a second truck roared up, apparently looking for the wayward duo, or also looking for a place to hunt. We wondered why no one had first walked up the driveway, to scout the area, before jeopardizing company vehicles and their time. Of course, walking, and especially walking up the inclined driveway might have been arduous owing to their average girth. Now, two huge trucks that had no business being at our house clogged our driveway. Thankfully, we did not have plans to go anywhere and we were not expecting anyone. If so, we could not go and no one could come. We could almost hear the traffic chopper reporting: "Everything looks clear, the main road has light traffic with one car heading east, and, what's this, there seems to be a bad snarl of large trucks at Morgan Spring. Oh, the infamy of it all." No, sorry, that was a different report. "Just as soon we can, we're going to take the chopper down for a closer look. Until then, back to you, Dave."

None of the drivers of the tree trucks liked it, but we were not allowing them to mess up the meadow. It took lots of backing up and driving forward in the small space we allotted them for turning around. After more back and forth and back and forth they were able to have the trucks pointing in the correct direction. We watched. We made sure no one hit the fence, the house, or did any damage to our tiny lawn and flowerbed. It would have been interesting if the proselytizers had been on their way up as the tree trimmers were on the way down. They might have both stopped and discussed the salient provisions of salvation and silviculture. Or, maybe they would discuss the two residents at the upper end of the driveway. If they had only called first, we could have saved a lot of time for lots of people.

CHAPTER 25

Shades of Gray

A few pages back, while pontificating examples of the ambiguousness of English names of a few animals and plants I wrote: "Sometimes it depends on what you grew up hearing." Not all jays are Blue Jays, even if Granddad from Ohio insisted they were. Any environmental rhetoric we might impart might be interpreted according to a listener's knowledge, their reaction to their peers, and even emotions. What does all that mean? It means some thoughts contrary to the status quo might cause unpleasantness or worse, and, depending on the individual, facts and theories may be colored with different shades of gray.

Here is the thing. Sometime after the Christmas snow at Morgan Spring, we developed a compendium of thoughts based on a few common threads from brief conversations with those neighbors we grew to love from the Morgan Spring region down to people from the sprawlopolis of the Rogue Valley floor. The first thread was one of friendliness and caring that is not readily forthcoming in much of the more crowded country. The closer we were to Morgan Spring the more genuine most people seemed, even if their ideas were not the same as ours. What is important is that their revelations about living in the region of Elk Creek were from openness and honesty, and help if we ever needed it.

This positive welcoming thread, merged with our earlier conversations, revealed people happy to live up in the mountains and trees. Lowland visitors often said, "we sure would like to live here." We knew that, given the opportunity, they would actually rather stay in the valley. As for our happy neighbors, we completely agreed; we are happy living in the mountains among the trees and believed anyone would want the same. Linda and I love the out-of-doors and therefore were on the same page as those also living in or wishing to live in our neighborhood. However, the love was not actually equal because our conversations, depending on who was involved, frequently had to avoid certain keywords. There were shades of gray separating us. For example, the word ecology, when used by us, seemed to elicit certain tells or behaviors that reveal the truth of what the person we were talking too actually believed. Gamblers look for tells from their opponents. A twitch, a nervous scratch, a bead of sweat on the brow and less obvious mannerisms are tells. The word ecology often elicited at least unexplained blinking, sometimes nothing, but most often something that revealed their discomfort. What were these newcomers from Washington, DC, going to say next? Who were they and where do they stand on environmental issues? Okay, by now any reader worth their salt is thinking we were not being totally honest. That is correct. We were feeling our way, just as almost anyone does in most meaningful conversations.

We were neither the Hatfields nor the McCoys. Those we talked to were likewise neither the Hatfields nor the McCoys. We hasten to add that many individuals were intellectually in tune with current conservation issues and generally realized that no one should stand idly by as nature shrinks and human population and greed expands. Nonetheless, the uncomfortable feeling of having to censure ourselves, while most others did not, felt to us sometimes like a feud. Again, we were feeling our way and hoping to avoid any black and white disagreements since almost all issues have shades of gray.

The word environment was not actually sounded out in conversations, usually. That word sometimes caused those standing to shift from side to side nervously. If we uttered the word conservation, we saw quickly folded arms. Oops, what transgression have we made? Upon hearing the word conservation, a few individuals reacted as if to say "I left a burner on my stove," or even more reactive as if, "my house is on fire, got to go." Almost any phrase was used to deftly terminate a conversation about conservation. Fortunately, a first uttering of the word conservation did not prohibit later conversations but we knew that in three strikes we might be out.

Not all but a few people we met were obviously unaware of of the importance of conserving the environment. They were used to the local rhetoric such that environmentalist would shutter the forests and take away their fishing poles and hunting rifles. Their suspicions, their shuttered minds, prevented them from even learning about the environmental movement. Unfortunately, contact with conservationists by local residents was limited as both sides disliked confrontation and some avoided contact out of fear. We had long heard that government vehicles traveled incognito to avoid trouble and that dead owls were placed in mailboxes of some known environmentalists. Of course, we hoped those were isolated incidents and certainly not the case concerning our neighbors. Nonetheless, based on personal experience, which is a different story altogether, I knew people in the law enforcement division of the Fish and Wildlife Service carried guns. There must be a reason for that. In the meantime, while people on one side of the fence or the other remained suspicious of each other, anyone going to their local barbershop or grocery store magazine rack would not be unduly exposed to Sierra Magazine or some other publication involving conservation. Such publications were rare even in a doctor's office down in the lowlands of the Rogue Valley. We also discovered that some individuals we met did not understand what the Sierra Club or similar organizations were all about but nevertheless hated the organizations. Linda felt sad that she had to make a decision whether to wear her Sierra Club cap or hang up her hat. Ignorance proliferated by what they were used to hearing from relatives and neighbors and thoughts were directed by who they liked and trusted. Science-based ideas did not represent truth. Just like later generations of the Hatfields or the McCoys, they would not be able to provide logical reasons for their beliefs but they knew they were right.

We did not mention names of publications or organizations we belonged to avoid consternation that the mere mention of those organizations might cause. Audubon Society was not too horrible to mention since a number of people associated it with pretty pictures and how to build a bird feeder or bird house. Mentioning the Wildlife Federation brought different reactions, probably because the name apparently suggested some association with the state game commission. Maybe the Wildlife Federation was something like Ducks Unlimited. The organization that buys habitats to save land from development, the Nature Conservancy, sounded suspicious even though some of the people might have habitat they would gladly sell to the organization in order to avoid commercialization. Being a member of the AOU, was accepted, but it was not nearly as good as being a member of the National Rifle Association. Two organizations definitely to avoid mentioning were Greenpeace and the Sierra Club.

Linda and I had decided during our arrival at Morgan Spring that we were not going to fight at the front but that we would soldier from the rear with attempts of subtle teaching if the subject lent itself to comfortable conversation. And, it had to be subtle. Most of the people we met love to hear the wind through the trees and breathe the crisp mountain air just as we do. However, not all, but a few of the same people think nothing of leaving hunting camps filthy, fouling streams, and most of all, do not understand the larger picture of the result of abusing our environment.

Not everyone is obtuse to our subtle message and the lessons put out by conservation organizations and concerned citizens. There were hunters that began spending more time aiming a camera than a gun, and ranchers that were trying harder to keep their open range cattle out of riparian vegetation. However, some cattle still trampled and munched the riparian areas, and some of the same people who were disgusted by clearcuts helped build more roads for the timber barons. In fairness to cattle people, lowly intelligent bovines will go wherever the grass is greener and where they can quench their thirst. Cattle owners cannot be everywhere to drive their bovines out of endangered watery habitats. Some owners do make the effort. Sometimes there is hope and other times the world is taking one step forward and two back, which is everyone's loss and our ultimate demise. That we may have already lost is not sufficient reason to stop trying.

We cannot predict what, if anything, might save us from ourselves. New information and innovative technologies should help. Something has to slow down global warming. Who knows what technologies may be devised that may help preserve the planet. When Linda and I met in February 1954, who would have thought we would even have the technology to perceive a hole in the ozone and know global warming was even happening. We have come along ways since marveling but not understanding the underlying trouble when an old timer tells of deep snow in his youth and briefly wonders just a little why the snow is no longer so deep. Of course, there have been technological achievements that allow us to tell better stories, but so has there been concurrent rampant burning of fossil fuels that contributed to climate change.

Nonetheless, some continue to ask is climate change real? That was an oft-asked question by some of our fellow conversationalists, the ones that have their arms folded; that what they cannot see cannot hurt them, or they doubt it even exists. Someone saw it, and it can hurt us all. Gentle persuasion does not always work, but pushing the envelope too much does not either. We could not have the label of being too interested in the environment since to the uninformed, an environmentalist was, in many minds, a *flaming* environmentalist. We did not want a hapless owl's corpse put in our mailbox, or worse, and we did not want to lose the hospitality or help if we needed it in this remote neck of the woods. Of course, we wanted our neighbors to know they could depend on us if they needed help and that we were not associated with the environmentalists that hid metal spikes in trees that were going to be chainsawed by some unsuspecting logger. However, some of the average people we encountered pooled the tree spikers and any other persons interested in conservation and ecology as "damn environmentalists." Actually, almost anyone who professed some use of the land that was contrary to theirs was a damn environmentalist.

Many landowners, many of whom moved to rural areas for the peace and solitude, became anxious to subdivide their properties into as small parcels as possible. Thankfully, Jackson County and Oregon state codes prevent some urban sprawl. Some of the want-to-be subdividers speak in disdainful tones and words about town people, speak of how many board feet is in a forest and drive further and further to have a decent place to camp, fish, and hike. Some of the people who have herds of cattle pounding the compacted stream banks and fouling the water and who vote for building dams blame others for the lack of fish, especially salmon.

There are ways that damn environmentalists are able to avoid the peer pressure of not being a good old boy. Ducks Unlimited promotes the wise use of wetlands for the benefit of ducks, and, of course, duck hunters. Wetlands, saved and maintained by funds from Ducks Unlimited, also provide habitat for a myriad of plants and animals. Donating a little to Ducks Unlimited and the Audubon Society, especially if the check is signed by the wife, won't get anyone thrown out of the local Elk or Moose lodges, and couldn't hurt kids in the 4-H. Even members of those organizations might want swallows or bluebirds nesting on the farm. Both birds are great insectivores, and most farmers have no love for insects, except bees. We have been on farms, and in parks too, that diligently placed numerous birdhouses everywhere, but alas, the entrance hole were wren-sized and much too small for their intended occupants. If the 4-H has a birdhouse building course, we hope someone teaches them to have the entrance hole 1.5 inches in diameter, just right for bluebirds and Tree Swallows and too small for annoying starlings. Anyway, helping out the Audubon Society is harmless because their members are just odd harmless birdwatchers.

Birdwatcher or birders, as we now call ourselves, should never presume to tell anyone how or what they should do on their land, regardless of what happens downstream. The should avoid getting to far into gray areas. Being a birdwatcher and former employee of the Biological Survey at Smithsonian was acceptable, however, revealing that my employer was actually the Fish and Wildlife Service was almost as bad as admitting to being a former employee of OSHA or the IRS. Well, maybe not quite, but I knew of Fish and Wildlife employees that found making friends with their neighbors, so to speak, was sometimes a little dicey. We would not be getting any dead owls in our mailbox but once we may have come close when a paper I wrote was published that was based on earlier museum work. Spotted Owls had been mentioned. We heard that as of 1991, logging on federal land was not permitted, but acres and acres by the hundreds were apparently available to the saw on private land. Still, some federal land was next to Morgan Spring. Was it our paranoia that caused us to believe our rural popularity went into decline once my profession was on the grapevine? What pictures our neighbors drew when sketching what they believed to be the people at Morgan Spring. It must not have been too bad since they seemed to tolerate us no matter their perceptions of our shortcomings, and we tried to reciprocate. Sometimes this was difficult, but as time went on, we believe our city-slicker, tree hugging and owl adoring reputation waned to being replaced with country living good folks who cared about the land and who liked to watch birds.

Actually, birders were the driving force in the early days of the Audubon Society. Birders make up a large part of their membership. The American Birding Association (ABA), founded in the 1960s, just six years after Linda and I met, is a strong force in teaching and conservation. Then there are the bird organizations such as Coopers' Ornithological Society, Wilson Society, and American Ornithologists' Union (AOU). (Cooper's Ornithological Society and AOU later merged to form the American Ornithological Society or AOS) All of these organizations, especially the AOU/AOS and ABA, are actively funding and lobbying for the benefit of birds and their habitats. They are a bunch of damn environmentalists. As it turns out, the love of birds has had possibly more influence to persuade citizenry to protect our environment than the plight of other animals or the need for clean air and water. The conservation movement of the National Audubon Society gave rise to countless state and local chapters. Good grief, I am divulging that the success of the Audubon Society, with its members of just a bunch of birdwatchers, was inspirational to individuals who helped found and are members of such unspeakable organizations as the Wildlife Federation, Nature Conservancy, and the dreaded Sierra Club. Who knew?

Having a bit more of a modicum of understanding about conservation than the average bear sometimes made us despair when we heard of wildlife practices counter to our own science-based knowledge. This was especially so concerning one of our neighbors had lived on the banks of Button Creek for decades. Who? He was none other than Mose Bush, who became a friend that Linda and I always enjoyed visiting. He kept his place neat and clean, no junked vehicles or forgotten trash heaps that were landmarks of some country dwellers outside the Morgan Spring region. Mose could have given others lessons in neatness. His woodpiles were almost prim and not a pine needle was out of place. There was nothing to trip over or that might cause you to wonder if your tetanus shot was up to date. Being a rural gentleman, he offered hospitality and stories about the region and its people. We delighted in listening but not always. Despite his towering age, he did not repeat himself often, but he often stated that he did not see as much wildlife in the area as he used to see. One of the reasons, aside from the obvious loss of habitat, was that he regarded anything with four legs or black feathers as a varmint. Sometimes he had learned, perhaps from a Hatfield or a McCoy, which varmints are to be hated. Varmints are nothing more than animals that eat other critters or their eggs, and especially like to eat chickens. It seems this competition for chickens gets many animals in trouble; not just four-legged and black-feathered varmints but also hawks and reptiles. Even in his age, Mose did not wear glasses and stood straight. He could easily hold a gun, and he did what he knew. He shot every varmint within the sight of his rifle, thus keeping his property neat. Whatever had been on his property was dead and whatever unsuspecting animal wandered down nearby Button Creek, if they didn't hurry or pass quietly on a dark moonless night, would not live another day. Nocturnal varmints were also not given reprieve since they were trapped. We never said a word to Mose. We did not even hint at the obvious. It was hard knowing about his war on critters, and it was especially difficult not saying anything.

We nurtured our low profile by venting to each other. Eventually venting evolved to calm discussions. We were learning that when the traffic is not moving, honking and yelling at the surrounding cars will have no effect except to enrage those hearing us. We strove to realize the many sides of every issue, with the many shades of gray, and appreciate our neighbors as students and as our teachers for what we might impart to them and what we could learn from them. We were not going to be aggressive drivers or aggressive conservationists, except in the voting booth, and with donations when we could afford them.

Most of the time we kept to ourselves, and when we did talk to neighbors we tried not to discuss the controversial issue of conservation. We hasten to add that many of the good people of our wonderful world were thoughtful and caring, but we were aware of the limits of tolerance and avoided stepping over the line. For example, there are gray areas concerning the concept of open range, which means allowing cattle to freely roam the countryside wherever they chose to graze. The fees to ranchers for open range, paid to federal or private landowners, is minimal, although some ranchers will say if it was higher they would go broke. Maybe so, but farming and ranching, not the pursuit of birds or music, is partly subsidized by taxpayers. Our conversations with neighbors were not going there. Had Linda or I brought up government subsidies, we probably would have stepped over a line. To our surprise, we learned that since 1974, Boise Cascade, the western lumber conglomerate, had lease agreements on over 22,000 acres at Elk Creek. The BLM and the Forest Service had historically operated the grazing program in the Elk Creek watershed, but in 1996, the year Linda and I arrived at Morgan Spring, Boise Cascade began a proactive program to determine how grazing is affecting vegetation, wildlife habitat, and water quality. We remained silent and withheld any sentiment that we might seem anti-American.

We should be more tolerant. After all, according to various governmental agencies administering adjacent land, the cattle are to be kept out of the riparian areas. One agency went a step further by reporting that there were no cattle observed eating riparian vegetation, compacting the soil, and sloshing and shitting in the streams. I suppose we had been seeing something yet to be discovered by science that was eating riparian vegetation, compacting soil, shitting in streams, and making utterances that suspiciously sounded like moo.

Our only overt action in regard to open range was to ask the county to put up some signs along the road designating the route as an open range zone. You know, the big yellowish sign with the perfect bovine looking impossibly smart and cute in its black silhouette. We thought the signs might encourage people to slow down, thus having the positive effect of fewer road-killed animals, including even, bovines. We were hesitant to admit to our neighbors that we might have actually done them a favor. Some just thought it was a little strange and perhaps frivolous of the county to put up the signs. Oh well.

CHAPTER 26

Smoke and Fire

Once, following a dry and sun drenched summer at Morgan Spring, we visited a wildfire above our house. The fire had originated on a 40-acre clear-cut. Our neighbors, who would not similarly abuse their own land by cutting every tree and then torching what remained, were appalled that someone would scar the mountainside so blatantly. Clear-cuts in your own back yard look different from those far away. We all knew the new eyesore might be a problem. Local run-off from winter rain might erode and flood the region. Linda and I knew that loss of vegetation would mean higher summer temperatures in the clear cut, which would ultimately contribute to the temperature of the air draining down the mountain that normally cooled our Morgan Spring home.

Linda and I had earlier witnessed the beginning of the fire when, on a hot dry September morning while hiking in the trees at the edge of the clear-cut, a couple of guys in a pickup roared up the road. We watched, horrified, as they jumped from their vehicle and scurried from one slash pile to another. They were setting the piles on fire! We were well aware that the ground was continuing to dry in the rainless autumn and the leaves and needles of the leftovers of logging were brown and brittle.

We watched from the sidelines, keeping quiet, refraining from any comment. We were concerned that the fires might spread to the uncut forest, especially because a couple of the slash piles were spilling over and extending beyond the clear-cut and into the forest. What if such piles ignited the remaining trees and took out the rest of the forest? We had seen the area before the clear-cut. There were tall firs and an occasional stately cedar. It was a beautiful landscape of green trees and dark cliffs spotted with mosses, lichen colonies, and wildlife. A small stream drained downward, and in winter, the burbling of intermittent creeks competed with the soothing wind bending the branches. We could watch the snow march down the hill; first it coated the higher trees, then the trees below, and soon the flakes were over Morgan Spring. All of that, the tranquil ecology of the forest was gone, now cut and much of it hauled away, and the ground where the trees once stood bared to the dehydrating rays of the sun.

The timber company even cut a bearing tree.]

As the fire starters drove away we worried. The weather prediction seemed unfavorable for such so-called controlled burning. Forest managers burn piles of slash every year, usually after the rainy season starts, and it is monitored so that fire doesn't spread to potentially harvestable timber. Have no illusion! Harvesting the timber is what it is all about. Money does the talking, and burning slash was part of forest management. However, we knew that controlled burns sometimes got out of control. In fact, the only truly controlled burn is one in a wood stove, and even then you have to be careful.

Because of our concern that the burning was less than a mile from Morgan Spring, we decided to monitor the area daily. It was an easy hike up the slope. We were the only people on the slope on our first day of checking on the burning slash. Wondering why and if and when someone from the timber company would be coming to check their forest managing practice, we drew a line in the sand. That is, we scraped a line with our boots that extended across the only road in and out of the clear cut. The next day our line was undisturbed, and some woody debris of the former forest floor was burning beyond the slash piles. Each day we checked the fire line and the line across the road. On each of those days, the fire grew and the line we scratched with our boots remained undisturbed. No one had entered the area by air. Any use of helicopters or planes would have been easily heard. No one had checked on the slash. We were definitely the only ones monitoring the fires.

One day we discovered our worst fear had come true. Material from some of the slash piles had acted as a fuse by connecting burning wood to the uncut forest. We called the Oregon Department of Forestry, who were apparently unaware of any problems. Telling the dispatcher that during the nights the smoke chocked the air that drains down the slope and that we could see glowing embers if the smoke wasn't too thick got their attention. Finally, one morning we looked up and the clear-cut was crawling with people and vehicles. Everyone was busy as a fire line was hastily built just outside the perimeter of the fire. By now the fire had encroached on the property of a different and larger timber conglomerate. We suspected that our phone call to the Oregon Department of Forestry connected enough dots with the timber companies and others. This was or should have been an embarrassing or potentially embarrassing moment in forest management, not to mention the larger company coming down on the smaller company. We have met forest managers that have a heartfelt concern for the future of our forests. The country is lucky to have these few. We recognize that their road is a tough road full of twists and twisted politicians who consider timber barons as constituents. Once again, it is all about money.

Early stage of the fire. In the evenings, smoke would drain down into the valley and engulf our home.

Donning our boots, we closed the house and made the all too short trek to the smoldering gray ash and debris. We soon determined that members of the small company representing the ones that started the fire told everyone that they had checked the status of the burning slash daily once the burning began. What about our line across the road? We never saw a track, be they human, Good Year, not even Fire Stone that crossed the line. Why had we not seen anyone while we were patrolling or seen anyone on the slope that was visible from our house? The small company also admitted that they were fooled by the weather forecast. Since when is a weather forecaster always accurate? Blame it on the messenger and lie.

One of the last people we talked to that day was a middle-aged man driving the ubiquitous white pickup. The newish truck was unmarked and the seated driver looked as if he might be in charge of something. Maybe he was a superior source. We told him that we lived downslope off Elk Creek Road, that it was too bad the fire got out of control, and that we were glad that it was being put out. We never revealed that we had been watching the whole process, from cutting down the forest to the slash fires burning out of control. We never mentioned conservation, not even bird-watching or the Audubon Society, and certainly not the Sierra Club. Thousands of perfectly good small tree trunks littered the ground, with enough poles to provide fence posts for a large portion of the giant King Ranch in Texas. We did not mention to the man the waste nor did we reveal we had pictures of those trees, dated photographs of slash burning into the forest floor and of the normally "do not cut" boundary tree sawed from its roots. As we talked the man seemed almost friendly, professional, and polite. Realizing that we might be impeding the man's work, we thought it best to end the conversation. Part of our salutation was an innocent and non-accusing phrase about the smoke. We reiterated that we were grateful that the fire was being suppressed, that the smoke was subsiding, and that everyone breathes the same air. He took in some of that same air and his face reddened, and his jaw tightened as if we had personally attacked him. He squinted his eyes, a frown appeared, and he mumbled something during an icy stare. Whatever he said was just as well unheard by us. The pickup's tires just missed our toes as he roared away.

Boy, was he mad that we so cavalierly believed that we shared the air on HIS land. "Damn environmentalist," he must have surmised. Whatever he thought, it is true that what gets into the atmosphere is mixed with the air we all breathe. And what about the barren land after the fire, the tire thrown into a ditch, the oil drained or leaked from some vehicle of a forest manager or other person, the cattle voiding their waste in streams, and the person that dumps their garbage and used appliances in a canyon? The rising smoke may release its pollutants locally or hundreds of miles from its source. And the solid particles, from dung to dust, are washed eventually down through our cities to the now polluted oceans. We are either downwind or upwind from everyone. We are all downstream from someone.

What would Linda and I have done had the wildfire spread? Too few years ago, we had realized we were moving into a forest that would be subject from time to time to runaway wildfires. In fact, not long before we moved to Morgan Spring, a fire in 1987 burned uncomfortably close to Button Creek. Since that year, Morgan Spring remained charcoal free. Like most who lived in our beloved former neighborhood, we thought about fire but wanted to deny the possibility. Nonetheless, a wildfire could occur. Given plenty of time to escape a fire, we would, of course, proceed down Elk Creek. It is difficult to imagine having to abandon our home, the view from our home, our Morgan Spring. What if we could not drive down Elk Creek Road? Escape might be possible by motoring up Grey Rock Road, then turn onto Needle Rock Road, which would take us eastward over the ridge. If the fire was near Needle Rock, we might have to stay on Grey Rock Road, pass Swanson Creek and Buzzard Mine and somehow escape past the county boundary near 5,147-foot Grey Rock. We would have then been faced with a myriad of forest service roads that would likely have gotten us lost. Maybe our maps would have helped, as would our coveted altimeter. Perhaps we would have driven past the tallest sugar pine marked on a Douglas County map. It is always a good idea to be prepared, to be ready for horrible events we hoped would never occur.

Luckily, the wildfire was eventually tamed and once the smoke cleared, we revisited the crime scene and pondered what that fire and so many others meant to the planet. Locally, and despite the season, the ravaged clear-cut was noticeably warmer than anywhere around our home and in the adjacent surviving forest. Loss of the 40 acres of trees is minuscule compared to deforestation either through harvesting trees for lumber or for clearing land to grow other crops. Multiply 40 acres of incinerated forests times a thousand, no a million or more and the picture should turn most everyone's hair a shade of gray. More lumber is needed to build homes for an unchecked burgeoning population and for such products as coffee, tea, soy, hamburger, and other endeavors that require open land. In the wake of global changes in weather that include continuing rises in temperature, should humans continue to practice unbridled procreation? Is having a large number of children and grandchildren a bragging right? Is the number of square feet in a home the measure of success? Did we once thrive without soy in almost everything we ate? We did, and we also could be just as happy by consuming less tea and coffee. As for all that deforested land, especially in such places as South America, that is now cattle land, there seems nothing to keep hamburger from becoming an item at the top of the food triangle. No, we are not forgetting bacon, but that is another story. One does not have to travel to South America to witness how hamburger on the hoof destroys forests and other natural vegetation. The destructive force of cattle upon the landscape is a historical landmark in Florida, the home of Florida crackers, originally the name for the cowboys there who cracked their whips to drive the cattle. All those cattle producing all those hamburgers helps grow the population and way too many of those well-fed people end up starting more wildlfires than thunder-struck clouds.

CHAPTER 27

Fixing Things

Mixed with watching out for fires and just as importantly birds and generally having too much fun, we occasionally, actually rarely and no matter the season, took part in fixing things. Doing so was something we were glad to do, that came with a since of pride and nourished our feeling of belonging to Morgan Spring. The residence at Morgan Spring was relatively new and not worse for wear such as some places Linda and I have lived. So, there would not be too many things to fix inside or out.

However, every now and then something breaks or might break that required a smorgasbord of things needing fixed. Sometimes it is even possible to predict when something is going to break. For example, the rotten snag leaning over the driveway might break and fall. Would it hit and possibly damage a vehicle or one of us as we walked down to our mailbox? Would we even hear the tree fall? I suppose one has to be there to hear the noise. For those paying attention, a small snag did fall across the driveway a few pages back. We did not have to worry about falling snags or the big pines next to the house. Fortunately, there are many less demanding and less dramatic things to fix than falling timber such as the cracking caulk around a bathtub, the leak around the garage door or sharpening the cutting business of the chainsaw.

My theory is to attempt to prevent trouble such as sharpening tools before they are needed, but that should not suggest I should be fixing something almost constantly. Of course, houses do need care. They need paint, caulking, a nail here and there where the siding starts to bow, and other touches to keep them from falling to their foundations. However, there is a difference between preventative maintenance and improvement. Some people never stop "improving" their house. That may be a good hobby for some but it is not for me. To me improving one's own house is making a place for a quiet and cozy warm bedroom, a place for books, CDs of good music, and a place to write and compose. Mind you, I am not against improvement but there is a fine line between improvement and fixing something before it is broken. There will always be situations either brought on by time wearing something out or an accident waiting to happen, but for the time, surrounding trees remained healthy, all caulking was water and airtight and fence crossings would not damage jeans or anything within them.

Perhaps the most important issue that worried Linda and I was obtaining water from Morgan Spring. Our water pump, the one boosting the water pressure from the spring, once suddenly stopped pumping one morning. The pump was a thing beyond our fixing capabilities and there was no one nearby to call for help. After several phone calls, a water pump specialist from miles away arrived and fixed the problem. That was the first time it went out. The pump would break again years later. The first time the pump went out seemed disastrous for us. We were, however, able to obtain water from the gravity-fed water line from the spring, which also provided a slow flow of water for flushing the toilet. The second time the pump broke was a problem of course, but we, like the parents with the second born child, took the situation much more in stride. By then we had weathered, so to speak, numerous electrical power outages, which might mean a water shortage unless we melted snow. We knew it was a matter of time when the pump would again need repairing.

Whether the trouble is a dry water pump, a cranky uncrankable chain saw motor, you name it, guys are expected to fix things, even things about which they are clueless. Clueless, not an inkling, do not have a manual, never saw or heard about the inside mechanism, or some other lack of knowledge was not a manly excuse. Whatever it is, it can be figured out. Suddenly some guys become carpenters, architects, machinists, yes, even physicists or engineers, who can fix anything before or after it breaks. Or else, the hardware store places you under suspicion if you cannot fix almost anything. It is something to do with preconceived notions that any male, especially taller ones, are capable of most repairs. Actually, Linda ranked several notches beyond many males' fixing abilities.

Lacking the proper tools is hardly ever an excuse for failing and fixing. Of course, it is an excuse to go buy a new tool. Our tool collection, not including shovels and gardening tools, were a claw hammer, a pair of pliers, a phillips screwdriver (I suppose phillips is capitalized but somehow it seems inappropriate for a type of screwdriver) and a regular screwdriver. That would be the one with the straight blade. It probably has a proper name too, and I suppose the business end of a screwdriver is not a blade. I probably will never know. We also had a small crescent wrench, a tiny ball-peen hammer, a coping saw and a rip saw, and a couple of bike tools that belonged to a bike ridden sometimes from Arlington, Virginia, to Smithsonian. We were later to acquire two power tools. Only two? That worked for us. The electric drill was very handy and the electric saw was useful for making birdhouses, cutting small pieces of firewood and trimming the addition's flooring. Oh, speaking of firewood, we added to our arsenal a double-bladed ax, a wedge, and surely a sledgehammer that I do not remember, and a smelly chain saw. Other than my old Boy Scout hunting knife purchased when I was 11, the most useful tool has been one of those screwdriver units that have different interchangeable types and sizes of heads (or is it blades?). My tool-man brother-in-law gave that to me one winter holiday.

So, with a limited but useful set of tools, the next thing was to fixing things or making something. Of course, if you did not know how or did not have the correct tool, you could hang out at the hardware store. Our closest hardware store was about 20 windy, mountainous miles away when we first moved to Morgan Spring but the establishment closed soon thereafter. Hardware was sold there again years later. In the meantime, fixin' stuff was dependent on one of those valley stores containing acres of tools, and almost every material required to repair or build something, even birdhouses. Linda bought numerous small plants, bulbs, seedling, and seeds there to decorate and landscape our nest at Morgan Spring. Planters were nailed together for the seedlings. The correct caulking to use around the tub and under the sliding glass door was at the big hardware store, waiting for discovery and purchase. Different caulking was required to patch holes where the part of the heat pump entered the house. The caulking was dried and cracking when we moved in and the gaping holes in places were easy to fix. Pasting over cracks around the hinged trap door leading from the outside to the attic were letting in outside air and apparently flying insects into the attic.

A nail here and there to tack down any boards that bowed from the weather and more caulking kept me busy during my fixing moments. Our addition was a major fixing job and after it was completed, it had to be painted. Unfortunately, our new paint did not exactly match the color of the original building, so we painted the new and the old parts of the house. The actual process of painting was relatively painless since my lowland-residing sister and her husband, the person who gifted me that wonderful any-size-fits-all screwdriver, with Linda and me, formed a painting party. But, and this is a really huge but, there was a major problem. As most people know, the color and texture of wet paint appear different when it becomes dry. The paint rolled on by one of us had dried on the vertical slab of the thirsty wood siding. The wider slab protruded slightly outward from the narrower vertical parts of the siding. The paint had to be brushed on these narrower parts. Fine, we thought as we moved around the corner. We were making great progress. Or so we believed. Hours later, we had a striped house! The person rolling on paint over the wider parts of the siding and the person brushing paint on the narrower parts of the siding was using paint from two different buckets. The paint was custom mixed but the color was supposed to be the same for all of the paint. Some of the walls looked like a designer zebra. Did I say pale brown? The differences were not the differences between light and dark chocolate. The differences were more towards ridiculous.

The dastardly paint came from one of those acres of tools and fixin' stuff stores where people are supposed to know how to repair or "improve" one's home. Having a striped house was not an improvement, especially in a beautifully forested environment. What I did not know was that custom color requires mixing by pouring it from their little buckets to larger buckets so that the mismatching colors may be blended. I suppose someone at the store could have instructed us on this fine point of mismatching colors, but being a guy, they assumed I surely knew what to do. On the other hand, maybe they thought I would rear up and spit or cuss at them for insulting my manhood. Whatever their reason, we still had a designer zebra at Morgan Spring. To make a long story short, I did call upon some of my baser manhood traits sans spitting, and got some new paint, compliments of the store. The house was well protected by all those coats of paint, the wrong one and the color we had chosen.

Naturally, there were a few other fixing moments. Most of them were connected to water. In fact, water, the staff of life, was both good and bad. Keeping water out or away from what we wanted to keep dry and directing water to have something green, to clean or drink occupied considerable time. To solve all these problems required certain apparatuses or tools of sorts. Tools such as water hoses and lawn and garden sprinklers that helped green the little lawn, eventually a garden, flowers, and other plants near the house, and a birdbath. The hoses were also potentially fire hoses in the event of a forest fire, an event we hoped would never rear its ugly head. Maybe the fire hose would be in use only for, well, nothing. We had an inside tool for fire, a good working fire extinguisher.

Runoff from heavy rain or rapid snowmelt sometimes became troublesome. Our steep, unpaved driveway was tightly packed earth and much of it covered with small crushed volcanic rock from the quarry just above Morgan Spring. When it rained, small rivulets would run down the driveway. If the rain fell rapidly enough and the individual raindrops were large enough, the rivulets would become creeklets. A creeklet is a small creek.

I think I made that up but probably someone out there used the term to describe a large rivulet or a small, embryonic creek. Of course, it is possible that a creeklet, if running year-round, could have a name, but more than likely the waterway would be some kind of creek. I have not seen Mississippi Creeklet or even Mississippi Rivulet. Maybe it depends on what one is accustomed to. Some parts of the country call creeks rivers and rivers creeks. It is all relative.

Anyway, these rivers washing down the driveway sometimes carried away enough of the crushed rock to create riverbeds. Actually, they were just rivulet beds or maybe creeklet beds. They never were so deep that most vehicles could not pass through or over them. Maybe they were too deep for a sports car. My old bug-eyed Sprite would never have made it. That was my car of choice during the college days. It was so low that I had to cross over a standard speed bump at a 45-degree angle instead of straight on. Our Morgan Spring vehicles were fairly close to the ground but speed bumps were not a problem. Our beater, the Brat, had a higher road clearance. I suppose we could have gotten one of those vehicles that require a ladder to get into but we opted to stay closer to earth. Besides, we noticed that those stratospheric vehicles somehow made some drivers appear somehow taller and concurrently sporting a smaller head. Regardless of the road clearance, optical illusions, or the actual size of one's head, we did not want the creeklets to become creeks. That meant filling in the holes, otherwise, given enough time, creation of a new grand canyon was a given.

Filling in the holes in our driveway required more appropriate tools. To some that might mean a backhoe, a steely blade pushed by a tractor with lugs aka bulldozer, or some other mechanical device that polluted with decibels and tiny solid particles spewing from an exhaust. Opting for simplicity, I chose a trusty shovel. The shovel was great for moving the alluvium back into the rivulet's canyons and also most useful to scatter crushed rock hauled to the injured driveway via the wheelbarrow or the back of the beater. The beater was also necessary for packing down the replaced crushed rock.

Drainage ditches on the sides of the upper driveway did not exist. Shallow ditches on the sides of the lower and steeper part of the driveway prevented water from running across the driveway. Those ditches were lined with rocks to prevent erosion. We routinely found it necessary to clear leaves, mostly from oak and madrone, and other debris from the ditches. When the driveway was covered with snow, we kept our fingers crossed that our vehicle would not slide into an unfilled or ill-repaired chasm along the sides of the narrow driveway. Keeping the driveway navigable was important.

Keeping the green metal gate closed certain times of the year, such as during hunting season and during cattle drives, was not difficult although we had to attempt to train, that is, fix the minds our non-open range visitors of the human ilk to close the gate once entering or exiting the grand bovine-less sanctuary of Morgan Spring. We were amused that some people just did not understand why we wanted the gate kept closed. Many of the few regular visitors did finally catch on as they began putting the latch on. Still, open range is a foreign concept to many.

Once, during our second summer, we heard some people yelling down the hill. They had stopped on the gravel road and opened our gate, drove four bovines through it, closed the gate and motored away in a cloud of dust. We guessed that it was someone with Open Range Deficit (ORD); they thought the cattle on the road were ours and somehow the four had managed to escape our fences. The people whooping and yelling thought they were doing us a favor. Or, it was someone who had a master's degree in open range and was playing a joke on the new people. We ended up chasing the fodder machines for about an hour until we finally were able to direct them through our gate. The not so dainty foursome went down Elk Creek Road even though we tried to get them to go the other and correct direc-tion. These seasoned open rangers forgot they were supposed to be eating that lush mountain grass where it was cooler and were fewer flies would interrupt their cud-chewing ways. That is right, those proto-hamburgers and future steaks regurgitate their food and chew it again! Actual cowboys on horses, but often by pick-up, with dogs that like nipping the heels of the bovines drive the cattle past the lower fence-line of Morgan Spring. Like the four driven in our gate, a few bovines sometimes missed their ques, ended up breaking through the fence and traveling their way uphill to the spring. Cattle had been in the meadow our first summer but not afterward. They could drink freely from the slow cool water that meandered through the bluish-purple camas and brilliant yellow buttercups until all colors, includ-ing green, were stomped into a black muddy muck by the prodding hoofs of the oblivious bovine, their feet, and legs making loud smacking sounds due to the sucking mud. Water in the moist meadow below Morgan Spring pooled in their tracks. Cattle sauntering along the road below the spring ei-ther remembered the overflow of Morgan Spring or they smelled the water. Memory is a doubtful possibility in bovines, but, at least according to old westerns on the big screen, cattle do smell distant water. Surely John Wayne spoke the truth. Maybe they smelled the water.

The olfactory talents of bovines are beyond my pay-grade, but their clumsy stealth when they broke through the rather rickety lower fence was within my purview. That is when I would give chase and eventually get the trespassing beasts on their way to open range. Sometimes open range cattle wandered downhill, hence the need to steer the steers and others out of the meadow. Although Linda and I enjoy a good hamburger or some other lean cut of beef occasionally, driving trespassers out of Morgan Spring property was doing all parties a favor. Trespassing cattle meant fence repairing.

The fences surrounding Morgan Spring were also subject to destruction by elk. These magnificent giants could walk through a well-maintained fence the same way a human might walk through a spider web. However, most of the time, the elk jumped over the fences. Deer sometimes jumped over fences, but sometimes managed to go under some barbed wire fences. Bobcats, coyotes, and probably other unknown mammals crossed the wiry boundaries in their own fashion. Fence destruction also was caused by two-legged mammals in the form of hunter who go over fences, not by jumping them. We saw hunters bring already weakened fences to the ground by standing on them. We rounded up signs befitting the season, appropriate nails, and a sturdy hammer to fix the problem. Our thought was that it does not require much intelligence to not trespass a posted area and even less ability to know how to not destroy a fence.

Although we were almost short on tools we were not entirely clueless about fixing fencing. There had been teenage summers working on a ranch and watching our dads repair fences. With our gloves, a pair of pliers, a claw hammer, and some assorted nails Linda and I could sometimes put broken fences together. With an old hand me down shovel, its handle weathered whitish and the blade worn thin and dull, we sometimes could get a broken fence post to stand vertically. If all else failed, the cause which was often without the proper tools, we used lifeless manzanita and other woody brush to build a wall that any self-respecting bovine would avoid and would keep the horses and mules at home.

What might might seem an awful lot of fixing so many things, we mostly did not mind taking care of home. Our collection of tools, cans of paint and collection of nails along with knowing we were caring for Morgan Spring gave us a good feeling, a feeling of belonging.

CHAPTER 28

Fish and Foul

Morgan Spring and surrounding territory is a wonderful place that has had its ups and downs, destructive forces such as wildfires, road building, and cattle that have fouled the ecology of streams, destroyed forests, and recoveries that have or will improve habitat for fish, protect the landscape, and continue to grow trees for following generations. The sought-after balance is to nourish what is there for the benefit of the future instead of over-feeding commercial income by focusing only on the present. This is conservation, wise use. There are many facets related to stewardship. One concerns fish, animals that are like the canaries of the mine but instead telegraph the health of waterways. The other subject regards negating the positive attributes of the environment, specifically Morgan Spring and territory. It is all too easy to foul our own nest, sometimes without even realizing it before it is too late.

Bragging about Morgan Spring being our retirement destination moved friends at Smithsonian to provide a nice fishing rod and reel rig among their many generous gifts during my going-away party. Years of fishing, mostly as a young Danny McSkunk, had long been abandoned for birding, but thinking about a fishy catch was dietarily inspiring. The Rogue River was just downstream from Morgan Spring, but Elk Creek or some its tributaries could be sites for hooking dinner.

Two of the kinds of fish swimming the waters of the Elk Creek watershed include non-migratory and migratory kinds. The migratory ones are known as anadromous fish that breed in fresh water but otherwise live in saltwater. Think salmon. People were thinking salmon in 1897 when a fish hatchery was built at the mouth of Elk Creek, but, as they say, that is history. So are so many dams that have had deleterious impacts on anadromous species. However, as time and improved understanding advanced, dams and other barriers have been removed from the paths of migratory fish. Although anadromous species are stopped in the Rogue River at Lost Creek Dam, a few miles below the dam, streams, depending on their size and health, offer potential habitat for breeding anadromous fish. Elk Creek was a good candidate for anadromous fish habitat, but a partially constructed dam on the lower part of the creek unnecessarily displaced people and prevented natural movements of migratory fish for about 20 years. Fish at the time were trucked around the dam, but that method reportedly did more harm than good. The dam was demolished in 2008. Elk Creek and its tributaries now provide spawning and rearing habitat for about 44 percent of coho salmon and 15 to 20 percent of steelhead breeding in the upper Rogue River watershed. Those are impressively important values.

Trout, salmon, and steelhead habitat was being improved in tributaries while Linda and I were enjoying the fruits of living Morgan Spring style. Logs were strategically placed to help create spawning beds in some of the tributaries of Elk Creek. Bitter Lick was one of the creeks. Our little Button Creek has a natural barrier about a quarter of a mile from the creek's mouth at Elk Creek, which, although I am not sure, seems too high and steep for even the best of Olympians among anadromous fish.

Salmon raised in the Elk Creek watershed will migrate to the sea or contribute to a good fish dinner. The watershed, its birthplace, someday will be a go-to place for sports fishing so long as the streams are healthy. As part of the health, the state of suitable habitat depends on water temperature. Removing shade warms the water just as do clear-cuts near a stream. That is where the next subject, foul, comes in. There are many ways to foul a stream, kill the fish, and ruin a watershed. One of the primary contributors to fouling watersheds, the cradle for Morgan Springs and other great locations, are people and cattle.

Now, we have nothing against cattle or people who raise cattle, especially so long as the bovines are not mucking up Morgan Spring and other waterways. Some Elk Creek residents may have thought our hand in asking the county to put up open range signs was for the safety of people and cattle. It was, and we were not anxious to hear the anguish mooing of some jay-walking bovine struck by a speedster or, as Mose said, "hear glass breaking or smell blood" the result of a vehicle and cattle occupying the same space. Again cattle are important. In fact, beef cattle and the American West go hand in hoof, but bovines are good, bad, and ugly in the United States, not to mention elsewhere, especially the Amazon Basin. That giant watershed creates its own weather and meteorologically influences the world. Unfortunately, the bovines there are rapidly depleting the vast basin's jungle. Loss of the forested Amazon Basin will forever alter our climate. Too many cattle is not limited to south of the border and is a problem in the temperate part of America where vast mesquite ranges cover the horizon as grim reminders of too much munching. The Texas Chisholm Trail was a place where cow-pokes once yelled "headem up, movem out" before driving the raw hides through once bountiful grasslands. Everybody was happy except the person bringing up the rear. All that dust and chewed product from the bountiful grass must have been something. Perhaps that era was the "good" because it was an important economic force driving the burgeoning country. It was also a "bad" time since cattle went stomping dusty trails to hard pack and denuding the route as they went. Maybe the "ugly" is what we so commonly see today, the fat little kids that become fat big adults who die a horrible and early death from all that fast food beef fat. Again, Linda and I appreciate a good hamburger, but not as a regular diet. Part of the reason is that it is a well-known fact that too much meat, especially red meat, is not healthy. Second, the obvious mark bovines leave on the environment is not good for the health of the planet. It is a two-pronged meat fork waiting to stick us into dire problems. Metaphors aside, the scar on the landscape left by cattle is a large one considering the amount of protein they provide. Cattle are inefficient food sources, taking inordinate amounts of feed and acres per pound of beef compared to chicken. Likewise, cattle produce considerably more pollution than chickens, but do not get me started.

Nonetheless, too many cattle have the capacity to create wastelands and stomp riparian vegetation to smithereens. That would be foul. Loss of stream side vegetation ultimately might lead to water disappearing from not just thirsty bovines, but from people scratching their heads while wondering what happened to the water. Thanks to fences and gates, large numbers of open range cattle did not settle near Morgan Spring. That is not to say the bovines would not have fouled Morgan Spring given the opportunity. Over the years, cattle that managed to encroach on the succulent marshy drainage of Morgan Spring were chased out of our domain. Linda and I found numerous places along most all of the tributaries where cattle had damaged riparian habitat. Our findings were contrary to those of a BLM employee, who was our guest for a few nights and who shall go nameless here.

Water quality deserves more attention. Surveys have revealed that streams become polluted from road run-off and cattle messing up the stream banks. Perhaps a better way to phrase that is that cattle do their mess in streams and streamsides. One of the most troubling facts is that deposits from cattle raise the *E. coli* count. That is *Escherichia coli*, the scientific name of a bacterium, for those who care to know. The generic name is almost always abbreviated, the *E.* might best be translated as "evil" since *E. coli* is

capable of killing or making one very sick. Not all forms of *E. coli* are harmful, but who wants to take a chance. In this time, only a foolish person would
drink from Elk Creek or its tributaries. Some people do use water from Elk
Creek for irrigation of gardens. Hopefully, they thoroughly wash what they
grew since the bacteria counts of *E. coli* are up. Not all of the increase can be
blamed on cattle. Domestic animals such as dogs and wildlife contributes
to increases in *E. coli* polluting streams. Remember, we are all downstream
from people and dogs.

Besides our concerns about cattle and pollution in general, we were
worried about wildfires, not just the one purposefully set above Morgan
Spring, but wildfires in general. Wildfires are yet another significant con-
tributor fouling the land. Hot dry summers with cumulus clouds in the sky
might produce lightning, and lightning could start a fire. Forests were tin-
der boxes, waiting for a spark. However, we worried just as much or more
about human-caused fires. Back in the day, 1900 to be more precise, only 11
percent of fires in the Elk Creek watershed were caused by lightning. The
remaining 89 percent were human-caused, mostly to increase treeless acres
to supposedly improve hunting and increase grazing acreage. According to
reports, the practice of clearing timberland by setting fires was used more by
white settler than by native people. More recently, most people avoid setting
fires, at least on purpose. Regardless of how a fire originates, fires in recent
decades burn more and more acres. A favorite forest management tool is
a "controlled burn," which is set on purpose with the aim of burning unwanted fuel such as a slash pile left behind after thinning or logging. There
is growing evidence that logging may actually be ineffective since the debris
left after an operation is such great kindling, average summer temperatures
go up and water tables go down, and too little effort is given to protecting
replanted trees from fast growing brush. Time, if we have it, will tell.

Today, the practice of "controlled" burning is in practice. The "controlled burn"near our home that predictably got out of control was not the
first fire in the Elk Creek watershed. Not surprisingly, years later, members
of a logging operation set fires to logging debris in late November that grew
into a wildfire of 125 acres in January. Not all fires in and around Morgan
Spring were alleged "controlled burns." For example, in 1910 more than
2,000 acres burned in the Bitter Lick Creek region. There were 300-acre
fires in the watershed in 1971 and 1972. Over 3,700 acres went up in smoke
around Burnt Peak in 1987. The lightning-caused Burnt Peak fire grew large
because most available fire suppression units were needed elsewhere. Settlers in 1915 were reported to be advocates of light burning. On the contrary, local residents in 1987 were active in fighting the Burnt Peak fire. That

fire, and others to come, put fear in the forefront for anyone living for miles around.

Residents of our region were aware that wildfires have occurred about every 15 years in the lower part of the Elk Creek watershed. A part of the upper reaches of the creek burn about every 35 years. Is that formula accurate today? Every summer, with the dehydrating sun baking a water-starved environment, people cringe as they wait for an errant spark that will set things ablaze. That spark could come from a lawn mower's blade striking a rock to lightning from a sulfur-and-brimstone storm that produces bolts of 50,000 degree lightning, which are hotter than the sun itself. While working at Crater Lake, the then rare fires were lightning-caused, and at ground zero were trees that exploded from the sudden electrical energy. The trees' sap boiled and evaporated so rapidly that huge chunks of wood, like war-zone shrapnel, rapidly spiraled in every direction. Huge chunks were propelled deep into the forest floor, others even into adjacent trees and many pieces scattered yards away from the lightning-struck tree. A few pieces of the exploded wood were burning and torching anything flammable.

The hotter and drier the fuel, the quicker and more severe the fire. By early July, Elk Creek Road was dusty. Poison oak, non-poisonous oaks, and other leafed plants, even grasses and wildflowers going to seed were coated by the grayish-brownish dust boiling up from the tires of vehicles. It was dry. It was too dry to park over anything flammable since catalytic converters of everyone's metal steed are capable of reaching over 1,500 degrees Fahrenheit. Matches burn at 600 to 800 degrees. The local environment was definitely too dry to ignite fireworks, which, unbelievably, were set off in several places in the watershed. Linda and I first experienced this level of stupidity near the confluence of Bitter Lick and Elk creeks. The forest service, or was it BLM, had even placed a sign warning against using fireworks. Yet, near several trees and yellowing grasses were fresh remnants of spent fireworks. We also discovered smoldering and abandoned campfires on several occasions. Most were found on a Monday, the day after someone's irresponsible weekend.

There are a plethora of reasons for saving the forests, one of which is logging. Logging was and is a way of life for a few, but the timber industry employs fewer workers than do fruit and health industries. Jackson County employees working in timber-based jobs make up only about 2 percent of the total county employment. However, depending on who one listens to or what newspaper one reads, it is possible to believe any reduction of timber harvest will be the death of us all. Of course, logging will continue, but exposing the forest floor ultimately leads to soil erosion, growth of flammable brush and slash, lowering of the water table, flash flooding, more roads, and other undeniable problems. Many of the considerations are imposed onto the industry by federal and state regulations. According to sources, the amount of tree harvest on federal and state properties since 1970 has slowed considerably. On the other hand, tree harvests on private property are currently only 22 percent of what was cut in the roaring days of the 1970s boom. That private property is mostly owned by timber companies headquartered far from the Elk Creek watershed that have less vested interest in the region than residents of the watershed. Of course, timber people on private property are supposed to follow certain rules also, but what we saw just above Morgan Spring and up Alder Creek demonstrated disregard of the forest, of adjacent landowners, and of Oregon Department of Forestry (ODF). Forests are finite resources and, although forest management is not an easy task, silviculturists must be on guard so that logging maintains the resource on which the industry and many others depend. It makes no sense to foul one's own nest and thereby render their way of living something of the past.

Evidence of soil erosion from logging and road building is easy to find.

Importantly, what happens to denuded acres, be they the result of a wildfire or a clearcut, is important to the future. Replanting is required by law in Oregon and must begin 12 months after, for lack of a better term, denudation. The ODF further states that planting should occur within 24 months and that in 6 years the blighted area be adequately stocked with what is called "free-to-grow" stands of trees. If all goes well, the replanted trees might, just might, become a forest, but only after decades of watching the trees grow.

All too often, at least in the past, replanted areas were left unattended, which allowed all kinds of competing vegetation to choke out the small planted trees. A clearcut might eventually look beautiful in the fall with the glowing embers of fall-colored leaves of pesky maples instead of green conifers. Competition causes slow growth or no growth of harvestable trees. Even in extant forests, removing small trees frequently allows the remaining trees to grow larger. The larger trees have less competition. Remarkably, larger, quick money-making trees, are preferred over trees with small wood-bearing trunks. Those very same large trees usually have thick, less flammable bark than the smaller, far more inflammable trees. In the longrun, looking at the big picture, the future, cutting, if required, of the smaller trees is far more of a win-win situation.

Considerable amounts of less valuable small trees are cut, but are not harvested.

Logging means roads and there are plenty of roads tracking throughout forests. In addition to the timber industrial complex, roads bring access for members of, for firefighters, for biologists, some studying Spotted Owls, for botanists, for recreation, even for exploring Morgan Spring residents. Besides every road mentioned thus far, Linda and I ranged up several other roads including Abbot Prairie, Elkhorn Ridge, Dodes Creek, and others. We drove near Gobblers Knob just south of Timber Creek. That region prob-ably burned in 2003. We summited Burnt Peak one mid-summer day, which gave us a different view of Morgan Spring. Of course, we drove Needle Rock Road on several occasions while on our way to Prospect. There were over 400 miles of road to choose for gaining access to the watershed. I use the word "were" since there are likely more miles of road as of this writing. The lower part of Elk Creek watershed and that of Button Creek have more than six miles of road per square mile. According to forest management reports, many of the roads were built during the housing boom after WWII when lumber was in greater demand, but many new roads were constructed in the early 1960s, and by 1970 there were roads up Bitter Lick and Sugar Pine creeks. About three-fourths of the roads in the Elk Creek watershed occupy places of potentially high erosion, which seems reasonable owing to the possibility of heavy rain, rapid snowmelt and the road surface material itself. There are a few roads, Sugar Pine Road included, that are actually paved. Travel elsewhere has revealed remnants of pavement such as on part of the so-called Ashland Loop Road or Mt. Ashland Road, aka forest road 20, west of the ski area in the south of the county. Money must have been more plentiful than it is today. In time, potholes in the old pavement will enlarge and roads will be bare. Many of those paved roads are in remote regions that are not inhabited and presently of little to no interest by the timber industry. Other roads once traveled become too rutted, with some spots showing potential for another grand canyon someday. Reports that Boise-Cascade Company is improving their roads are welcomed although I have noticed over the decades that forest road improvement is frequently a prelude to tree harvests.

Like Emperor Joseph II, who, speaking about Mozart, complained there were too many notes, the US Forest Service and BLM every now and then think of closing some of the too many roads. This is especially true in regions called Federal Riparian Reserves. By definition, Federal Ripar-ian Reserves "consist of the stream and the area on each side of the stream extending from the edges of the active stream channel to the top of the inner gorge, or to the outer edges of the 100-year floodplain, or to the outer edges of riparian vegetation, or to a distance equal to the height of two site-poten-tial trees, or 300 feet slope distance (600 feet total, including both sides of the stream channel, whichever is greatest." Those are the rules for streams that have fish; rules are modified for other classes of streams. Definition of site-potential trees and their significance is beyond my wheelhouse. At any rate, the rules remind me of instructions for filing taxes and often seem to be understood by logging operations at a level that would cause the IRS to levy a penalty. That is to say, I have witnessed many cases of abuse that are beyond an oops moment when chain saws slipped and cut trees down the bank of a stream. I can hear the retort "Sorry Mr. Forest Ranger, I didn't see the stream, I just saw big juicy trees needing cut." Part of the problem in such situations goes beyond greed, to harvest the "juicy trees," and could be improved by education and enforcement. Returning to the subject of roads, the last time I checked, there were 170 miles of roads in Federal Riparian Reserves primarily within the upper parts of the Elk Creek watershed. Button Creek is excluded. On the other side of the coin was a comment, or was it a complaint, that the Timber Rock Fire originated in an essentially roadless area. Would a road or two have allowed firefighters access and thus prevented the spread of the fire? Or, would such a road, actually, any one of the numerous forest roads, have allowed a careless camper to forget to extinguish last night's campfire where they might have set off fireworks near their steaming hot catalytic converter? Maybe, maybe not.

Questions outnumber answers, but the primary point of inquiry might be as we fish for answers, why do we continue to foul our own nests?

CHAPTER 29

Gifts

No matter what might happen to the glorious land, we could feel in our bones that Morgan Spring is a treasure of beauty and beasts from sunsets to trees and wildlife. Morgan Spring is a gift. It would be difficult to ignore the lessons from the privilege of living at Morgan Spring. Time at Morgan Spring brought humility, humor and great memories.

We continued to see the humor in some of the names of Morgan Spring creatures, be they jays of some hue of blue or by some proper name such as Steller's Jays. Did I say proper? Yes, that is a specific jay, not just any old jay. We, that is followers of the American Ornithologists' Union's official check-list of birds, capitalize English names of birds since they are proper nouns. That's the rule. Proper English names should be capitalized. We would never write rogue river, oregon, or morgan spring in lower case letters. What about cats? One animal that even the fiercest eagle, the Bald Eagle, not bald eagle, would not eat is a mammal known by several names, but by any name, it is becoming endangered in much of its range and in some regions of the country a legal target for hunters. As humans encroach on more and more of what is left of Mountain Lion country, more lions are often observed by people, sometimes in suburban regions. The animals are hungry sometimes forage in what was once their domain but is now humanized with paved streets. The big cats are losing natural territory daily and, at the very least, deserve a proper name. Why not? Mountain Lions are also known by such names as Cougar, Puma, Panther, and Golden Retriever. That is correct. Golden Retriever. We suspect, although, with some tongue in cheek, that there were reported increases of sightings of Cougar, or cougar according to newspapers, before and during discussions about whether and how they should be hunted. How could Cougar populations otherwise

spike at the convenience of discussions weighing the good and bad of being Cougar? Were some of the reported cats actually dogs? Could golden
retrievers by proxy be Cougars? Wait. Shouldn't that be Golden Retrievers?

It is interesting to us that visual sightings of Mountain Lions, aka
Cougars, infrequently had a cascading effect on different communities. For
example, an animal was seen at point x, then, suddenly, following a report
of it in the regional newspaper; three more cats were at y, and two at z. How
could that be? What was happening, we believe, were reports by mostly
honest people that wanted to see a Mountain Lion so badly that they did,
even though they really did not. Maybe a distant Golden Retriever morphed
into a Mountain Lion. We have tried and tried to see Mountain Lions but
to no avail. Individuals left tracks but we never were able to see this cat that
is a lion. We wonder, does a wild cat become a lion and when does a golden
retriever become a Mountain Lion? And, how to forget that nostril hair
singeing smell of a Mountain Lion marking its territory at Morgan Spring.
It was so awful as to be funny.

There is certainly humor elsewhere, including in nomenclature that
went beyond capitalization. How could we forget that a controlled burn is
sometimes not under sufficient control? That a fair amount might equal an
unfair amount. That a clean-cut look had noting to do with hygiene and that
long hair was not a dirty cut look.

How could we forget that mules, at least old Fred, hates cats, or at
least Cat? Could we possibly know without first experiencing being up such
a fine creek, that admitting we all breathe the same air would elicit such
anger? Would we know for sure that a litter of skunks, just like in the Disney
films, follow their mother in a single file? They do, or at least that was the
way one family proudly sauntered by our dwelling. What about drawing
building plans, dealing with the county to authorize those plans and waiting for building inspectors to nod their approval; what about construction
without hospital-rated injury, playing the stereo as loud as possible and not
being arrested, and sporting no tan line and also not being arrested? Those
were gifts.

Animals taught some good lessons. Almost anyone will agree to
practice caution when confronting animals stronger and larger than you.
Actually, most mammals bigger than a mouse should be given a respectful
distance otherwise expect to bitten or at least scratched beyond comfort.
That applies to dogs, horses, and mules, and definitely to elk, those very
same beasts Linda and I crept much too close to near the beginning of residing at Morgan Spring. What were we thinking? The answer: I was not
thinking of being pummeled to smithereens, to not live another day. When
my daughter visited, a similar mistake was made. She and I went for a walk

near Skunk Road, her very young son being left with Linda and his keen interest in the weather channel. In short order, I glimpsed three elk walking several yards ahead of us. They were mostly hidden by surrounding trees and bushes. I asked my daughter if she would like to see an elk. She said she would, and I instructed her to continue on the route while I ran through the woods as quietly as possible. The elk were heading perpendicular to the main trail and I reasoned I could drive them across the more open trail and in front of my approaching daughter. Imagining myself younger and more agile than reality, I managed to get behind the elk and herd them toward the main trail. The effort paid off, my daughter had a close view of the elk that fortunately did not turn around and interrupt my plans for the gift of living.

I learned splitting green madrone is a dumb idea. Because snow was more constant than any place we earlier resided, improvements for driving in it increased. Snow or no snow, during trips to the valley, we learned to be on the alert when a vehicle made a turn at an intersection of a driveway. Many drivers turning right would set up their turn by first inching left, often invading the lane to their left, before actually turning right. Except for very large trucks, such a maneuver by cars and pickups was completely unnecessary. I know, since have been driving for decades, including a 23-foot RV all over cities, towns, and the countryside. Turning even a skosh, let alone sometimes a foot, to the left before turning right was not required. Running over the curb at the corner did not happen. We observed the first left, then right, maneuvers performed by all sorts of drivers, including short little ladies, and drivers who might or might not be former log truck drivers who might have picked up the habit. Observing people and learning from them, which might mean an evasive turn of the steering wheel, was a warning and another gift.

Some people we knew, when not cautioning us against quicksand and hungry Cougars, warned us about traffic. It is true, traffic in the lowlands occasionally was problematic, but mainly because of driving habits rather than the number of cars on the road. Coming from the Washington, DC metropolitan region had provided us with sufficient practice in not just Traffic 101. We had earned graduate degrees navigating the capitol byways. Many drivers in the Rogue Valley held up the flow of traffic by making those left then right turns, rubbernecking, not taking advantage of openings for making lane changes, turning too slowly as if fearing the vehicle might tip over, and more. We surmised that eventually, and sadly, Rogue residents would get the hang of driving in heavy traffic.

Linda and I were wrong about several issues. One almost happening moment was at the split second the world's clocks might have timed us out. That moment was called Y2K, the year 2000. A large contingent of people was convinced a digital bug concerning the clock, the computer time-piece that is important in driving the comings and goings of all those teeny-tiny ones and zeros would reap disaster. Would there be trouble at a split second after midnight on 31 December 1999? Would computers be capable of recognizing the first millisecond of 1 January 2000? Would computers suddenly stop the flow of electricity? If not, what then? Would planes fall out of the sky, ATMs not cash out, hospital equipment fail? Huge lines of people did withdraw their savings and patients likely worried about being wheeled into operating rooms before midnight. Y2K was receiving attention from our president, from people across the country, it was on minds internationally. Could the problem be averted? Was there actually a problem? Should we worry? Of course, we should worry, but to what extent? We discussed at length whether to purchase an electric generator. Thousands, maybe more, purchased electric generators, along with dried food and other survival stuff. A generator would have been a big expenditure on our budget. Probably most households along Button Creek were variously prepared, which is to say, some homes probably already had generators and were prepared for at least short-lived hardships. Others, as did many people around the globe, scoffed at the idea of Y2K. However, what if? What if electricity stopped surging? Would a generator only be a stopgap? We would take our chances and follow the calm of our neighbors. However, just in case, we stocked the pantry up to its brim and, like people worldwide, waited. The answer came with a tick-tock, and one second after midnight, the first moment of 1 January 2000, we were all okay. That was a relief, but had the worst come to fruition, we knew the best place to be would be at Morgan Spring.

We worried, but only slightly, that living remotely would cause difficulty. We were definitely wrong about that. We appreciated our neighbors and we definitely enjoyed our solitude together.

Of course, more time visiting with neighbors meant less time for other activities, including birding Morgan Spring and filling in some of the gaps about birds in the county. The back story here is that about two decades earlier, I published what was then known about the distribution and occurrence of birds found in Jackson County and region. My compilation relied heavily on data from myself and others, but most birders then lived and birded in the lower part of the Rogue Valley. Birds of Morgan Spring and its region had never been documented, and now living in the unexplored location offered the opportunity to collect data on the birds of the region. Just off the cuff, I believe the distribution of a few species differ from previous generalities, but, as we ornithologists say, more study is required.

The growing list of birds Linda and I detected around Morgan Spring surpassed 84 species, which is a reasonably good total for a backyard checklist. Would there be more? In time, more birds would come. In the meantime, we knew the limited types of habitat excluded most water birds and most species found in the valley. We did have a few surprises such as migrant flocks of high-flying White-fronted Geese on two occasions and winter-visiting Pygmy Nuthatches. High flying flocks of migrating Sandhill Cranes did not happen often enough and we never tired of hearing them communicate with their trumpeting calls. From a negative point of view, the absence of so many species of flycatchers was surprising. Could that have been from the lack of preferred insects? Many of the same species of flycatchers could be detected with relative ease elsewhere in the county. Also surprising was our singular record of Orange-crowned Warbler, one of the more abundant species in most suitable habitats in southwestern Oregon. Was Morgan Spring at the wrong elevation for those warblers? The next season might bring something new. Again, more study is required.

Morgan Spring was asking questions and gifting us with many answers, but never completely revealing all the best questions or all of the correct answers. That would require time, introspection and definitely more of what Morgan Spring might offer. That was something to look forward to, but little did we know what was around the corner.

CHAPTER 30

Departure

Years ago, on the summer day when Linda and I discovered Morgan Spring was the day we thought we had found the place where we might enjoy living. On the fall afternoon when we arrived at Morgan Spring, we thought we would stay many years,. After passage of a short time, we knew Morgan Spring should be our home forever. Morgan Spring was peace of mind, peace and time for work since I was not suited to actually retire, and a place to savor the playful side of living unencumbered by so many societal demands.

The last winter at Morgan Spring.

Little did we realize that after only six years in paradise that we would find ourselves moving away from the spot we could not help but love. Leaving Morgan Spring was not voluntary. Our departure rested on more than one reason. Our parents' failing health required us to travel more frequently to the valley. Each trip down to their homes meant more deer and cattle to avoid colliding with during each rush to the lowlands. Coveted time at Morgan Spring was diminished as we spent more and more time away from our home, and once frequent walks above the meadow and around the mountains became more and more elusive. There was less and less time to watch the elk, feed the juncos, listen to Steller's Jays talking, to hear wind singing in the conifers, observe a pair of devoted ravens watching over us as we attempted to tend events close to the affairs of living at Morgan Spring. It was good that our garden was small since the time for our domestic obligations was fleeting. How can one ignore loving a parent?

While struggling to decide whether or not to leave Morgan Spring, we began to notice changes. The quiet hush we so long enjoyed during our early days and nights was regrettably broken by an increase in vehicular traffic. We were not sure why. At the same time, we detected a decline in wildlife, especially mammalian. It was subtle, but by comparing our nearly constant observations, we knew, at least subjectively, something was scaring away animals that earlier roamed past our view. Was Morgan Spring changing? Should we stay and hope any outside forces would eventually allow Morgan Spring to return to the normal which we loved?

The enduring sounds from nature that we so long enjoyed during our early days and nights, we regret, was broken several years after our arrival, not by traffic or hunters, but by our closest, albeit unseen, neighbors. They decided to build and fill kennels with barking dogs. We noticed a decline in wildlife that we attribute to the scary sounds of the mutant wolves down the hill. In fact, studies fortified our conclusions that the mere sound of dogs, even the sight of dogs on a leash, contributes to wildlife's primeval fear and eventual avoidance of dogs or places dogs habituate. We found the barking hard to ignore, but the clear air, with bright starry nights and the crisp taste of Morgan Spring almost was enough to overpower our need to be more able to help our parents and ignore the new sounds of Morgan Spring.

We did not want to abandon Morgan Spring, but it seemed the responsible thing to do. We could have endured the ever-increasing commutes to help our parents, but the hounds below barked our decision favoring us to move. Could we live at Morgan Spring and do the right thing for our parents? We believed we could not. Linda and I wept the day we knew we had to leave. Packing was nothing like those nights after work just before retiring. Then, we were excited, anxious and looking forward to moving to

Morgan Spring. Packing to move from our beloved mountain home was not exciting and we were anxious only in wondering what the next years away from Morgan Spring might bring.

The day we left Morgan Spring could not have been more cheerless. We cried, with large tears and painful sobs released from deep in ourselves. Emotions were full of regret jumbled with failure. Our lives torn, we reluctantly moved to a spot not far from the Rogue River. From our new home, we looked north and imagined Morgan Spring hidden a few ridges over from our stare. We were painfully only a few miles from our old home, but should the phone ring, the route to aid our parents would now be easier, safer, and quicker, with winter snow unlikely. From our new purchase, we could see a couple of our neighbors and hear their lawnmowers. Of course, they had dogs, but luckily, the animals rarely made a sound. There would be little to no opportunity for four-legged animals to roam our new place and far fewer birds to cheer us. The inspiring meadow was far out of sight. Our real home seemed so far away.

Epilogue

After moving from Morgan Spring and before settling into our place near the Rogue River below Lost Creek Reservoir, a horrible wildfire began eating acres of forest dangerously close to Morgan Spring. The fire, officially designated the Timbered Rock Fire, began from a lightning strike on 13 June 2002. Timbered Rock is in rough steep terrain at 4,740 feet in elevation near north-central Jackson County and southern Douglas County. The promontory is near the headwaters of Flat Creek and only 8.75 miles northwest of Morgan Spring. Separate fires that together were part of the Timber Rock Fire were not detected until days after the discovery the initial fire. Could strategically placed lookouts have helped decrease the number of acres burned? A fire lookout built in 1933 on 4,748-foot Ragsdale Butte north of the headwaters of the West Branch of Elk Creek might have seen it all, but it was burned (on purpose) in 1962. From our proximity along the Rogue River, we could see smoke billowing into the sky and ash falling at our new door. We feared Morgan Spring might burn and kept a daily lookout, including frequent drives to Shady Cove to get the latest fire information. We could easily see the awful anxiety of people examining the current maps showing the boundaries of the rampaging inferno. The fire exploded from 161 acres on 23 July to 27,090 acres on 5 August, burning approximately 27,100 acres. Timbered Rock Fire was officially contained on 9 August (basically, a fire line of 63.2 miles contained it) and it was declared controlled on 14 September when mop-up procedures were completed. Smoldering continued into winter.

The Timbered Rock Fire definitely left its mark, not just on the thousands of acres burned, it caused the evacuation of the population living along Elk Creek Road. The stress of leaving everything behind and not knowing about tomorrow must have shaved years off the longevity of some. Knowing about the fire was definitely stressful for our health. The fire ended up impacting about 32 percent of the Elk Creek watershed, mostly on private and BLM land, but indirectly smoke put its stranglehold on many, including the lungs of tourists and residents downstream in the Rogue Valley. Once the fire was snuffed out was not the end of the story. In many ways, it was the beginning; work to rehabilitate the region had to begin, partly in order to avoid exposed soil from eroding, soil that had been moved while building fire lines and access roads, and soil burned so severely that it lost its nutrient value. Attention and money had to be directed toward potential erosion and destruction to roads, and prevention of wayward soil and burn duff clogging culverts and silt chocking anadromous fish breeding sites. That was just the beginning. Cattle grazing on private and public land would be suspended for two years to prevent burned stream banks from being trampled. Concerns about soil quality or lack thereof and the commercial worth of unburned timber precipitated discussions about salvaging trees killed but not burned by the fire, and reforestation efforts continued for years.

Knowing that the wildfire in 2002 had burned so much of the forested ridges along the route to Morgan Spring did not invite us to revisit the hurt environment. After the passage of more time, we drove a few miles up Elk Creek Road, but could not bring ourselves to the final destination. More years passed. We continued to mourn not being able to view a once beautiful route. Finally, one day we managed to achieve a visit to Morgan Spring. Our beloved Morgan Spring looked different and it looked the same. It was a welcoming old friend ready to pick up the conversation where it ended, but we could not talk. What had become our way of life was a candle we could not and did not want to extinguish. Choking with tears, we again said goodbye. In our hearts, Morgan Spring is home forever.

www.ingramcontent.com/pod-product-compliance
Lightning Source LLC
Chambersburg PA
CBHW071049280326
41928CB00050B/2147